Daddy's Girl, Mama's Boy

Other Books by the Authors

The Divorced Catholic
A Catechism for Divorced Catholics
   by Dr. James J. Rue and Louise Shanahan

The Ups and Downs of Marriage
All About Adam . . . and Eve
   by Louise Shanahan

The Nine Most Common Marriage Problems and How to Overcome Them
   by Dr. James J. Rue

Daddy's Girl, Mama's Boy

by Dr. James J. Rue and Louise Shanahan

The Bobbs-Merrill Company, Inc.
Indianapolis/New York

Library of Congress Cataloging in Publication Data

Rue, James J.
  Daddy's girl, mama's boy.

  1. Mothers and sons.   2. Fathers and daughters.   3. Oedipus
complex.   I. Shanahan, Louise, joint author.   II. Title.
HQ755.R85   301.42′7   77-15435
ISBN 0-672-52348-5

To our Mothers and Fathers, with love and affection. Their guidance and inspiration through the years made this book possible.

Acknowledgment

We wish to thank our respective families, who have made possible the writing of this book by their encouragement, cooperation, and understanding.

Our thanks and appreciation also go to those individuals and families who participated in the counseling programs that we have used as the basis for our data.

Finally, we are sincerely thankful to Susan Suffes, whose superb analytical and editorial skills have clarified the theme of our book.

Contents

Foreword

The importance of parent-child relationships during the early years of life has been a recurring theme of psychological literature for decades. Few aspects of child development have been more thoroughly documented than the emotional vulnerability of boys and girls during their formative years at home. But now, Dr. James Rue and Louise Shanahan have added significantly to our understanding of human nature by showing *how* those early influences affect a developing personality. Of no surprise to those who read the title of their book, the critical factor turns out to involve the delicate relationship between a child and his or her parent of the opposite sex.

Specifically, the authors contend that the image of Mama remains long after junior is grown, influencing his sex life, his relationships with people, and especially his marriage (or decision not to marry). Likewise, a girl's memories of Daddy persist and impinge on all her later experiences. (These conclusions are perfectly consistent with my own observations in counseling.) There is no doubt that girls who had loving, supportive relationships with their fathers are more likely to enter into healthy marriages. The same concept applies to boys and their mothers. As Rue and Shanahan have written, "The parent figure of the opposite sex is the unconscious model for all future romantic encounters."

I can recommend DADDY'S GIRL, MAMA'S BOY enthusiastically to parents, to professors, and to people who want to understand their own hidden motives. In my view, the book's emphasis on personal application represents its most valuable contribution. To facilitate this self-analysis, separate rating scales are included for men and women. Perhaps their use will help us avoid repeating the mistakes of our parents in dealing with our own little ones.

Finally, let me commend James Rue and Louise Shanahan for the traditional values they have woven into their manuscript. They have resisted the temptation to endorse the avant-garde life styles that their contemporaries have embraced, including extramarital affairs, cohabitation and homosexuality. Instead, they have prepared a solid, well-written text that will take its place in the annals of human understanding. It is my honor to have been asked to write the foreword for this significant book.

James C. Dobson, Ph.D.
Associate Clinical Professor of Pediatrics
University of Southern California School of Medicine
Author of *Dare to Discipline,*
Hide or Seek, and *The Strong Willed Child*

Introduction

This book grew out of our recognition of the influence Daddy and Mama have had on the husbands and wives, parents, adolescents, children, and homosexuals and heterosexuals we have encountered in counseling sessions. All had become aware of an aching need for love-security that they had failed to satisfy in one futile or tragic relationship after another.

Our approach is based on our counseling experience and our conviction that an altruistic sense of responsibility toward one's mate and oneself is the foundation of a happy marriage. And this capacity for altruism is developed in the childhood relationship with Daddy and Mama.

The Daddy's girl/Mama's boy theme is so obvious and so often taken for granted in our society that its power for good and evil has been obscured by its commonness. Whether we repudiate or imitate our experiences in this early relationship, each of us is undeniably and irrevocably Daddy's girl or Mama's boy.

Consider the fascinating and almost infinite number of variations of this relationship. Recall for a moment all those men and women who in middle age refer to their mates as Daddy or Mama. Remember, too, those adolescents who are so eager to substitute the more mature words Dad and Mother as symbols of their independence. And look to the noteworthy and infamous of the past and present, and see how their personalities have been formed by their parents.

In today's world, there are abundant blueprints for marital happiness. All offer glittering promises for approaches that require little effort. We believe that such misrepresentations constitute a disservice to those men and women who have struggled to achieve love-security in their lives. We do not offer popular solutions to marital unhappiness. Extramarital affairs, living together without marriage, or other alternative life styles will not change the person. But no matter where you are in your life journey, you can initiate the process of self-understanding, which is the beginning of wisdom and personal happiness. You are not doomed to a mindless repetition of an early unhappy relationship with Daddy or Mama. Nor does a loving and secure childhood guarantee you a life of marital happiness if you fail to commit yourself to love-service. The profound, philosophical and psychological implications of the parent-child relationship are constantly molding our personal responses and affecting our capacity to love and share.

This book, then, is a guide to self-discovery and self-direction. With it, we believe you can transform your most intimate relationships by beginning, courageously, with yourself.

James J. Rue, Ph.D.
Louise Shanahan
Los Angeles, California

Daddy's Girl, Mama's Boy

1   A Life for a Life

Hidden within each of us is a yearning for the love-security we found in our childhood relationship with Daddy or Mama. Why is it hidden? A partial answer might be that as adults we are embarrassed to admit that these yearnings from our childhood days still cling to us and influence our lives.

Throughout life, from the moment of birth until death, the image of Daddy or Mama looms as a primordial force which determines all romantic episodes, all sexual encounters, our choice of a marriage partner or partners, and, to some degree, all other interpersonal relationships.

For the most part we are not conscious of this yearning, this endless quest. We tend to deny its existence and its impact on our sexual and marital choices.

The nomad who sprints from one sexual misadventure to another is just as certainly seeking the love-security of his/her relationship with a parent of the opposite sex as is the monogamous husband or wife who has found contentment and love-security in a mature marriage. Vehement protestations, however, may arise from husbands and wives. "My husband is the exact opposite of my father." "My wife could never be mistaken for my mother." These remarks may be only too true.

At the crux of this opposition lies the same search for love-security, a love-security that was in some way denied or distorted in childhood. Daddy's girl or Mama's boy spends a lifetime in an unconscious pursuit of the satisfaction he or she did not have in childhood.

Who is a Daddy's girl or a Mama's boy?

All of us.

Our adult lives are manifestations of those particles of love each of us absorbed day by day in childhood. The unpretentious beginnings of a Daddy's girl or a Mama's boy are found in the everyday activities all of us have known.

What little girl has not cherished an expensive dress that Daddy bought for her? And didn't she joyously kiss Daddy to reward him?

What little boy cannot recall a time when Mama intervened in order to protect him from a well-deserved punishment from Daddy? Upon recollection the boy may remember his tears of gratitude or the shy kiss he bestowed on Mama's cheek.

Now look at the young adult man or woman. See how Daddy's girl attempts to recapture the love-security of her youth by her unconscious choice of an older man as husband. Or how a young man chooses a domineering wife and then makes an unhappy discovery years later. Why did he select exactly this woman to be his wife?

Look to Mama.

For instance, Sigmund Freud received great sustenance from early love-security. The first of Amalia Freud's children, he was adored by his mother and occupied a preeminent position in her life. Knowing that he was especially favored by his mother constituted the basis of his inner strength and hence his success in later life. In fact, he wrote, "The indisputable favorite of his mother keeps for life the feeling of a conqueror."

A Mama's boy, therefore, is not always a term of deprecation. The fortitude derived from the first intense love relationship may catapault a son into accomplishments which bring worldly recognition and power.

History is filled with examples that lend validity to Freud's perceptive observation. Franklin Delano Roosevelt and his mother provide an excellent example of the compelling influence of a unique mother-son relationship. Whether mother and son are bound together by love or by hate, the impact of the bond is manifested in a struggle for political power. It is no accident or coincidence, but rather a verification of the need each human being has for love-security.

If Daddy or Mama was our first love, is the rest of our life then determined by this childish and childlike relationship? If Daddy or Mama was our first object of hatred, are we then enslaved in our future lives by the uncontrollable outbursts of rage or hatred expressed in childhood?

If we become Daddy's girls or Mama's boys unwillingly, before we realize what is happening to us, how and why do Daddy and Mama weave the tangled skeins of bondage that manipulate our future emotional lives?

What are some of the forces acting on Daddy and Mama to cause them to develop this specific kind of relationship with a daughter or son? For although there are traces of this relationship in all of us, there are, in some of us, attachments so unique that they affect all our attitudes toward our partners.

The future sexual adjustment and interpersonal adaptation of an individual has its roots in his or her childhood relationship with Daddy or Mama. The seeds sown in this childhood relationship may determine whether one will suffer the self-perpetuating tragedy of sequential monogamy or enjoy faithfulness to and happiness with one mate. Whether a son or daughter's adult life will be blighted or rewarding will depend on this initial Daddy's girl or Mama's boy relationship.

The Daddy's girl and Mama's boy relationships were first dramatized in the Greek tragedies by Aeschylus, Sophocles and Euripides.

The ultimate calamity, an incestuous relationship, is detailed in *Oedipus Rex* and *Electra*. Sexual attraction generates acts of murder, revenge and, finally, incest. The inevitable consequence of incest is the blinding of Oedipus. Electra, too, in her implacable hatred of her mother, reflects for all future generations this distortion of sex which results in tragedy.

How this sexual attraction for the parent of the opposite sex is deflected and redirected into normal avenues of sexual growth, or encouraged and arrested at an infantile level, has been the subject of much modern dramatic literature.

In *Strange Interlude*, Eugene O'Neill dramatizes the torment of the Electra complex in a readily identifiable context. The simplicity of the New England setting intensifies the complexity of the interior psychological deterioration of Nina Leeds, daughter of Professor Leeds.

Professor Leeds characteristically opposes his daughter's marriage to Gordon, a young man who is later killed in war. In his own words

Professor Leeds reveals a glaring Daddy trait: "I was opposed at first . . . I think, for the boy, for all his good looks . . . really came of common people and had no money of his own, except as he made a career for himself."

Professor Leeds expresses his naked motives to Nina: "I wanted to be comforted by your love until the end. In short, I am a man who happens to be your father."

And Nina, after her father's death, punishes herself mercilessly for her strange relationship with him.

His books . . . his chair . . . he always sat there . . . there's his table . . . Little Nina was never allowed to touch anything . . . she used to sit on his lap . . . cuddle against him . . . dreaming into the dark beyond the windows . . . warm in his arms before the fireplace . . . dreams like sparks soaring up to die in the cold dark . . . warm in his love, safe-drifting into sleep . . . "Daddy's girl, aren't you?"

Our Inherited Value System

Despite the fact that there have been intermittent periods when females have dominated society, by and large Western civilization has been and continues to be male-dominated.

In *Women as Force in History,* Mary Beard documents the significance of woman's position in society. She notes that during the Middle Ages it was the lady of the household who managed the estate when the lords had gone off to war.

A sprinkling of female abilities were evident in certain learned areas. In the Middle Ages women were allowed to study law and medicine in Bologna. Moreover, in the city of Frankfurt, no less than fifteen women were practicing medicine. Such minor victories did not tilt the seesaw of domination in favor of the female, however. The elements prolonging and protecting male-dominated society assured man an almost totally unchallenged position until the middle of the nineteenth century.

Jean Jacques Rousseau, the father of the Romantic Revolution, blasted the opening fusillade in the war over the equality of women. He stated that women existed chiefly to please men. Rousseau's premise that women should find happiness in pleasing men met with violent reaction; inherent in this thesis is the subjection of women to men.

In *Emile,* Rousseau wrote:

> *Woman is expressly formed to please the man. . . . This, I must confess, is not one of the refined maxims of love; it is, however, one of the laws of nature, prior to love itself. If a woman be formed to please and be subjected to man, it is her place, doubtless, to render herself agreeable to him, instead of challenging his passion. The violence of his desires depends on her charms; it is by means of these she should urge him to the exertion of those powers which nature hath given him.*

Naturally such an arrogant attitude of masculine superiority did not go unnoticed by the female sex. A powerful rebuttal issued from the pen of Mary Wollstonecraft in *Vindication of the Rights of Women.*

She rearranged Rousseau's thesis to please herself. Her creed was, "Woman is everywhere in chains, but I propose to show her the road to freedom."

Her efforts were valiant, and she is idolized by feminists, but Rousseau's concept of the relationship of the sexes prevailed.

In the nineteenth century a male advocate arose to present the true lot of womanhood. In 1869 John Stuart Mill published *The Subjection of Women.* Mill's interpretation of the role of woman and of her frustrations in marriage was clearly stated. He declared that the existing marital relationship in which the female was subordinate to the male was morally indefensible.

On such terms the institution of marriage was virtually a paradise for man and hell for woman, since the male was able to express his interests and his tastes, while the woman was expected merely to be a reflection of the man. Mill believed that a woman was held in a perpetual state of bondage to men, first her father, later her husband. Such repression has consequences, and Mill hinted at them. Refusing to allow her personality opportunity for growth was perilous, for if woman were not permitted a normal avenue of expression, she might seek malevolent, dark compensations.

Mill suggested that male-dominated marriage forced women to find expression through their children. And in what way? The assertion of power, control and direction of their lives.

Mill stated:

> . . . a married woman's appetite for power is to be found in her relations with her children. This is the most obvious source of relief and compensation for a mother who is disappointed of self-realization and those energies cannot flow freely outward on equal terms with others. This is the relationship which is the obvious target for corruption by emotions soured and starved in the marital and social roles by the principle of female subordination. The children can so easily become living objects for the receipt of "affections" compounded of disappointed pride or crushed self-respect or rejected love. Under what more innocent cloak than maternal love could such bruised and thwarted emotions find a seemingly more legitimate release?

John Stuart Mill's shrewd prognostication regarding woman's use of a cloak of maternal love to hide her control of her children's lives finds corroboration from an unlikely source.

Sigmund Freud, who accepted the nineteenth-century thesis of male supremacy, nevertheless comprehended the profundity of the influence of a mother over her children's lives.

Freud's interpretation suggested the possibility of a benign rather than a malignant mother-child relationship. Specifically with respect to the mother-son relationship, Freud wrote:

> A mother is only brought unlimited satisfaction by her relation to a son; this is altogether the most perfect, the most free from ambivalence of all human relationships. A mother can transfer to her son the ambition which she has been obliged to suppress in herself, and she can expect from him the satisfaction of all that has been left over in her of her masculinity complex.

Although these words may arouse fury in feminists, this insight into the diversion of repressed feminine ambition into a son is one of the keys to understanding the Mama's boy relationship. Its range, as indicated by Freud and intimated by Mill, may include the concentration of female energies for the ego fulfillment of the mother or the son.

When Mama is immature, her ego needs are so great that her son merely functions as an extension and reflection of her own personality. Thus the attachment may have some pathological aspect to it, because the son's psychological development is arrested at an infantile level as a consequence of Mama's destructive control.

Should Mama recognize the relationship of her frustration and ego needs to her son's emotional development, she may transcend these limitations and utilize her thwarted personal energies in a constructive manner. Naturally this benign influence requires considerable personal maturity. As will become evident, not all Mama's boy relationships are destructive.

Freud's interpretation of the perfection of the mother-son relationship goes one step further and includes the sexual aspect of marriage.

He wrote, "Even a marriage is not made secure until the wife has succeeded in making her husband her child as well and in acting as a mother to him. . . ."

This was the situation in his own life.

Protests of indignation will undoubtedly arise as a consequence of Freud's concept of the husband-wife/mother relationship in marriage. He is, however, describing a phenomenon which was very prevalent in the nineteenth century.

This wife/Mama-husband/boy marital relationship, which was rein- forced through social, religious and cultural conditioning of men and women, by no means reflects any of the changes suggested by Mill in his earlier analysis of woman's subject position. Its implications are self- evident. If woman was deadlocked according to Mill's evaluation, Freud was pointing the way to power for women—through the mother-son and wife/Mama-husband/boy relationships.

The hidden sexual influences in the Mama's boy relationship distin- guish it from the Daddy's girl relationship. Rarely, even under the most wretched and sexually disappointing circumstances in marriage, does a woman resort to seduction of her son. However, the converse is not true. There is a high incidence of incest in father-daughter relationships.

The alternative, which is obviously more socially acceptable, is the decision on the part of a woman to have a younger lover, thus psychologically fulfilling her sexual ego needs in this disguised Mama's boy relationship. Such relationships were particularly common in the artistic and literary world of the nineteenth century, when women lived under the severe constraints established for them by a male-dominated society.

Consider, for instance, the salons of Paris, a vehicle for displaying the glittering talents of poets, painters, musicians and writers. Madame Jeanne de Loynes was one of the reigning queens of the artistic world when, at the age of fifty, she met and fell passionately in love with Jules Lemaître, a writer of thirty-three whose star was then in ascendancy.

In Madame de Loynes's salon Lemaître received the pampered adoration his heart desired. His fervent ardor was reciprocated beyond his wildest yearnings. Madame de Loynes knew how to make life intensely joyous for him.

Lemaître visited Jeanne de Loynes every day for twenty years without missing one day. Her salon functioned solely for him. She recognized his literary talents, and, through her salon, she gave him every opportunity to meet those people who could advance his career. Each realized the benefits of the Mama's boy relationship.

Another observer of marriage, G. B. Shaw, offered his cynical and devastating analysis of the disappointments he felt women could expect from the male-dominated institution of matrimony. Like Mill and Freud, Shaw perceived the relationship between a woman's disillusionment with her husband and her subsequent efforts, through her children, to gain a measure of self-esteem. In *Getting Married,* Shaw presented a humiliating portrait of marriage. It is, he proposes, a relationship which gives legitimacy to the basest drive of man: the sex drive.

It is not a coincidence that Shaw's relationship with his mother formed the basis of his future attitudes toward sex and marriage. With his parents separated, Shaw lived a haphazard, cheerless boyhood which gave him a chilly attitude toward sex that had tragic repercussions in Shaw's later life. He believed he had been treated with contempt and neglect by his mother, and hence his view of women and marriage was sour and contemptuous.

Shaw reiterated the lessons of lovelessness learned in childhood in his dramatic works and essays. He wrote, "It is not surprising that our society being directly dominated by men, comes to regard Woman, not as an end in herself like Man, but solely as a means of ministering to his appetite. The ideal wife is one who does everything that the ideal husband likes, and nothing else."

Shaw was unable or unwilling to comprehend the significance of a marital sexual relationship beyond the level of male exploitation of the female. With such a foundation to marriage, he felt that a wife was likely to begin to feel "used." Therefore, she had to find some way to mitigate her unhappiness.

Shaw observed, "Her business is to sit there (at home) and mope until she is wanted. . . . Then what can she do? If she complains, he is the self-helper, he can do without her; while she is dependent on him for her position, her livelihood, her place in society, her home, her name, her very bread."

Indeed, what can a woman do?

Shaw reached the same conclusion that Mill and Freud did, although each interpretation is unique to the personality of the analyst.

Shaw offered a glimmering of hope to women. He wrote, "The self-respect she has lost as a wife she regains as a mother, in which capacity her use in the community compare favorably with those of most men of business. She is wanted in the home . . . wanted by the children. . . . And so, though she is completely disillusioned of the subject of ideal love, yet . . . it has not turned out so badly after all."

Thus woman had an arena of compensation to mollify her. The children, especially her sons, were avenues of fulfillment through which she could realize her secret ambitions and dreams of achievement.

The male-dominated society of the nineteenth century contributed other object lessons to the female who grew restive under the constraints of marital domesticity.

The central fact of a married woman's existence during this period was that her husband was the breadwinner. By extension, his authority in his own home reached almost omnipotence.

The average woman was occupied totally in non-moneymaking domestic chores, unless she came from the lowest class, in which case she was employed in a domestic capacity by members of the upper classes.

Her day was filled with washing, cleaning, mending, baking, child care. Because modern appliances had not yet been invented, a woman's calendar might read: Monday, washing; Tuesday, ironing; Wednesday, mending; and so on.

It is no wonder that a woman felt distinctly inferior to a male. She lived a narrow menial life in comparison to that of her husband, whose sense of superiority appeared to be based chiefly on the fact that he brought home wages. If she suffered, she suffered in silence.

As the Industrial Revolution transformed the lives of ordinary men and women, the cleavage between the two became manifest. In order to survive, the husband was forced to spend long hours away at his work. The wife and children were relegated to the background of his life. If he was ambitious, he was also intensely preoccupied with his work. His wife was not able to understand his work, because Victorian husbands did not bother the little woman about the practicalities of moneymaking. Hence, she lived in a dismal vacuum.

His attitude reinforced her feelings of dependency, and his feelings of authority and superiority. As he earned more money, his self-esteem grew, and her feelings of dependency increased proportionately. The male's sense of superiority was inextricably bound up in his earning ability. He tended to regard this money as "his," and he might lord it over his wife since she had not earned any of it. Therefore, money became another weapon in the male arsenal.

Since there was such a serious divisiveness between husband and wife, of what real value was a woman?

The Victorian wife was imperceptibly becoming the prototype for the status-symbol wife of contemporary life. Her physical beauty and grace, her clothes (which her husband probably selected or approved), her gentility were all reflections of what his money could buy.

While this may appear to be a harsh analysis, women, nevertheless, submitted to it, since there was really no other choice except the singular life of a spinster.

Gradually such a woman's charm became influential in the maintenance of her husband's business success. In essence, the dependent wife moved into a kind of playgirl role. She was gorgeous for her husband. He quite literally paid for her, since she was not paying her own way in the marriage, and he issued the commands.

Any thinking woman very naturally found this interpretation of marriage repugnant, for it made her an object instead of a human being. She had become, in a very real sense, Daddy's girl, all because of the fact that he was the moneymaker and she was the nonentity.

The Daddy Image

"Surely you're not serious. You must be old enough to be her father" (or even her grandfather).

Such a daring confrontation (or compliment) suggests the epitome of sexual success for the older male. It is a coup of the greatest magnitude.

The Daddy who needs this kind of ego satisfaction carefully ignores or blinds himself to the fact that his prowess is directly related to his wealth. Under such circumstances, who will complain of a little sexual embezzlement?

In almost every Daddy's girl relationship, whether it is an older man seeking sexual pleasures from a much younger woman or a father seeking to control an "uncontrollable" daughter, the elements of sex, money and power are related to varying degrees. These controls may be exerted in a subtle or blatant fashion, depending on the personalities of the male and female.

Nowhere was this intricate and tangled relationship more adroitly drawn than in the Daddy Browning—Peaches episode. The ingredients of sex, money and power exploded in this fatuous relationship.

Daddy Browning was millionaire Edward West Browning, who had made his fortune in New York real estate in the Roaring Twenties. His propensity for young girls made delicious gossip for the scandal sheets of that day. He was in his mid-fifties when a mad, impetuous passion swept over him as he looked upon plump, cuddlesome fifteen-year-old Frances Belle Heenan, an adorable flapper.

He instructed her, "Call me Daddy. I'm going to call you Peaches because you look like peaches and cream to me."

The two were married amidst a jungle of reporters, photographers and envious little girls who had missed this once-in-a-lifetime opportunity.

Like most Daddy's girl episodes, this one was shortlived. Six months after the wedding Daddy Browning found himself without his little girl.

Peaches decided to sue Daddy to find out just how rich he was. Daddy was no fool though, and his imposing courtroom appearance was in sharp contrast to Peaches's hysterical crying. The judge decided that Daddy was not going to be taken by this greedy flapper in spite of his lecherous urges.

Although Daddy and Peaches may be relegated to the absurd, their story points out the essential elements of a Daddy's girl relationship. If Daddy's sexuality is waning, then his earning abilities may be burgeoning because of his concentration on financial success. Prestige and power compensate for any shortage of virility. He is running the show. Regardless of his age, this composite of tangible and intangible assets allows him to tantalize or intimidate the female into a pattern of behavior that is in accord with his desires.

The Mama Image

If power in any of its various forms is the ultimate technique of male combat, then the opposite—powerlessness or weakness—is one of the most effective female tactics. This trait, in combination with sexual appeal, is one of the most lethal weapons at a woman's command. Almost all variations of Mama's grand strategy are related to one or both of these tactics.

In spite of the struggle for equality, the Victorian attitude of patriarchal supremacy is still very much in effect in male-female interrelationships. In reality, the average man's and woman's life is oriented principally by the vast residual influence of the concepts elucidated by Freud, Mill, and Shaw.

One of the most ardent feminists, Mary Wollstonecraft, understood only too well the unexpected avenues of expression that female sexuality takes in a stratified milieu. If a woman has been taught to spend all her time charming and pleasing her husband, what happens when familiarity dulls his ardor and enthusiasm? What is a woman to do?

The disappointed wife, Mary Wollstonecraft observed (and Shaw later confirmed), turns her charms on other males. What other males? Her sons offer her the best opportunity to exert her powers of persuasion and influence. Should a woman be indifferent to the consequences of infidelity, she can and on occasion does turn to younger men.

The Mama image necessarily conveys more subtle sexual implications than does the Daddy image. A woman functions in her Mama role in a gentler, more subdued fashion, despite the fact that her conduct may range from pathological authoritarianism to the power of helplessness or martyrdom.

Mama is more likely to say of her relationship with her son, "I have given my life for him." And this evaluation may indicate either the essence of altruism or the suffocating attachment inherent in immature ego satisfaction. In contrast, Daddy is inclined to interpret all female relationships—with mother, wife and daughter—in terms of his own sexual needs.

This fundamental difference arouses many of the competitive feelings that begin as sexual fascination, evolve in marriage into unresolved conflicts, and finally deepen into disappointment with a husband or wife. These dormant frustrations seek expression by way of a relationship with a son or daughter.

The cultivation of bonds of affection has its foundation in the highly complex forces of our cultural heritage, social conditioning, economic system and biological differences. None of these contributing factors have been nullified to any large extent, despite the struggles of women for equality and the modification of woman's role brought about by the biological revolution.

A Life for a Life?

The love-security that each human being finds in his childhood relationship with the parent of the opposite sex remains the key to his future sexual adjustment in marriage, regardless of all clamor for reversal of role playing in marriage and all unisexual attempts to blur the distinctions between Daddy and Mama.

When a man assumes the Daddy's role in a Daddy's girl relationship, or a woman does the same with respect to a son, there is an enormous range of possible emotional mutations.

Ego satisfactions are most urgently needed by the Daddy or Mama who is narcissistic, insecure or unable to cope with his or her sexual frustrations in a mature manner. This kind of Daddy or Mama parasitically attaches himself/herself to a daughter or son with such a frightening bond that "a life for a life" characterizes this relationship. Daddy or Mama subtly destroys the possibility of the daughter or son's achieving a future normal love relationship in marriage. An insidious pathological attachment is unwittingly cultivated under the camouflage of love for a child of the opposite sex.

However, there is another avenue of expression which Daddy or Mama may pursue. Not all Daddy's girl or Mama's boy relationships are detrimental. Some are beneficial. Although there is a peripheral sexual influence on the son or daughter's later emotional life, the primary impact is manifested in the subsequent contributions that the son/daughter makes to mankind in general.

Great intellectual achievements by a son/daughter may be the culmination of the altruistic sublimation of Daddy or Mama's sexual energies into a creative outlet through their offspring. Thus, in such instances, Daddy or Mama is selflessly deflecting ego satisfaction away from himself/herself and encouraging deep ego satisfaction in a son/daughter. The proud Daddy or Mama whose daughter/son receives recognition in school is one example. In these circumstances, love-security is achieved in an abstract, unemotional way.

From generation to generation, Daddy's girl or Mama's boy behavior continues in some modified form in each of us. The consequence, or harvest, is manifested in the interpersonal relationships each of us establishes in adult life.

2   The Hand That Rocks the Cradle

Variations of the Daddy's girl/Mama's boy theme are expressed in dramatic literature, novels, lyrics of popular songs, mythology. All represent the cultural acceptance of this phenomenon in human relationships.

Daddy

Daddy is intriguing. He has perplexing disguises. He is mentor, director, persuader. Daddy can take care of everything and make even the worst catastrophe in the life of his little girl appear absurd and even funny. There are moments in the life of every female when she would like to have Daddy smooth out all the knotty problems of her existence. Thus the Daddy's girl relationship flourishes because it affords varying degrees of emotional satisfaction to Daddy and his little girl.

G. B. Shaw understood the nuances of this relationship perfectly. In *Pygmalion,* Shaw explored the universal fascination of Daddy (Professor Higgins) for his little girl Eliza. With a knowing heart he delineated their all too human attraction for each other.

Professor Henry Higgins, an educated gentleman and master of phonetics, needs no introduction. Eliza Doolittle, the sharp-tongued Cockney flower girl, is an extraordinary match for him. The twenty years' difference in their ages enhances the muted sexual intrigue.

Never admitting his attachment to Eliza, Professor Higgins proceeds to transform her from a guttersnipe into a lady. She responds beautifully.

He dominates, insults, wheedles and browbeats her until she becomes a person utterly unlike her former self. Eliza becomes, under Professor Higgins's tutelage, a perfect lady.

During the metamorphosis Professor Higgins finds himself assuming the Daddy role. In fact, he assures her, "I'll adopt you as my daughter and settle money on you if you'd like. Or would you rather marry Pickering?"

Higgins is quite aware of the absurdity of his sly suggestion. That is why he confidently proposes the notion to Eliza.

She is disturbed and miserable. Her shopgirl's dreams of romance vanish in the brittle reality of Professor Higgins's unexpected shield of playful mockery.

Higgins protects himself from his true feelings by evasions. He tells Eliza, "Five minutes ago you were like a millstone round my neck. Now you're a tower of strength: a consort battleship. You and I and Pickering will be three old bachelors instead of only two men and a silly girl."

Obviously Professor Higgins is not that obtuse. He needs Eliza desperately. He needs to dominate and bully her. He enjoys the ego satisfaction of having her carry out his smallest whim on the pretext that it will aid in her transformation. He is, however, equally determined to avoid marriage. Why does he respond so skittishly?

One must remember the ever-loving Mrs. Higgins, who is as adroit as her son at weaving charismatic attachments. Professor Higgins cannot detach himself from her. Nonetheless, Henry Higgins has played Daddy to Eliza so long that he cannot and will not give her up without a struggle. He refuses to believe that she is leaving him.

So in his complacent arrogance he continues to order her about. As Eliza is bidding him farewell, he demands blithely, "Oh, by the way, Eliza, order a ham and a Stilton cheese, will you. And buy me a pair of reindeer gloves, number eights, and a tie to match that new suit of mine. You can choose the color. . . ."

Eliza will not permit Professor Higgins to have the last word. Indeed, her transformation has suffused her personality with self-confidence, so she answers in kind.

She says disdainfully, "Number eights are too small for you if you want them lined with lamb's wool. You have three new ties that you have forgotten in the drawer of your washstand. Colonel Pickering prefers double Gloucester to Stilton; and you don't notice the difference. I telephoned Mrs. Pearce this morning not to forget the ham. What you are going to do without me I cannot imagine." She sweeps out.

Shaw understood the idiosyncrasies of the human heart on the subliminal level, where decisions affecting human relationships are truly made. In accord with his character, Professor Higgins has savored his Daddy role to the hilt, and now there is a cruel wrench away from Eliza. What alternative does he have? Mrs. Higgins, his dearest Mama, has made life so pleasurable for him that he will revert back to the love-security she has always provided for him. He is not an unwilling captive.

Professor Higgins's unhappiness is only temporary; Shaw diagnoses his malady with unerring cunning. Eliza could never hope to corral Higgins into marriage because Mama came between them. Under Shaw's acrimonious scrutiny, a subtle array of Daddy traits are dramatized.

However, not all males who play Daddy have the incomparable charm of Professor Higgins. They offer a counterfeit love-security. And the little girl, whether she is child or woman, gravitates toward this ersatz satisfaction, for she is unaware of the profundity of genuine love.

Not until later in life when she is seeking adult relationships and possibly marriage does such a woman realize that her emotional destiny has been warped by Daddy. This poisoning is accomplished in a very gentle way with society's approval. For what is acceptable to society in the form of tradition, customs and mores is reflected in its literature, art and music.

The Daddy's girl theme is winkingly encouraged, for example, in lyrics of popular songs. "My Heart Belongs to Daddy" was made famous not only by Mary Martin's rendition of the lyrics, but by the relationship implicit in the title. So, too, was the magnetism of the relationship popularized by "Santa, Baby," sung by Eartha Kitt. And for a variation of this theme, Maurice Chevalier immortalized "Thank Heaven for Little Girls."

The abundance of such material indicates the potent force of this theme. It is so obvious and so often taken for granted that its power for good or evil tends to be obscured by its commonness. Particularly when ambivalent love-hate manifestations torment Daddy into expressing his needs for ego satisfaction does this power make its impact felt on his little girl.

Elizabeth Barrett Browning and her father Edward had just such an ambivalent relationship. Unfortunately, the authoritarian aspect of Edward Barrett's personality has been so strongly emphasized in dramatic literature that it has almost been forgotten that he was a loving and benevolent father according to Victorian standards.

If he needed to make Elizabeth an invalid for his own psychological satisfaction so that she would always be dependent on him, Edward Barrett also encouraged her early poetic efforts. He was proud of her creative abilities because they were a reflection of his good taste. Moreover, the fact that she could do nothing without him, or so he believed, enhanced his feelings of possessiveness.

Like all girls enmeshed in Daddy's subtle bondage, Elizabeth felt both love and constraint. Not until she met Robert Browning did she understand the profound harm of that constraint.

Edward Barrett's uncompromising prohibition against marriage for any of his children indicates one of the pathological possibilities in a Daddy's girl relationship. Here was an unusually sensitive, complex, authoritarian man who believed in Daddyhood by divine right. He could make or break the lives of his children, and indeed this is what he actually did by refusing to permit them to marry.

Despite Edward Barrett's protests and threats, Elizabeth Barrett did, of course, marry Robert Browning. She was the first of his children to overthrow the shackles he had imposed. At the same time she was very disturbed by her act of defiance. Elizabeth loved this unyielding man and apparently did not comprehend the insatiable depths of his ego needs.

After her marriage Elizabeth wrote to him, and he responded by forever rejecting her. Edward Barrett assuaged his ego wounds by denying her existence from that time on. She was as dead to him as if she had never been born. Shortly before his death he sent a packet of her letters to Robert Browning. They were unopened. Upon receiving news of Edward Barrett's death, Elizabeth collapsed completely.

This psychological retaliation on the part of Edward Barrett is not uncommon in a Daddy's girl relationship. There are those, like Elizabeth, who break the bonds and survive, and even blossom in an extraordinary love relationship, but there are others who are emotionally destroyed and merely wander from one Daddy to another for the rest of their adult lives.

In exchange for a promise of love-security, Daddy's girl accepts a muddled future.

Daddy is big and strong, and he becomes proportionately more powerful the more his little girl needs him and is dependent on him. This relationship affords Daddy abundant ego satisfaction at the expense of partial or total arrest of his little girl's psycho-sexual development. She is, therefore, conditioned not only to please the male, but to rely on him, never developing her own capacities for self-reliance.

Daddy is cast in the role of a giver, a protector, one who bestows material advantages in exchange for ego caresses. The more pleasurable the relationship is to him, the more he needs to control his little girl. Thus early in life the little girl develops a feminine response which she later repeats in relationships with other men.

It is Daddy who ties her shoe, washes a smudge off her face, kisses away a tear. It is Daddy who buys the cradle, and it is Daddy who is her first big date. It is Daddy who teaches her about men as no other man ever will. His responses to her establish the tenor of her future emotional and sexual life. He is a model of the man she will unconsciously yearn for when it is time to choose a husband. She is literally putty in his hands, and Daddy truly relishes the feelings of omnipotence. It is an elixir to his ego.

In her childhood days he may tweak her vulnerable ego with petty reproaches, neglect or derision, or he may satisfy his ego needs by intermittently lavishing flattery, gifts or expensive vacations on her in return for total submission. In either case the hurt may later explode in psychological maladies.

As his little girl grows from infancy to adolescence, Daddy reveals other facets of his character. If his wife has not cherished him as he had hoped she would, he turns his bruised ego to his little girl. She will make him feel marvelous.

Her awakening sexual and maternal instincts are exploited by Daddy.

He urges her to wait on him hand and foot if he can get away with it. She may begin to cook gourmet delicacies for him. He will teach her how to mix his favorite cocktail. A weary Daddy may grandly lay at her feet hints of sweeping victories at the office. This approach will confound her innocence and give Daddy a deep sense of virility.

Throughout the years, Daddy refuses to guide his little girl or to teach her values of any kind upon which to build her future life. That is not his department, he claims blithely, washing his hands of such nuisance tasks.

Unconscious captive that she is, Daddy's little girl insidiously assimilates his attitudes toward her. The relationship may purr along for years, and she may be aware only of the fact that she is Daddy's favorite. There is no comprehension of the gradual psychological maiming that is taking place.

Sometimes a very seriously disturbed parent will prepare his little girl for physical seduction, but this is usually preceded by psychological seduction. Such events may take place when a child is relatively young. The shock of such a calamity may be denied because of the shame and revulsion implicit in the act. As a consequence, Daddy's little girl may be irretrievably disturbed in all future relationships with men.

While Daddy may rely heavily on masculine charm to ensnare his unsuspecting little girl, there are other equally effective ways to exert his superiority and dominance, more lethal ways which enslave his victim by arousing feelings of dread, fear, anxiety and even hatred. These responses, like uncritical adoration and submission, provide a certain ego satisfaction which sustains Daddy.

Nowhere does a man have more power than in the domain of his own home. There all disguises, pretenses, simulations are shed. Daddy reveals himself as he is in all his humanness. And for the man who demands unconscious compensation for his lack of recognition or success in business or professional life, this humanness may involve feelings of bitterness and skepticism and a basic inability to cope with life. If he cannot achieve ego satisfaction in the world of his work, he may turn his attention to those most vulnerable to his demands, namely, his daughters.

He may fasten them to himself by eliciting pity from them at a very early age. This love substitute, Daddy knows, is extremely powerful. He may imbue his little girl with the attitude that the world is against him. And for good measure he will declare that his little girl's mother does not understand him either. This conspiracy of discontent may deepen through the years, as Daddy continuously nurtures the seeds of pity. Unaware of her exploitation, the little girl views life through Daddy's self-pitying haze.

If Daddy cannot bind her to him by this means, he may find satisfaction in other ways. For example, he may manacle his little girl to him by financial tyranny. Daddy may dole out money in such a miserly fashion that she comes to dread these encounters because she feels humiliated. He may further indoctrinate her over the years by suggesting that if she does something for him—namely, submit to his every demand—she might be given something in return. There are many varieties of emotional blackmail. He may hint that, should she refuse to submit to his demands, she will be sorry.

From her earliest years Daddy may convey to her the feeling that she is a financial burden to him. He may, as his little girl grows older, suggest that she may have to repay him for all the sacrifices he has made on her behalf. Thus a sense of vast, inescapable responsibility lurks in the shadowy future. Indeed, she may brood about her future life, fearful that somehow Daddy will always be there.

A sense of her own unworthiness having been established, Daddy's little girl dutifully walks the treadmill of bondage he has planned for her. If her feelings are less than love, they are not exactly hatred, because he has indoctrinated her with a sense of duty almost beyond her comprehension. The Daddy who seeks compensatory control of a daughter is alert to all opportunities for deprecation of any achievement which brings her recognition. Unconsciously Daddy is fighting a threat to his quavering ego. In order to be master of the situation, Daddy must appear to be superior to all females.

Hence, if there is even a remote possibility that his little girl is becoming seriously dedicated to work of any kind which could conceivably bring rewards, Daddy stifles her efforts and denounces her. He may attempt to frighten her by declaring that the use of her mind is a repudiation of her femininity. Daddy may, if all else fails, withhold financial aid for the education necessary to fulfill her potential.

So far we have been discussing Daddy at home. But what about those men who are emotionally or literally absent from the home? What impact do they have on their little girl? What happens when Daddy still lives at home although his sex life is a world apart? Then what are the consequences or repercussions in the life of his daughter? Daddy may have a second ménage complete with mistress if he can afford it. Or Daddy may be a Don Juan and sprint from one little girl to another so long as his energy and money hold out. In either case he probably will not seek to establish a relationship of bondage with a daughter, because his ego satisfactions are already being fulfilled in an affair with a woman who plays the little girl to his Daddy.

His natural daughter tends to be emotionally neglected. She may be bereft of love-security. Her view of Daddy is ambivalent and filled with sour doubts. Her unconscious response to him is to feel that this is the way it is with men, take it or leave it. Such a Daddy may offer crumbs of affection, such as gifts of expensive clothes, designed to soothe his guilty conscience. It is not unusual for him to advise her to grow up and accept men as they are instead of as she wishes them to be.

In essence, Daddy demolishes her burgeoning sensitivity and attraction to young men. He may do this when she is at an age where she is desperately, but unknowingly, yearning for love-security from a Daddy substitute. Her adolescence, as a consequence, may be filled with one sexual escapade after another, each ending in greater disillusionment. She does not feel promiscuous. She feels miserable. And Daddy may cruelly deliver the emotional death blow by referring to his little girl as a tramp while he continues to prance along his merry way.

The divorced Daddy may victimize his daughter by prevailing upon her to become cook/housekeeper/girlfriend if she is old enough. He may coax her into moving in with him, promising financial security for her future. Should he remarry or find a mistress, he may just as callously advise her to return home. His little girl has served his purpose.

Daddy is a product of a complex heritage: his personal genetic inheritance, religion, culture, tradition, education, the folklore and fads and mythology of his generation. Rarely does Daddy understand why he acts the way he does. Society has conditioned him to believe that if he is not in a position of dominance he lacks manliness.

Nonetheless Daddy is very real, and his sphere of influence over his little girl is intricate and tangled. If his primary concern is the satisfaction of his own ego needs, Daddy will mold a muddled, confused little girl who has substantial psycho-sexual problems.

She may be led to believe that she loves Daddy, and indeed she may, or she may have ambivalent feelings toward him or even hate him. All of her responses to him are the expression of her search for love-security, and Daddy, if he has fulfilled his ego needs at the expense of her emotional development, has ensured that her search for love-security will invariably end in disappointment.

Mama

Mama's ways are labyrinthine. She is a connoisseur of the checkmate stratagem.

Beneath the rustling satin and velvet of Freud's and Shaw's day and the denim skirts of today lurks the very same Mama, a little leaner perhaps, but as calculating and devious as ever.

As Daddy is a reflection of the thesis of male supremacy, Mama has been conditioned by the dilemma of biological destiny. Suddenly, with the eruption of women's liberation and the biological revolution, it seems that the female has been transformed beyond her wildest imagination.

Let us look back in order to look forward to learn just how much motherhood has changed.

Freud's theory of the perfection of the mother-son relationship was far-reaching and stimulated much dramatic writing.

Moreover, both Shaw's and Mill's astuteness in identifying marital and sexual disappointment as the influence on the mother-child relationship was delineated in considerable detail by liberationists in an earlier struggle for women's rights during the first part of the twentieth century.

One of the writers of this period, Sidney Howard, wrote a classic play called *The Silver Cord* on the mother-son theme, exposing the complex nuances of the tragic frustrations forced on women by the constraints imposed on them by society.

Mrs. Phelps, the mother, is at once grotesque, diabolical and tragic, a caricature of Freud's perfect mother. Although there is no doubt about her malefic influence on her two sons, there is another side to her nature.

Mrs. Phelps is a mother who has loved, but unwisely. She has been disappointed in marriage. Like some other miserable women, she has decided unconsciously to destroy the lives of her sons in order to enshrine her own ego. Mrs. Phelps believes that because she has been deprived of all other happiness in life, she will have to have her sons with her always.

She resents the marriage of her son David to an educated woman, Christina. Refusing to admit that they have any sex life, Mrs. Phelps sends them to separate bedrooms in the opening scene of the play. Quite fervently she demands recognition from Christina for her role as mother. Mrs. Phelps says, "Give us our due, Christina, . . . we made a great profession which I fear may be in some danger of vanishing from the face of the earth. We made a profession of motherhood. That may sound old-fashioned to you. Believe me, it had its value. I was trained to be a wife that I might become a mother. . . . For twenty-four years, since my husband died, I've given all my life, all my strength to Dave and Rob. They've taken the place of husband and friends for me. . . . I'm asking you, my dear Christina, not to take all my boy's heart."

Her dialogue throughout the play is one long rhapsody of self-delusion.

"David's always had my ideas. And they're very sound ones. . . ."

". . . No mother should expect any woman to love her son as she loves him."

"You're not going to let your happiness crowd me out entirely, are you, Dave, boy?"

". . . Let Dave find out for himself what he's done. She won't be able to hold him. She won't have time for a home and children. She won't take any more interest in him than Hester takes in you. But you, Robin, you can still be saved! I want to save you from throwing yourself away as Dave has. . . ."

". . . And you must remember what David, in his blindness, has forgotten: that mother love suffereth long and is kind; envieth not, is not puffed up, is not easily provoked; beareth all things; believeth all things; hopeth all things. . . . At least, I think my love does?"

And Robin, Mrs. Phelps's younger son, responds dutifully, "Yes, Mother."

Has there been a total metamorphosis in the role of motherhood since *The Silver Cord* was produced in 1926? Have the sex manuals, the contraceptives, the ideal two-child family, and higher education offered women greater fulfillment and thus stopped them from abusing the privilege of motherhood? Particularly in the rearing of male children, have any radical changes occurred that invalidate the observations made by Freud, Shaw and Mill with respect to the mother-child relationship?

Certainly the shift in emphasis from a male-dominated authoritarian marriage to a more democratic equalitarian relationship has tended to modify the husband's and wife's roles. Women's liberation has altered some of the externals of marriage and family life. A woman may pursue higher education and career opportunities which were heretofore closed to her. She may decide to accept or reject motherhood. Some women today choose motherhood without marriage, while the vast majority prefer marriage without the responsibilities of parenthood.

None of these changes, however, remove the risk inherent in every marriage relationship. The imposition of external social changes does not guarantee a transformation of inner attitudes, nor does it obliterate fundamental and vital biological differences.

Therefore, the woman of today is almost as vulnerable to emotional problems and obstacles as her grandmother or great-grandmother was. The modification in her maternal role brought about by higher education does grant her a certain area of self-fulfillment. If she is inclined to utilize this avenue of expression, it is possible that she may not feel the inner need to entangle her son in a Mama's boy relationship in order to satisfy her own frustrated ambitions.

However, the ego satisfactions—whether they are constructive or destructive—found in human relationships within marriage and the family can never be totally equated with career fulfillment outside the home, for the two ego needs are entirely different. Career fulfillment cannot compensate for failure to fulfill the complex personality needs of a woman.

Hence, Mama's needs today are as vital as ever, although they may appear in altered form. There is a unique quality about every mother-son relationship which makes it different from every other. At the same time, certain effects are common to almost all mother-son relationships, varying primarily in intensity, duration and the specific conditions within a family.

Mama tends to mold her son's personality within two very broad categories within which, from a psychological point of view, there are almost endless variations.

There is the conqueror, or aggressive, personality (which Freud recognized) and the passive, or dependent, personality.

Mama's world may appear to have been circumscribed in past generations, but her unrecognized scope of power lay in indirect tactics. Whether Mama works or is at home, the emotional climate of the lives of young children is still her very special domain, as it was in the past. It is Mama who interprets the world and its human relationships for her boy.

It is Mama who gives or withholds love. She is the image her boy will yearn for or avoid in all future relationships with women. It is Mama who will enable him to live the life of a normal male in marriage, or prevent him from realizing emotional satisfaction in his adult life. She may have dreams of greatness for her sons, born of her own suppressed ambitions and/or marital unhappiness. Sometimes Mama rears a conqueror because her husband is mediocre and hence she has been denied ego satisfaction—this is not necessarily a deleterious influence on her son's life. Although she may sow the seeds of the conqueror in her boy's life, he may still be unable to realize the love-security that can be found in a mature relationship because his psychic energies have been deflected to other areas of ego satisfaction.

Mama's ambitious proclivities are frequently mingled with hostile reactions to any other woman whom her son may love. Fearful of losing him, Mama indoctrinates him from boyhood with the concept that he needs her, whereas the truth of the matter is that she needs him for her own ego satisfaction. Such a Mama may advocate career achievement at the expense of emotional satisfaction in marriage.

By using subtle forms of discouragement and creating feelings of guilt in her son, she may dissuade him from a normal interest in sex and marriage. Mama may ridicule or deny her son's need for a marriage relationship, or she may express revulsion at the notion of an active sexual life for her son.

"No woman is good enough for my son" is the tentacle approach Mama employs to ward off all other females, whom she considers enemies. This Mama may indeed spur her son on to extraordinary achievement, but the price she demands is pedestal tribute.

There are many men of phenomenal achievement who married late in life or relinquished marriage entirely because of Mama's influence.

Andrew Carnegie, for instance, was forty-four when he finally became enamored of a young girl of twenty-two. Not until his mother had been dead for a year did he dare to marry—at the advanced age of fifty-two.

And Mackenzie King, former Prime Minister of Canada, was raised by a forceful Mama who was determined that her son would become a man of destiny. Quite inconsiderately, and not at all according to Mama's plans, Mackenzie King fell in love with a young nurse while he was studying for his degree in Chicago. Mama so effectively dominated his life that he found himself apologizing to her for considering marriage. He poured out 21,000 words of regret in a letter to her and remained unmarried.

When Mama creates a conqueror within her son she establishes a pattern of emotional response that may continue unmodified throughout his life. Essentially what Mama gives to him is an uncommon degree of self-confidence based on her uncritical admiration of him. Thus, from childhood days on, such a son will seek complete idolatry from the women in his life. Should a woman attempt to express herself as an individual and cease to be a reflection of his ego wishes, the relationship ends.

The conqueror son requires constant adulation and affirmation. Any contrary expression constitutes treason. Unfortunately Mama has instilled this trait in him with such consummate skill that he does not realize the emotional problems he brings to marriage.

Another facet of Mama's idolatry is revealed in her attitude "My son, right or wrong." This is her concept of love. Such nurturing can cause a son to develop a wayward personality; a son raised under this influence may be brutal and exploitative in his relationships with women.

As an adult he may interpret a relationship only in terms of what a woman can do for him sexually, never considering his responsibility. He may demand subservience in all areas of marriage, treating his wife like a frightened private while he plays commanding general. Not surprisingly, he does not find the love-security he seeks. The constant thwarting of this desire may cause him to wander from one woman to another all his life, never aware of the source of his unhappiness.

Mama's stratagems may also mold a passive, dependent son. Instead of concentrating her energies on producing a conquering, aggressive male, Mama may find her greatest ego satisfaction in overprotecting her son. She may prevent him from realizing his masculinity by binding him to her so forcefully that he cannot escape.

Such a son may manifest an amazing variety of traits, many of which may appeal to a young woman considering marriage to him. He is boyish and charming. He appeals to her maternal instincts. She may find him irresistible and good-natured because he lets her have her way. She feels a need to do things for him, primarily because he leaves things undone.

He appears devoted to Mama, and this trait a young woman interprets in terms of herself. He will also be kind and gentle in marriage, she believes. It does not occur to her, when she is assessing his personality, that he may run home to Mama under stress. Under the mask of docility fester gradations of frustration, anger, resentment, vindictiveness and hatred. Mama evokes ambivalent feelings at best, but her boy hides such emotions even from himself, except under crisis conditions.

He feels victimized, and he tries to perpetuate these same feelings in his adult relationships with women. He is unable to perceive any other latent traits in his character, for he fears that if he breaks the bonds of attachment to Mama, she may never recover.

Frequently a Mama enslaves her son by overprotecting him during childhood illnesses. She may exploit a temporary malady, turning it into a permanent state of convalescence. Mama treats him psychologically like an invalid until he becomes one. The more ego satisfaction she derives from his feelings of dependency, the more she encourages this tragic response from him.

Mama's needs are not always expressed in hovering, smothering caresses and overbearing decisions. More serious personality disturbances result from interpersonal relationships characterized by neglect, indifference, rejection, alcoholism or other character disorders.

Then Mama's boy may develop responses of contempt, disgust and hatred, which he may reveal only later in life by acts of sexual delinquency, aggression, rape or murder. Such acts may be combined with a life of promiscuity, so that while he appears to have found counterfeit love-security in the role of a gigolo, Don Juan or deviate, he is actually acting out his childhood frustrations in violence against women.

Mama may express shock, indignation or grief at her boy's adult behavior. She will honestly feel that it runs counter to everything she has taught him. For she will believe that she has given him love, despite the fact that she has created for him a network of duplicity, guilt, martyrdom and unrequited sexual feelings from which he does not know how to escape, except by venting these very same emotions in a relationship with another woman.

Should Mama be castigated? Has she created swaggering, arrogant, frightened brutes and effeminate, trembling, agitated eunuchs?

Are Mama and Daddy villains wreaking immeasurable havoc in the lives of their boys and girls? Or are they repeating mindlessly the patterns of past generations?

In Western civilization marriage has evolved into an essentially materialistic, competitive contract which fails to recognize the emotional and spiritual facets of human nature. Husband and wife are locked into a rivalry from which only one mate can emerge the winner; the other mate eventually concedes defeat and accepts inferiority.

The logical results of such a competitive approach to marriage are manifested in the psycho-sexual wounds the protagonists bequeath to their children. Ego satisfaction for Daddy and Mama, who are stalemated in a furious battle for sexual love and/or power, can only be purchased at the price of arrested psycho-sexual development of the child.

The love-security that each child yearns for can be realized only if Daddy and Mama change their competitive approach to a cooperative one. In this way they can concentrate their efforts on nurturing the child's psycho-sexual development by providing him with the love-security he needs.

3

Authority and Freedom: Beyond Daddy and Mama

As the child matures, he ventures into the world outside of the home, and his relationship with Daddy/Mama becomes part of a larger, more complex frame of reference. He is constantly adjusting his personality to fit the requirements of externally imposed authority symbolized by law and institutions. His personal freedom, internally monitored and modified by a value system that is religious/philosophical in nature, is not as easily adapted.

The child's primary experience center beyond Daddy and Mama is the school setting. It is important to remember that the child is also gradually building his self-image in this ever-widening sphere of influence. His initial attitude toward himself comes with him from the parental milieu.

The child is unconsciously saying to his teacher and classmates, "This is what I learned at home. This is how I feel about myself because this is the way Daddy and Mama treat me." Thus the healthy or adverse effects of Daddy's and Mama's response to the child, the stepping-stones to future life adaptation or maladaptation, are brought out in the classroom. The attitudes the child ultimately develops toward authority, freedom and frustration come from both the home and the school.

In order for a child to establish the foundation of self-worth based on his own individuality and his relationships with other human beings, he needs to develop a proper understanding of authority and freedom. The purpose of authority, from a psychological point of view, is the ultimate development of self-direction and self-regulation so that an individual may live a resourceful and abundant life. Rarely is the concept of authority interpreted in this way. Instead, today we live in an era in which all of authority's symbolic and practical manifestations are suspect. Authority has become equated with tyranny and is considered to be an unalloyed evil. From the child's point of view (and that of those adults who never developed a mature attitude) authority constitutes an oppressive human condition whereby an individual or institution compels one to conform arbitrarily to a set of objective rules or a particular standard of conduct.

Authority is thought of as a burden implacably opposed to freedom, personal happiness and love-security. The notion that a society, and specifically the individuals within that society, may begin to experience deterioration without adherence to some sort of legitimate authority is perceived only gradually in adolescence and early adulthood.

The role of authority as a transitional link between Daddy and Mama and the school setting is frequently misinterpreted. To many individuals, authority equals discipline equals punishment or severe arbitrary restrictions imposed in order to "teach a lesson" (i.e., compel one not to repeat some undesirable activity). A common and unexamined notion embraces this punitive and limiting aspect to such an extent that the role of legitimate authority in leading the human personality toward self-regulation and self-direction is ignored or repudiated.

Daddy and Mama and teachers may begin an early victimization of a daughter/son by passing off punitive discipline as authority. The effects on the child's personality responses in later human relationships may be difficult or impossible to modify.

Consider, for example, the Mama who slaps her four-year-old son into hysterical tears because the child inadvertently drops a glass container on a supermarket aisle when the two are shopping.

Look at the proud intellectual Daddy whose ten-year-old daughter simply does not understand math. "You stupid idiot," he growls at her.

Or consider the teacher who refuses to allow a child to use a bathroom because it is within his authority to "lay down the law."

Authority has fallen into contempt as a legitimate vehicle for developing the human personality, partly because of the personality problems of many of the individuals who are in a position to administer it. As a consequence, authority is often associated with punitive harshness, restriction and victimization, and in this form is utilized to misshape and misdirect human lives.

Properly applied, however, authority facilitates the child's gradual movement *away* from the normal dependence on Daddy and Mama and *toward* the eventual self-direction and self-regulation of satisfying adult interpersonal relationships. Any other application is a distortion and can, by limiting normal growth and development, cause personality problems.

In contrast, freedom is assumed to be an unequivocal good. The child's inner comprehension may be translated as, "When I grow up, I'll do exactly as I please." One of the child's conclusions is, then, that one's happiness and love-security are proportionate to the degree of freedom one enjoys. The complexities of freedom are, however, still veiled; they remain to be learned in the course of various life experiences. The child does not plan ahead (one facet of freedom of choice); he cannot yet envision the rewards or consequences of his actions. These factors are constantly being monitored for him by Daddy/Mama and teachers.

Without the compensating balance of legitimate authority, freedom may, in fact, be hazardous to the human personality. Psychological and historical data suggest that an individual reared in a permissive milieu will sometimes utilize unlimited freedom to exploit or harm others. Conversely, too much authoritarianism, as distinguished from legitimate authority, acts as a deterrent to the normal development of self-direction in the individual and can be an obstacle to the forming of wholesome and happy personal relationships.

Coping with this tension between authority and freedom (the yearning to determine one's own destiny through satisfying human relationships) requires an ongoing process of adjustment, integration and reevaluation. Crucial to this life process is a reconciliation, on the most intimate levels of human interaction, of the needs for authority and freedom. Only this will provide a basis for the constellation of traits that constitute love-security.

The capacity to reconcile the tension between authority and freedom is, to a great extent, an unconscious process of assimilating parental attitudes toward frustration. The manner in which the child learns to respond to the inevitable frustrations of life as they exist within this authority/freedom context will be crucial in shaping his future life and his future relations with others. A simple definition of frustration might be our reaction to all those unexpected and undesired life circumstances in which "we don't get our own way."

Although there are a great many human responses to frustration, the child begins to take his cues from Daddy/Mama before he comprehends the long-range effects of this assimilative process. If Daddy has a low tolerance for frustration and manifests his feelings in angry outbursts or other destructive behavior, a daughter may adopt some variation of this maladaptation. Should Mama whine or "develop a headache" and lie in bed all day because of frustration of some sort, it is possible that her son will develop similar techniques for protecting himself from reality.

Conversely, when parents utilize frustration constructively to overcome societal and personal obstacles, the child will be receptive to alternative solutions as a means of growth. A son/daughter can begin to perceive in preschool years that just because one does not get one's own way, the world still goes on, and in order to adapt to it through interpersonal relationships, one must make an effort to surmount frustration and redirect energy.

These concepts—the balancing of authority and freedom and the capacity to utilize frustration in a constructive or destructive manner—serve as a bridge from the home environment to the school, where further complex personality adjustments will unfold, foretelling the child's eventual interpersonal adaptation.

Childhood

The child's self-esteem is undergoing impalpable change and development as he ventures into the school milieu. Two continuing experiences give dimension to his world. One is his positive or negative adaptation to the school situation. The second is his growing awareness of Daddy and Mama as mere human beings, possessing considerably less than godlike authority.

Freedom of choice becomes an awesome reality when the child enters the classroom. No longer is Daddy or Mama supervising every waking moment. A new symbol of authority, the teacher, becomes an extension of the familiar parental figure.

New horizons seem to appear. The child perceives that he now has individual decisions to make, although they are still defined by the parent/teacher authority frame of reference. Will he do his homework? Will he read? Watch television? Practice his music lesson? There are countless possibilities.

But within the world of the home it is really Daddy and Mama who determine the success or failure of the child's adaptation in school. Do they care whether he learns to read and to understand math? Are they too busy to care about his struggling efforts? Is life at home full of explosive quarrels, desertions, egocentric forays? Or is life at home comfortable and secure? Do Daddy and Mama have time to share and examine the day's school lessons? Do they scold, threaten, abuse, ignore the child? Do they encourage, stimulate, comfort, guide, love?

There are multiple nuances of response which tell the child whether his school life is important or irrelevant to Daddy/Mama. Although the child cannot identify his experiences in complicated language, he responds with "I like" or "I feel," and he knows whether the school environment is a dreaded or desired experience.

The future school dropout, the delinquent, the achiever, the feminist, the latent misogynist, the scholar sit side by side in the early years, innocently unaware of the future. What do they think? See? Feel? Stand in the corner. Shame on you. Why can't you learn? What's the matter with you? Why do you fight all the time? Why do you let the other kids push you around?

Daddy and Mama reenter their own childhood vicariously. The academic and character potentialities of the child constitute a powerful stimulus for the parent who is genuinely concerned with the delicate balance between authority and freedom. The mature and benevolent Daddy and Mama do not envision the child as a sort of alter ego who exists solely to fulfill their expectations. Instead, they understand that cooperation with the school and continuous supportiveness of the child comprise a secure foundation which will encourage gradual movement toward self-direction and self-regulation. With his parents' help the child develops inner strength and self-esteem. He learns that temporary setbacks and even failure are a part of the life experience first unfolded in the school setting. Instead of yielding to frustration by manifesting self-destructive and antisocial behavior, he attempts alternative courses of action. For this is the pattern that Daddy and Mama established for him.

Moreover, this pattern is not an isolated intellectual experience, but includes the child's most profound feelings about himself. The child will not withdraw from the effort to grow toward self-direction and self-regulation if he understands, with his feelings, that Daddy and Mama do care about him and will not abandon him, figuratively speaking, during these early attempts.

A temporary learning setback or an actual failure constitutes a crucial test of frustration reactions; Daddy and Mama's misunderstanding of authority may first emerge at such a time. The overprotective parent—or the one who threatens, ignores, discourages or manifests any other sort of powerful negative response—initiates an emotional alignment within the child which is later very difficult to restructure. The negative parental response usually occurs within the framework of restrictive or punitive authority. The child is subjected to humiliation of some sort (which may include physical punishment), and he loses a measure of self-esteem, which further reinforces the harsh experience of frustration.

As a consequence, frustration becomes a totally negative experience, one that is resisted passively or defied aggressively. This attitude is later manifested in antisocial behavior. Self-direction and self-regulation are thwarted, and the child unconsciously develops a hostile attitude toward authority. At the same time, the child unintentionally deceives himself by telling himself that he will not try in school (and later in life) so that he cannot be forced to submit to humiliation or external restraints because of some degree of failure.

A second vital area of perception is changing at the same time: the child is becoming aware of the humanness and fallibility of Daddy and

Mama. They are still indispensable creatures, but they have their moments of doubt, anxiety and impatience. They make mistakes.

Moreover, the child realizes that Daddy and Mama have a distinct life of their own. Sometimes he discovers that this separate life is so all-absorbing that there is little time left for him. Or he may find that there is only Daddy or Mama to care for him. Through desertion, death or divorce, the other parent is no longer present in his everyday life. At any rate, the child becomes accustomed to a certain kind of parenting and the feeling of being loved or unloved. The child's attitude toward his sexual self is mingled with his attitudes toward school, teacher, classmates and all that the world beyond the home symbolizes.

If the child is fortunate, his parents love him and accept him as he is, without qualifications, and exhibit this love by helping him achieve a balanced attitude toward authority and freedom and some understanding of the nature of frustration in interpersonal relationships.

By the time the child enters adolescence, certain patterns of response toward authority and freedom will have become apparent, and these will serve as the model for his more complex adolescent self still to develop.

In every case, it is Daddy and Mama who, by their altruism or egocentricity, provide a pattern of response for the child to emulate. This pattern either enables him to take the next step in developing interpersonal relationships or impedes his progress by setting up emotional barriers in the form of destructive or antisocial characteristics.

A well-adapted child exhibits a proper understanding of freedom and of authority, including acceptance of a religious/philosophical value system. The son/daughter who will eventually be capable of self-regulation and self-direction utilizes frustration as a means of growth and development.

Conversely, the child who will emerge as a troubled, withdrawn, extremely aggressive, antisocial, delinquent or sexually precocious adolescent will indicate maladaptation in the early school setting. The primary contributing factor can always be found in the child's family life: there has invariably been some extreme distortion of the concepts of authority and freedom. Frustration has developed into a self-destructive vehicle because Daddy/Mama has acted out—either through some manner of direct abuse of the child or through his/her individual traits (alcoholism, random promiscuity, unstable job record)—a negative behavior pattern which acts to restrict the normal maturation potential of the child.

Problem children almost always have problem parents and a serious lack of comprehension of the function of authority and freedom as it is related to human interaction.

Similarly, the manner in which frustration is managed by Daddy/Mama will be reflected in the child's social behavior and in his academic progress in the school milieu. If Daddy/Mama patiently guides the child's emotional development, stressing the idea that frustration is an everyday life experience that can be managed constructively for the growth of an individual, desirable personality traits and academic achievement can be anticipated.

Adolescence

During adolescence a pattern of adaptation or maladaptation is taking shape. The struggle for freedom, self-direction and self-regulation may become the prime battleground in families where there is a disturbed marital or parent-child relationship.

The adolescent is eager to grasp adult privileges and rewards, while still retaining the security and supportiveness of Daddy/Mama. As he experiments with freedom and self-regulation, he enters into a world of more complex and subtle frustrations. The adolescent's emerging maturity or immaturity is very definitely related to certain profound life conditions, which are continuing to mold his capacity to adapt to enduring interpersonal relationships.

One of these conditions is his success or failure adaptation in the school setting. This pattern is usually a continuation of his earlier adjustment in elementary school. However, there are additional ramifications. The adolescent now understands more clearly that there is a relationship between his efforts and future educational accomplishments/career recognition. If academic achievement is not very important to Daddy/Mama, the adolescent may take the line of least resistance unless there is some influential teacher or other adult who encourages him to pursue another course of action.

If an adolescent understands that his/her parents value an achievement pattern in academic life, and Daddy and Mama have encouraged self-direction and self-regulation, a son/daughter grows into responsibility and an appreciation of selective freedom. That is, the adolescent is more inclined to respect Daddy/Mama's experiences and judgment as guides in developing his own self-direction. The transitional adjustment to self-regulation can be achieved with a minimum of parent-child tension if freedom is encouraged in proportion to the child's ability to deal with gradually emerging complex life situations. Naturally, this ideal situation implies that there is optimum understanding between Daddy/Mama and the adolescent.

The adolescent is also aligning himself with a peer group that shares his success or failure adaptation. At this phase of development, boys and girls who are achievement-oriented are establishing friendships with those of their peers who have comparable goals; such friendships will strengthen self-esteem and promote a constructive life adaptation. Conversely, those adolescents who are developing serious personality problems (reflected in occasional or even continuing antisocial acts) generally seek out unhappy and confused peers as associates. This is not, of course, surprising, but it does portend a pattern of development that can be averted if Daddy and Mama understand how they are contributing to the formation of a problem-ridden future.

There are tangible examples of Daddies and Mamas who unwittingly support such development. For instance, Nancy, age sixteen, is given a new car as a birthday present by her doting Daddy even though she is failing in school. Or Mama promotes her seventeen-year-old son's precocious sexual activities so that he will be occupied with girls and then she can devote time to her live-in lover. Daddy refuses to attend a school science fair where his daughter won first prize because he believes that science is a man's world. Mama promises her son that she will remain sober long enough to watch him compete on the school debate team, but she shows up in an alcoholic haze.

The adolescent who is aware of parental indifference to his success or failure in school is likely to turn to antisocial expressions of retaliation. The fifteen-year-old girl who is pregnant frequently has an absentee or unsupportive father. The seventeen-year-old adolescent who is picked up on a felony charge may find that his escalating antisocial behavior is the only way he can "get even" with Mama for either her extreme authoritarianism or her extreme permissiveness, either of which tells him that she does not care what happens to him.

Thus, whether the adolescent succeeds or fails in this primary arena of self-direction and self-regulation outside the home depends on the degree of supportiveness and the quality of the role-model behavior provided by Daddy and Mama.

A second major environmental factor shaping the adolescent personality at this time is the actual strength or weakness of Daddy and Mama as marital partners. By this time the parental marriage will either have grown in cohesiveness and loyalty or else have become deadlocked in a controversy that will eventually result in divorce. The adolescent is either learning that human beings in intimate relationships can strengthen each other in all sorts of unforeseeable life circumstances, or serving as a reluctant witness to the use of desertion or divorce as a means of ending relationships that are no longer pleasurable or meaningful.

The emotional stresses on Daddy and Mama as husband and wife have a profound impact on the capacities of the adolescent for self-regulation and self-direction. A daughter/son begins to comprehend the more subtle uses of frustration in interpersonal relationships.

If Daddy or Mama will not tolerate any degree of frustration in the marital relationship and seeks a no-fault solution, the adolescent is susceptible to a similar pattern of adaptation. Frustration becomes a negative vehicle of personality expression. Instead of being a means of personal growth, it causes the adolescent to circumscribe his/her latent capacities for emotional growth. He/she is guided solely by the desire to avoid frustrating experiences and refuses to recognize that frustration has any constructive function in interpersonal relationships.

Thus the parental marriage either enhances the self-esteem of the daughter/son or frightens the adolescent about intimate relationships. He can learn that Daddy and Mama are mature people who grow closer together as they face life's adversities. Or else the adolescent may be misled by the egocentric behavior of one or both parents to believe that relationships are meant to be temporary.

The transition to self-regulation/direction must also be examined within a third context of adaptation. This is the adolescent's coming to terms with his/her sexual self. Once again in this sphere a child's success or failure adaptation will reveal exactly the sort of impact Daddy and Mama have had on the daughter/son in the childhood and early adolescent years. The adolescent's religious/philosophical value system, any effects of parental narcissism or altruism, his way of coping with frustration—all these factors converge in the individual adolescent's attitude toward his sexual self.

Here he/she is on the brink of aligning himself/herself with a pattern of sexual decisions which will probably characterize his/her future adult life. Seeking love, appreciation and an acknowledgment of his manhood/her womanhood, the adolescent ventures forth in a quest for reassurance. By this time some mode of adaptation or maladaptation is already evident.

The adolescent who engages in random sexual activity because he/she "cannot help himself/herself" is revealing a pattern of ineffective self-regulation and self-direction. He/she may have been misdirected by the parental pattern. Or the societal pressure to conform by engaging in precocious sexual activity may have tipped the scales in favor of a behavior pattern that will lead to later personality problems and confusion.

There are variations of the constructive and destructive patterns of adaptation with respect to the sexual self. The adolescent may participate in sexual activities not so much to assure himself/herself that he/she is loved as out of a belief in the "sex for sex's sake" pattern, which is characteristic of our current narcissistic interpretation of individuality. Not only is the adolescent unaware of the long-range consequences of such a self-destructive pattern, but he may find that these actions have the immediate consequence of compelling him to reexamine the concepts of self-regulation, self-direction and frustration.

In other words, the adolescent perceives once again that he/she is not merely a physical being. He/she begins to understand that sexual responses and satisfactions cannot be isolated from the larger context of his/her total personality. Paradoxically, while his/her awareness of sexual possibilities is deepening, he/she is also venturing into the more sophisticated terrain of his/her emerging adult personality, which necessarily will include an acceptance or a rejection of some kind of religious/philosophical value system.

Thus the child's personality comes full cycle, and he/she enters into his/her own selfhood. He/she is the young man/woman Daddy and Mama have, in effect, created by the influence of their personalities on the child's ultimate self-regulation and self-direction.

The adult man/woman now has an essential pattern of attitudes, learned consciously and unconsciously, with which to deal effectively or ineffectively with other human beings. This does not mean, of course, that his/her personality is irrevocably unmodifiable if he/she discovers that certain personality deficiencies are preventing him/her from leading an abundant life. Rather, the significance of this essential pattern of attitudes lies in those latent capacities which are continuously unfolding at every stage of human life and which can conceivably function for the benefit of human relationships if they are called into use.

One way of understanding the gradual self-regulation and self-direction process is to evaluate a child's behavior at any given age in the light of Daddy's and Mama's influence. Parental behavior which is excessively authoritarian and disregards the child's unique nature will result in a pattern of concealed frustration, anger and even hatred. So, too, will parental behavior that reflects a narcissistic personality. The son/daughter will be incapable of assuming any sort of self-regulation and self-direction because he/she will have been too heavily manipulated by Daddy/Mama's personality deficiencies. Hence these important psychological developments may be obstructed indefinitely, or they may occur later on in life as a result of a specific crisis. Family or individual therapy may restore this capacity for self-regulation/direction.

The altruistic Daddy and Mama provide a congenial family life which promotes self-regulation/direction at each stage of the child's development. Parental awareness implies that there is continuing love-security expressed through supportiveness, compassion and legitimate authority instead of restrictive authoritarianism. A crucial determinant of such a philosophy of child-rearing is respect for the child and an understanding that he/she is a unique human being.

There are, of course, gradations of the abusive authority/power pattern. Daddy and Mama may grow in maturity and develop an ability to deal with frustration that may eventually prove advantageous to the child. Or they may believe that they can do with their children whatever they wish. This can lead to many types of disturbed behavior ranging from sadistic exploitation to an equally misdirected attitude of total permissiveness. The child's capacity to develop his/her potential for self-regulation and self-direction is related to Daddy's and Mama's ability to exercise legitimate authority.

4

The Single Life Style

In this era of relationships uncluttered by the impediments of law, marriage—with its prize of love-security and exclusivity of sex—is dimming as a chosen goal.

Sex without marriage is unhampered by the confining restrictions of law, society and custom. Odious comparisons between those who marry and those who do not have almost vanished from our contemporary world of meaningful relationships. Yet upon examination, we find that beneath the perfunctory interpretation lie unconscious reasons and explanations for the popularity of the single life style.

The man or woman who chooses to ignore the religious/cultural heritage of Western civilization by not marrying does so apparently out of a belief in experimental relationships. Is this a genuine repudiation of all past tradition? Or is it merely a tentative and temporary solution, for want of a more penetrating analysis of the individual search for love-security? Has the unmarried man or woman found a superior or at least an equally satisfying way of meeting his human needs?

Beneath the euphemisms with which people explain their decision not to marry are hidden tangled and profound unconscious reasons directly related to a son's or daughter's early relationship with Mama/Daddy.

From youth to old age, those who do not marry repeat a pattern based on a self-imposed restriction against marriage. The decision not to marry is deliberate, but unconscious; sometimes it is the result of an unhappy marriage that has indelibly scarred a person's attitudes. Daddy's girl and Mama's boy are shackled to their solitary lives by socially inappropriate feelings of revulsion, contempt, pity, psychological indebtedness, fear and worthlessness in varying degrees of intensity.

Adults can often create a façade that will pass superficial scrutiny, but a probe beneath its surface will find the seething, festering passions of a wounded childhood that make marriage a psychological impossibility.

In some families one son will marry and another will not. A daughter may marry several times because of divorce or widowhood or a combination of both. Another daughter will never marry. Is an individual's life direction entirely fortuitous?

During early adulthood it is the exceptionally perceptive man or woman who can accurately predict the nature of his future—marital or solitary. In this phase of life the state of being "in love" is common to those who will marry and to those who will not. Rarely does a young adult express on a conscious level his intention not to marry, unless he or she is going into a form of religious life which requires a vow of chastity and precludes the possibility of marriage.

The need to experience love-security is as intense in those men and women who do not marry as it is in those who do. But because of their relationship with their parents, and particularly the parent of the opposite sex, their quest for emotional fulfillment is unconsciously directed away from marriage. Usually they have been inhibited by searing experiences in their relationship with Daddy or Mama. These are the individuals whose arrested psychological development has maimed their capacity to enjoy love-security in its fullest expression.

Such sons and daughters may move away from the parental home during their college years never to return again, or to return only at a time of crisis, such as a terminal illness. Or such sons and daughters may remain in the parental home long after youth has passed, their true feelings disguised under the obligation of duty.

Whether the result is physical proximity or separation, the psychological reverberations of childhood always weave an ensnaring cocoon of emotional bondage.

Such Daddy's girls and Mama's boys have never achieved that degree of psychological liberation which would enable them to find love-security in marriage. Unconsciously, they are led by their feelings for

Daddy or Mama to fear marriage and, at times, childbirth and child-rearing.

Contempt

More than depth of emotional response separates those who marry from those who do not marry. By the time early adulthood is reached, one has already acquired a complex network of learned behaviors; this network may include an unconscious admonition to be suspicious of or to avoid marriage.

The love-security quest often veers away from marriage because of one's hidden response to a parent of the opposite sex. At the same time, feelings of contempt, hostility and buried rage against Daddy/Mama may also need to be satisfied. Thus two divergent and conflicting passions battle for supremacy.

Love-security will be sought in a sexual relationship, but the relationship will not culminate in marriage. Often the first partner of a man with this emotional heritage will be a slightly older woman, and she may initially seduce him. A young woman who has powerful unconscious feelings of contempt for Daddy will often "choose" an older man, who will temporarily satisfy her insatiable need for love-security. In either situation, the promise of marriage may be mockingly offered, although the sexual partners have no intention of making a legal marriage.

The need to punish Daddy or Mama is built into the sex-without-marriage relationship, even if it endures for an extraordinary length of time.

Typically, an individual's feelings of contempt are eventually manifested in the relationship with the current sexual partner. Unconsciously, the emotions of childhood are transmitted and reconstructed.

At what point do they emerge, since the love-security need is satisfied with sex? Moreover, why should a man or woman ostensibly fulfilled in a relationship without commitment proceed to subtly destroy its foundations? The unconscious compels him/her to "punish" over and over again the "guilty" Daddy/Mama of childhood.

Premonitions of sexual discontent occur. The relationship may not be as intense as the man wishes it to be. Or he may seek the variety of two partners at a time, an older woman who acts as surrogate mother/mistress and a younger woman who naively hopes for a marriage that will never take place. Trapped in his self-created maze of sexual futility, a man may indeed begin to feel victimized, especially if one or both women are demanding marriage.

In order to extricate himself from such a tangled triangle, he unconsciously employs the emotional weapons of contempt and rage in a multitude of disguises. His unconscious wish to terminate the relationships is justified in his conscious thinking by the disagreeable demands of marriage that are being made upon him.

Characteristically, this pattern is repeated with imaginative variations throughout the man or woman's life so frequently that he or she does not learn from any of these sexual episodes. He or she feels victimized and unhappy, but completely justified in his or her maimed attitudes toward members of the opposite sex.

As age and desperation intensify the need for love-security, such a man or woman may drift recklessly from one relationship to another, becoming more and more deeply mired in feelings of self-contempt. The original need to punish Daddy or Mama has been blurred by time and repetitious affairs with no enduring love-security.

In some instances the death of Daddy or Mama severs the cord, and a now aging son or daughter may stumble into a "new" relationship, hoping to find the love-security he/she feels has been denied him/her all through life. In the majority of cases, not even death unravels the complex emotions enough to relieve the self-inflicted agony of the man or woman who has tragically nurtured the seeds of an unfulfilled life.

Love-security substitutes, such as money, power and status, are sought after and secured by men and women who do not fulfill their human needs in enduring relationships. Vast material possessions are successfully acquired by these individuals, who unconsciously yearn instead for warmth and abiding closeness.

The unexamined inner void is never filled, and the emotional life of such a man or woman is mute testimony to the ravages of the childhood relationship with Daddy or Mama.

Exploitation

Arrested psychological development may predispose a man or woman toward unconscious exploitation of sexual partners. The emotional malaise manifests itself in paradoxical activities.

An individual may appear to have a normal desire to marry. Many dates and appointments with seemingly marriageable men or women fill his or her social calendar. Engagements may be announced—and then very discreetly broken. The reasons are hidden in rumors. No one, neither family nor friends, can be sure exactly why the relationships were terminated.

During the individual's twenties and thirties, when most of his peers are marrying, he may manifest antisocial tendencies from time to time, but there may not be any clearly defined pattern of sexual exploitation.

Without comprehending the psychological dichotomy that urges him to seek love-security outside of marriage, a man, for example, will boastfully proclaim that he is eager to marry and settle down.

At the same time, he will conveniently choose non-marriageable (to him) women as his sexual partners. He may fall in love with a divorcee who has children, but he will not marry her. If the truth were known, he would prefer to marry a virgin. However, he is perfectly willing to exploit a woman sexually until he tires of the relationship and finds another partner who is equally non-marriageable from his point of view.

Then, although still consciously searching for someone to marry, he may choose a young woman who is not able to have children. He manipulates this strategic lack to his own advantage by announcing to everyone that he *would* marry her, but he cannot because he wants a woman who can bear him sons and daughters.

And this pattern continues. All the while he is deluding himself and frantically searching for the love-security he is unable to find. Such a response is somewhat similar to that of the man who visits prostitutes regularly, all the while complaining that the marriage which he desperately seeks is growing more unattainable. The exploitative male chooses prostitutes in order to vent his feelings of rage/hatred toward a female figure (mother) whom he unconsciously despises. Yet, at the same time, in the act of demeaning her (the prostitute), he is unaware that this action is the epitome of love/hate directed against the maternal figure.

Examine a man's relationship with Mama and you will find the key that unlocks this bewildering array of personality disturbances.

Some Daddy's girls, especially the liberation-oriented ones, tend to consider marriage a form of slavery. Despite their proclivity to repudiate marriage, they will not admit that they never intend to marry. Such an admission would exhume from their past the transcendent relationship with Daddy, which is far more profound in its impact than the women's liberation movement.

Antisocial or severely unsettled responses to a love relationship have been permitted to women in the past because custom and tradition have considered an intensely emotional life part of the feminine heritage, whereas men have been considerably more restricted in expression. Thus identifying this form of behavior in the female is a more difficult process.

Exploitation wears many disguises. A woman may seek love-security from a substantially older man who will provide her with a pampered life, for example, in exchange for sex. Mutual exploitation is a characteristic of such a relationship, for feelings of contempt are also mingled in her camouflaged aggressiveness. A man may wish to marry her despite her personality problems; but she will avoid marriage, rationalizing her motives so that to lover and friends they appear acceptable. Her career is giving her the recognition she desires. Or she doesn't want to move to another city, where her prospective mate's business interests would take her away from her own. Or she may be weary of the subtle pressures exerted in the direction of marriage. If she is true to her innermost conflicting needs, she will not surrender to marriage.

In another instance, a woman may assert that she cannot find the right man. Because her unconscious compels her to seek the "perfect" mate, she fails to cultivate friendships that would normally lead to marriage. Or, she may find herself drawn into a relationship that provides her with the love-security she needs, but the uncomfortable proximity to marriage fills her with a yearning to accept and at the same time to escape. A woman may continue in this pattern of responses until she withdraws into self-imposed loneliness or even regressive behavior.

Her need for love-security remains as potent a force in her life as it was when she was young. But the likelihood of fulfillment narrows, sometimes causing her personality to deteriorate still further. All that remains of her sexual encounters is a disorderly collection of erotic memories, hurried assignations, exhilaration followed by despondency, the vain search for serenity, an imperceptible acceptance of the back streets of life.

As the exploitative woman faces middle age, she avoids interpretations of her past life and denies vehemently that she might have married if she had honestly wished to do so. Her career, lack of suitable marriage opportunities, the necessity of assisting a younger brother or sister through college, all were obstacles. She may murmur sadly that it was not possible. Oddly enough, she speaks the truth. Nestled in her unconscious is a Daddy who has irrevocably charted her adult decision not to marry.

Pity

"Of all the paths that lead to a woman's love, Pity's the straightest," wrote Beaumont and Fletcher, two Renaissance dramatists.

Pity is the oblique expression of love-security gone awry. Its imitative response is unconsciously acceptable to men and women who have learned in childhood that substitutes are better than nothing in the quest for love.

Pity can comprise tenderness, sensitivity and sexual satisfaction and still be devastatingly inadequate for those who yearn for love. That pity is acceptable to so many men and women as a love substitute is not surprising, for it is a normal human expression to feel pity for those who appear to be less fortunate than ourselves.

The critical difference, however, lies in the fact that pity of this sort does not form the proper basis for a man-woman relationship in adult life.

When Daddy, for example, molds the childhood relationship so that pity is his daughter's central response, he lays the groundwork for her to become unconsciously receptive to this kind of relationship in adult life.

She searches for a man who will provide her with an emotional milieu that will allow her to express these same feelings of pity for him.

Daddy's negative reaction to marriage also emerges in his daughter's emotional life. Although she may have given pity freely, she tends to yearn for a masculine response that she cannot really identify because she has not experienced it in her relationship with Daddy. Pity compels her to find a lover who will allow her to unburden herself of her confused feelings toward Daddy.

A common example is a nurse-patient relationship that continues long after hospitalization. A woman brought up pitying Daddy is especially vulnerable to men with minor physical infirmities. She can take care of them in the same way that she took care of Daddy. By absorbing herself in her tasks of service and sacrificial sex, she relieves herself of the emotional debris of childhood.

Pity softens the reality that frightens her. In her psychologically disoriented state she cannot accept as a husband a man who offers love-security, because she herself is unable to fulfill his needs.

Struggling to find an abiding relationship, yet fighting against it because she unconsciously loathes the love substitute of childhood, a woman may compulsively seek yet another kind of sexual partner—the man who may be characterized as a loser in life. His life history is a repetitious pattern of failure, or at least minor defeats, over the years. He never seems to find himself in work or in love. An incredible variety of obstacles have accumulated, and he is in need of someone who will restore his sagging ego.

The similarity between her lover and Daddy is there, but her discordant feelings do not warn her of it. She lacks insight. This is particularly true of the woman who finds alcoholic men irresistible because she pities them.

The attraction-repulsion response of pity eventually ends in disaster for a woman. When her lover wants to terminate the relationship, which he usually does after he has had his fill of pity for the time being, he will endearingly tell her that he does not deserve anyone as wonderful as she is, and thus perpetuate her lack of self-understanding.

Although women are more inclined to unconsciously seek out a relationship that offers pity as a love substitute, men are not immune from the attractions of such a liaison.

The most celebrated fictional relationship of this sort is in Somerset Maugham's *Of Human Bondage*. Pity, rather than love-security, is explored in all its mutations with despairing sensitivity. Philip, with his clubfoot, elicits pity from Mildred, and she arouses in him an eloquent, horrendous passion because at last he has found someone more pitiable than himself.

Philip even considers marriage to Mildred, but, typically, shrinks from such a decision. The relationship increases pathologically in its intensity. When Mildred mocks Philip, he despises himself for needing her so desperately, yet he is unable to comprehend the hidden basis of his need. He believes it to be sexual attraction alone. Mildred's mesmeric influence draws him into a whirlpool of self-hatred. Philip's satisfaction is an absence of happiness, and the presence of anguish born of pity and self-pity.

Of all the unconscious motives for not marrying, pity is the most difficult to identify because of its similarity to affirmative personality traits that are not obstacles in the path of marriage. It appears enshrined in feelings of nobility, self-sacrifice and exaggerated self-effacement.

A son or daughter who is unconsciously taught this pattern in childhood by a parent of the opposite sex may receive considerable social approval for his response to Daddy or Mama. He is being "good" to the parent who wishes to receive this counterfeit form of love. As a consequence, when his adult love life is not normal, there is only shock or astonishment. Of all the unmarried sons or daughters, this individual seems to be most deserving of married love.

Psychological Indebtedness

The feeling of never being able to repay a parent in gratitude or gifts of material value for his or her contribution to a child's life haunts many adult men and women and is an intangible psychological obstacle to marriage.

A man who is inadequately prepared for fatherhood may overwhelm his daughter by unconsciously indoctrinating her with the notion that the financial cost of her upbringing was an enormous burden, and vaguely suggest that when she reaches adulthood it will be time to compensate Daddy.

More commonly it is Mama who corrals her son by reiterating what he knows only too well. He would not be where he is today if it were not for Mama's endless sacrifices. Although this may be true, the Mama who restrains her son from seeking a normal love-security relationship in marriage is desirous of more than recognition of her contributions. She is unconsciously demanding that her son enter a state of perpetual indenture, that he never under any circumstances give homage to any other woman. Thus restricted, a son or daughter will seek unconsciously to avoid relationships with commitment.

Significantly, the concept of sharing, which is central to marriage, becomes a psychological barrier. The subtle coercion expressed in Daddy's or Mama's attitude focuses unnatural attention on money and material possessions, and this emphasis tends to demean, but not set aside, the individual need for love-security.

Confused and unhappy, an adult son or daughter will wish to escape from this emotional climate. A man will not seek marriage, because he does not wish to be reproached for all that he owes to a woman. He may establish a non-marital relationship that will seem to satisfy him.

A woman's response to this situation may differ somewhat. She is inclined to search for a lover who will be lavish with gifts—the exact opposite of Daddy—but will make her feel indebted to him in other primarily sexual ways. He may be so possessive that she loses her sense of individuality. He may invade and completely dominate every aspect of her life. A woman owes this much to him, so the lover will reason, if he is providing her with a luxurious life.

Occasionally, an adult son or daughter may feel so indebted to a parent that he/she will dutifully live at home but will secretly establish a second ménage with a mistress or lover for evenings and weekends.

Gradually feelings of debasement and prostitution emerge in these relationships because there is so much emphasis on the use of money and material gifts to mitigate the pattern of psychological indebtedness.

A woman is likely to rebel eventually against the exorbitant demands

of her lover. It is as frustrating a relationship as was the one with Daddy.
From her point of view, she is giving more than she is receiving, because
her psychological needs are never really satisfied, despite the release of
sexual tension.

Inevitably a man, too, will become disenchanted. He may divert his
energies away from a mistress into a business or professional endeavor,
because there he will not experience the same frightening pattern of
demands (indebtedness) that he can never repay. He may come to believe
that all emotional relationships with women are disappointing. Therefore, he may compromise by maintaining a sexual relationship only until
he is presented with an ultimatum to marry. Then, because of his intense
psychological distress, he will escape.

The feeling that one is somehow prohibited from living one's own life
because of prior obligations to Daddy or Mama can become a constant
goad, ultimately influencing all actions and decisions in the realm of a
man-woman relationship. There is also the possibility of still more serious
personality problems. Unintentionally, Daddy and Mama have distorted
love and have perpetuated the concept of gratitude and parental obligation as insurance against a lonely old age. Disappointed with each other,
Daddy and Mama reach out with suffocating precision to bend an
unsuspecting child to their implacable needs.

Blindly and obediently the child does as he is commanded until his
entire life is built on a wracking sense of duty and indebtedness. The maze
becomes more complex as the emotional needs go unsatisfied or ignored.

When, a man/woman may wonder, is it my turn to live?

Feelings of Worthlessness, Fear and Inadequacy

Lack of self-esteem is a learned behavior pattern communicated to the
child by Daddy or Mama through punishment, ridicule, humiliation or
rejection. Daddy or Mama satisfies certain ego needs of his/her own by
destroying the child's sense of worth. The child may be referred to as
"stupid" or "a bumbling idiot," or he may have physical indignities
heaped upon him.

Daddy or Mama may bait the child with love offerings such as gifts, movies, clothes or a car in exchange for renunciation of his/her psychological development.

Repressed anger toward Daddy or Mama is mingled with feelings of fear and inadequacy. Typically, a son or daughter becomes passive, clinging and dependent in his/her general response to life situations. He is unable to make decisions for himself because he has been taught he is not capable of doing so. The more limitations Daddy or Mama imposes on him, the more inadequate he believes himself to be. The thought of marriage fills him with dread. What if he cannot perform sexually? Life is a series of blunders that add to his burden of worthlessness.

A daughter reared in such an atmosphere is a prime candidate for sexual seduction. She does not believe herself worthy of marriage, although she may have a complicated fantasy life in which she is married to the man of her dreams. Her feelings of worthlessness, combined with fear and a sense of inadequacy, make her susceptible to the exploitative male. Secretly dreaming of marriage and yet fearful of it, she accepts sexual relationships that allow her to relive her childhood feelings. Frequently she becomes an unmarried mother without ever understanding why.

Invariably, this woman is deserted or jilted in adult life. Astonishment is her response, for, although she may have been dissatisfied with the sexual relationship, she had been clinging to her partner for fear that no other man would want her. Consideration of her own deepest feelings seems to be absent from her evaluation of self, for she is accustomed to Daddy's interpretation of her personality. Thus repetitive frustrations and dwindling experiences of love-security via sex are her circumscribed lot in life.

In a man, such feelings of inferiority may be hidden behind a mask of arrogance. He may drift from job to job, alleging that no one appreciates his superior talents. But he refuses to accept work that is demanding because he is fearful of failure. His feelings of inadequacy make him a susceptible target for the aggressive, exploitative woman. He, too, is susceptible to casual seduction because of his lack of self-esteem. If he is good-looking and has agreeable manners, he may become the escort of a series of wealthy, lonely women.

A fragmented sexual life is characteristic of a son or daughter steeped in feelings of worthlessness. He or she "takes what he/she can get" out of life. Deeply grateful for any sexual satisfaction in lieu of love-security, such a man or woman may be preyed on by more seriously disturbed antisocial individuals.

Daddy or Mama tends to remain a psychological obstacle in the life of such a son or daughter, because the feelings of inadequacy are so profound that an independent life is seldom considered.

Intermittent excursions may occasionally be attempted, such as an apartment of one's own, an independent vacation, a change of job made without consulting Daddy or Mama, but the possibility of failure is so imminent that these treacherous mature decisions are rarely carried out. These men and women have to struggle to overcome the emotional shackles of childhood in various non-sexual ways as well as various sexual ways.

Should Daddy or Mama die, the dependent man or woman may either go into a state of suicidal depression or cling to a married brother or sister who extends affectionate support. He or she will unconsciously search for an instant replacement for the absent parent. Being compelled to live independently is the crisis that may prove to be a blessing in disguise. At this juncture in life, the passive, dependent, non-marrying man or woman is faced with an astonishing possibility. He is psychologically free to marry. Whether or not he will marry introduces him to a new concept of self which can be developed by psychological reconditioning.

The vicarious love-security experiences he has accepted in the past may be recognized for what they are—love substitutes—and the crisis that follows the death of Daddy or Mama may challenge him to explore alternatives.

Why Not Marriage?

Those who do not marry are struggling in a labyrinth of emotional conflicts that reach back to a childhood relationship with Daddy or Mama. In our society the excuses for not marrying are plentiful, but rarely do they allude to arrested psycho-sexual development.

Those reasons proposed as major obstacles are usually of minor significance. Beneath the seemingly logical reasons—supporting an elderly parent, helping a brother or sister complete his education, repaying debts for one's own education—there lies hidden a deeper motive. Often it has been so carefully forgotten by the individual's conscious mind that he would resent the truth if he were confronted with it.

Probably the single most compelling reason for avoiding marriage is an unhappy relationship with the parent of the opposite sex. Daddy or Mama not only did not provide love-security for a son or daughter, but in its place created an emotional atmosphere where predominantly negative and harmful feelings prevailed. Daddy or Mama bound a daughter or son to him/her in a relationship where feelings of affection were negligible, or were offered as a bribe for suitable behavior on the part of the child. Instead of developing a pattern of love-security, the parent, because of his own disenchantment with marriage, demanded temporary ego satisfactions. And neither Daddy nor Mama was ever aware of the havoc he/she was creating.

An opposition to marriage develops in the son's or daughter's unconscious. Daddy's girl or Mama's boy becomes an instrument of distortion with the latent potential for an antisocial or tragic adult life. On the conscious level, neither parents nor children will admit that such a confusion of normal human needs is developing.

Feelings of hatred, contempt, hostility, pity and a multiplicity of other powerful negative emotions are nurtured. The prevailing emotional life directed by Daddy or Mama may spell his or her own doom when the adult son or daughter explodes in a frenzy of destruction. The shocking murder of a parent of the opposite sex is not unrelated to this pattern of arrested development.

More commonly, however, the negative feelings are dispersed, and major tragedies are averted. Instead, a series of actions carried out over a long period of adult life reveal evidence of profound unhappiness.

Sometimes a son or daughter may give expensive gifts to a parent he despises in order to soothe his guilt feelings. Or, on the other hand, he may refuse to visit a parent who is dying of cancer.

The resulting inner conflict is expressed in self-repudiation. Feelings of worthlessness, self-contempt and self-hatred serve to further limit the possibility of marriage. In order to alleviate these feelings of unhappiness, a son or daughter seeks love-security in a sexual relationship without marriage. Because of Daddy's or Mama's disappointments, he/she is already certain that marriage is not the path to happiness. Marriage is for those who are "stupid," for those who "get caught." It is a trap that should be meticulously avoided. The unconscious equation is "marriage equals bondage equals misery."

What the non-marrying man/woman does not realize is that his/her unconscious motives will betray him/her, because they are infantile. He misappropriates his sexual energies in relationships that reflect his conflicting feelings toward Daddy/Mama. The emphasis is on egocentric sexual "getting," because the individual believes he has never had his share of love-security from Daddy or Mama. Some variation of sexual exploitation and/or dependency will inevitably terminate the relationship.

Successive sexual encounters intensify the search for the emotional satisfaction of love-security. Each relationship fails to satisfy the ego needs, because a transference and perpetuation of the Daddy's girl or Mama's boy relationship eventually leads to the destruction of the sex-without-marriage liaison.

Cynicism, rancor and other negative emotions "justify" the non-marrying man's or woman's attitude toward the opposite sex. At the same time, these feelings cause progressive deterioration of the personality unless the individual seeks redirection of these feelings through psychological counseling or therapy.

Tragically, he is not aware of these grotesque changes in his personality which are preventing him from entering into marriage. All he "knows" is what he feels, and his feelings distress and torment him. In an effort to escape from himself, he enters into liaisons with other individuals on whom he places the burden for his happiness.

Superficially he may appear dynamic and exciting to a woman who is not perceptive. He may be a remarkably successful bachelor, sought after by many women. Elusive and charming, he hides behind a façade of shallow luster. Those who know him intimately see manifestations of his contempt for women. Perhaps a woman left her husband for him. Or maybe a young girl took an overdose of drugs after he ended their liaison in order to continue his insatiable search for love-security.

Daddy's girl is hidden behind an alluring exterior. Her obvious erotic attractions are revealed as sham when the camouflage is removed; her essential self is turbulent, frightened and angry. She is going to "get even" with all the men in her life because of the way Daddy treated her as a child.

Escape from marriage is considered the ultimate triumphant maneuver by these unhappy men and women.

"I love you as much as I am able to love anyone" is the inarticulate credo of these non-marrying men and women. And who can say that they are "at fault"? This is the way Daddy and Mama loved them.

Creative Sublimation— The Altruistic Love Life

The altruistic love life is distinguished from the egocentric or sexually oriented love life by certain characteristics which are sometimes apologetically advanced as too difficult for the average man or woman to achieve.

What are some of these characteristics? And does this interpretation of love have any validity for those who do not marry? Does Daddy or Mama influence a son or daughter toward this avenue of love expression?

Creative sublimation is a redirection of the sexual energies for the positive good of mankind, in relationships and activities that transcend the one-to-one relationship characteristic of egocentric sexual love.

Altruistic love is not sexually repressive; it is a more comprehensive love experience, free from the limitations of sexual desire. Its central tenet is not to love merely those who are lovable, but to love all human beings.

Altruistic love is motivated by will, a faculty of the mind, in contrast to egocentric love, which is fed by emotions and the sensory faculties. A conscious decision and a conscious effort are involved in creative sublimation. It is not an expression of love that a man or woman drifts into after having exhausted the satisfactions of egocentric love.

Altruistic love, in contrast to egocentric sexual love, concentrates on giving without concern for receiving. Its dimensions are not limited by sensory knowledge or desire or sexual magnetism. Egocentric sexual love unconsciously demands an accounting of satisfaction for satisfaction. The most familiar expression of creative sublimation is found in men and women who are religiously oriented or non-materialistic in their philosophical attitudes toward life.

In Western civilization the Judaeo-Christian philosophy has promulgated the doctrine of altruistic love as the ultimate good in man's relationship with his fellowman. Its essential source is God's love for mankind. St. Paul offers the definitive concept of altruistic love (1 Corinthians):

Love is patient and kind; love is not jealous or boastful; it is not arrogant or rude. Love does not insist on its own way; it is not irritable or resentful; it does not rejoice at wrong but rejoices in the right. Love bears all things, believes all things, hopes all things, endures all things. Love never ends. . . .

Those who do not marry occasionally choose the path of creative sublimation, not because it is an alternative for those who fear sex, but because Daddy or Mama has provided the affirmative influences required for such a decision.

In these circumstances Daddy or Mama has relinquished immature ego satisfactions for himself/herself in order to obtain certain psychological satisfactions for the child. The son or daughter is the fortunate recipient. Thus a son or daughter sees acts of altruistic love directed toward the well-being of other human beings beyond the boundaries of the family. He learns to comprehend the value of love for the sake of love, with all of its intangible psychological and spiritual satisfactions. Teaching the child to live and love beyond the self is the ultimate gift a Daddy or Mama can transmit to a child.

It is not impossible for egocentric sexual love to coexist with altruistic love in one individual.

In its highest form, altruistic love constitutes the zenith of spiritual and psychological development. Religious, humanitarian and social services of all kinds are thought of as appropriate expressions of altruistic love. A son or daughter so motivated deliberately chooses to improve the physical and spiritual condition of other human beings.

A son may choose to become a rabbi/minister/priest or missionary worker in a community far away from family and friends expressly in order to serve God by serving mankind. His rewards, in a material sense, are nonexistent. As he serves, his altruistic capacities expand to include a vision of love that is not limited by human understanding.

A daughter may offer her talents in a service role that brings her into contact with the most hopeless segments of humanity. What material gain would warrant such sacrifice? But if we look more closely we see that this is the essence of altruistic love: she is ministering to those human beings most in need of love because they have been rejected by their fellowman.

In these instances, a Daddy or Mama is an instrument of love-security of the highest order. Such a parent transmits an interpretation of love that goes beyond the exhilaration and frustrations of egocentric sexual love. Egotism thus creatively sublimated unleashes a vast potential for human good that would otherwise never come into being.

5   The Happy and Enduring Marriage

Every marriage, whether it is enduring or temporary, must come to terms with the Daddy's girl/Mama's boy pattern of response.

Inevitably, a man marries a woman with a past. That past—her particular collection of childhood responses to Daddy—will form the basis of her marital relationship with her husband. Her very choice of a husband, whether she is aware of it or not, is a reflection of this early relationship. In selecting a mate she will unconsciously seek to re-create the pattern of love-security she knew as a child, be it wholesome or warped.

If her Daddy's girl pattern is fundamentally altruistic rather than egocentric, she will seek to duplicate that aura of psychological satisfaction. Her husband, in fact, may bear an astonishing physical resemblance to her father. Or he may have the same professional background. Most significantly, the psychological climate he will create for her in marriage will embody the same profound love-security she had in her life with Daddy.

Similarly, a man will seek a woman whose emotional responses give him the comfort he knew in his childhood relationship with Mama. If Mama has established an altruistic pattern, the chosen wife will evoke memories of Mama's physical warmth, tenderness, sympathy, encouragement and approval. A man will unconsciously yearn for a wife whose total femininity is reminiscent of Mama's. This is not to say that the marital relationship is essentially maternal or paternal, but rather that the Mama's boy/Daddy's girl response governs the overall marital pattern, including sexual intimacy.

The mystery of human attraction is complex. Yet despite the seem-ingly diverse and confusing responses of men and women in search of love-security, there remains a singular basis of clarification. The desire to find what one lacks in the self, what one wishes to be or to have, constitutes the crux of human attraction. In choosing a mate, one attempts to complete oneself not only sexually, but psychologically, aesthetically and spiritually.

The parent figure of the opposite sex is the unconscious model for all future romantic encounters. If Daddy has established an altruistic pattern with his daughter, she, as a young woman, will desire a man whose psychological heritage reflects Daddy's. Conversely, if Daddy's egocentric pattern has arrested his daughter's psycho-sexual development, she will repudiate, in part or in whole, any male who bears a psychological resemblance to him. Instead she will unconsciously yearn for a man who is everything her father lacks. Her choice of a husband will indicate her disavowal of Daddy as a transmitter of love-security.

It is through this repudiation that Daddy's girl and Mama's boy become involved in the confusion of motives and desires that always leads them to choose an inappropriate marriage partner. Indeed, opposites do attract. This disastrous choice is based on a need to escape from Daddy or Mama.

When the parent figure of the opposite sex is absent because of death, desertion or divorce, the child's need for love-security is intensified. There are several major ways this can later affect a marriage.

There is a tendency to idealize and romanticize the absentee Daddy or Mama. He or she symbolizes to the child an altruistic perfection that, under the circumstances of absenteeism, can never be measured against the reality of daily life. This romanticism comes to fruition in adult life, when a son or daughter chooses a mate substantially older than himself or herself. This choice is merely an externalized admission of the child's intense need for love-security and his/her inner conviction that this relationship can only be realized with a man or woman who is nearly or actually of the same generation as the absentee parent figure.

However, a substantial age difference does not necessarily imply an inappropriate marital choice. These marriages may endure as long as the vast majority of marriages. The so-called December-May marriages are a declaration of the powerful Daddy's girl/Mama's boy need in everyone for love-security.

The Pattern of Imitation or Repudiation

The enduring marriage constitutes a triumph of altruism over egocentricity. Both altruism and egocentricity are learned in the childhood relationship with the parent of the opposite sex.

An inner psychological balance, or emotional core of stability, manifests itself in responses imitative of parental altruism, and in marriage these responses are supportive and sustaining in times of crisis. The emphasis is on giving for the ultimate good of one's mate. If Daddy or Mama revealed a capacity to give and to grow, the child, now an adult, imitates the pattern of love-security in his relationship with his mate.

Repudiation, conversely, is an expression of egocentricity. It is evidence of ambivalent yearnings within a man or woman whose Daddy's or Mama's love-security pattern was a unilateral seeking of ego satisfaction.

An egocentric husband will not be inclined, in times of crisis in marriage, to be emotionally supportive or to sustain his mate. Typically, his response will be destructive. He will be concerned primarily with his own satisfactions and pleasures, irrespective of his mate's needs or wishes.

How did Daddy solve his marital frustrations? Drink? Have an affair? Gamble? A variety of psychological escapes will also occur to Daddy's girl, who has learned his pattern of egocentricity. At the same time that she wishes to escape from marital crises, however, she also desires love-security. Her inner conflict becomes externalized in acts of repudiation of her mate.

Thus a Daddy's girl or Mama's boy who repudiates his/her mate in imitation of the parental example will tend to have more emotional problems in marriage because of the tangled legacy of egocentricity. Unless this pattern of repudiation is coupled with a positive redirection of emotional energies through a process of learning "new" responses, a marriage will tend to deteriorate. It will become another temporary interlude in the search for love-security.

In a marital crisis, this means that a wife cannot become Daddy's girl when her husband needs to be Mama's boy—both partners cannot return to the love-security of childhood at the same time. If both husband and wife respond according to an egocentric pattern, the marriage will totter. Both will demand emotional support and sustenance, and neither will be capable of the needed altruism.

In the enduring marital relationship, one mate (if not both) is capable of calling forth the strength that only a childhood based on parental altruism can provide. He has learned to receive psychological satisfaction from giving to his mate.

Because altruism and egocentricity are mingled in the human personality, each marriage has a unique interrelationship of traits, strengths and weaknesses that comes to the fore in time of crisis.

Every crisis is a struggle between altruism and egocentricity. No marriage is a succession of continuous victories or defeats. Experiences and emotions are jostled together, accumulated and unconsciously evaluated, always in terms of the individual need for love-security.

Disparities in Externals— Age, Sex, Money/Power

Why does a young man or woman choose a marital partner substantially older or younger than himself or herself?

Moreover, why, after this choice is made, do some of these marriages endure while others fall apart?

What essential ingredients are present in one or both mates?

A woman who chooses a man substantially older than herself as a husband does so to satisfy a combination of profound psycho-sexual needs that were unfulfilled in her relationship with her biological father. The absence of a father, as previously indicated, arouses deep yearning for a masculine figure who will provide the love-security a child needs.

Daddy is the man who can "make everything all right," providing the reassurance a daughter needs as a child. This norm creates an unconscious criterion the daughter will employ in her search for love-security in adult relationships with men. A young woman whose norm is closer to destructive egocentricity than altruism has more pronounced needs and tends to choose a literal father figure as a husband. This does not apply, however, to cases where Daddy is totally absent in childhood. Idealism and romanticism then shape, to a large extent, the motivational needs of such a young woman.

When Daddy is present, he conveys to his daughter by his pattern of egocentricity the portrait of an emotionally indigent man. His satisfactions take precedence over his daughter's psycho-sexual development, creating an ambivalent pattern that will come into play when she chooses a husband. Daddy's response to his daughter may be characterized by harshness, austerity, excessive physical discipline, and a total or at least considerable absence of physical affection. His response to her conveys the notion that she is somehow worthless, inferior, not deserving of masculine attention.

Therefore, as she grows into womanhood, she unconsciously craves to please an older man. Such a daughter may repudiate her father's emotional tyranny, but she will also feel that she was not a "success" with the first masculine figure in her life. Her intense need to vindicate herself will become manifest in the choice of an older husband who can provide, in a sense, a "second chance" to satisfy her legitimate love-security needs, which had been so inadequately dealt with in the initial relationship.

A woman who chooses a younger husband has generally had a childhood relationship with Daddy that followed a predominantly altruistic pattern. Her psycho-sexual development has generally flourished in this beneficent emotional climate. It is usually something related to the nurturing process that caused her to favor younger men. Typically, she developed in an environment where there was a decided emphasis on caring for younger children, or perhaps a child who was ill for a long period of time. Caring for those who needed her aroused a maternal response which gave her profound satisfaction. As an adult woman she may unconsciously seek to reestablish the pattern of her childhood.

The young woman who is hostile to or rebels against the mother role may have an egocentric paternal figure in her emotional background. If the father-daughter relationship is unsatisfactory, the child cannot proceed in the altruistic pattern that would eventually allow her to accept responsibility for those who need her care.

It should be pointed out that not every woman who chooses a younger man for her husband does so because of an abundance of emotional resources. Sometimes such a woman, like the older male in the reverse relationship, chooses a partner who will enhance her waning sexuality. Although this selection is unconscious, there is, on the conscious level, a deliberate attempt by the man or woman to manipulate "assets" (sex, age, money/power) for his or her own egocentric satisfaction. But since this unilateral seeking of love-security is self-defeating, these marriages do not endure.

Because our society is male-dominated, the love/power theme has infiltrated the majority of marriages in one way or another. Generally speaking, the male, more than the female, has been conditioned by a collection of social, cultural and economic forces to seek love-security in love/power. (Religion has modified this credo somewhat by introducing the concept of love/service within an altruistic frame of reference.)

The masculine interpretation of love is power over one's mate. If a man can get a woman to do things for him, he is reassured of his love/power over her. If he can persuade her to let him make love to her on his terms, the male is convinced of his love/power. But love/power is egocentric, in contrast to love-security, which is altruistic. Love/power is a preeminent trait of temporary marriages. In the enduring marriage, love is interpreted as service to one's mate.

The male who chooses a much younger woman as his wife is partially influenced by this love/power motive. Such a marriage will endure only if the love/power motive is modified by a certain altruistic force learned in his boyhood relationship with Mama—the ability to unconsciously accept the roles of protector, mentor, and provider, all of which are conditioned altruistically rather than egocentrically.

This male has a good maternal image, and his choice of a younger wife is attributable, to a large measure, to his unconscious wish to reverse the roles of childhood. He wishes to love and protect Mama because she was the source of his love-security in childhood. Because this is not socially acceptable, he yearns for a wife who may bear an astonishing similarity to the first maternal figure in his life. Thus his sexuality combines successfully with Daddy traits to provide his much younger wife with the love-security she seeks. This pattern is unique to the enduring marriage.

A son with an egocentric mother and a much younger wife will exploit the love/power motif and eventually destroy the marriage—or at least seriously threaten it—in his unilateral search for ego satisfaction.

Latent Conflicts in "Equally Matched" Mates

In all marriages there are latent conflict areas that relate back to the childhood relationship with the parent of the opposite sex. When the husband and wife appear to be "equally matched" in age, sexual attractiveness, money/power and economic, educational and religious/philosophical backgrounds, the dimensions of conflict are much more nebulous. These are the marriages that would seem to have the greatest likelihood of enduring for a lifetime.

The latent conflict, however, is hidden in the pattern of similarities. The critical difference between the happy and enduring marriage and the temporary marriage lies in the emotional resources of the more altruistic mate. Husband and wife may not really be equally matched in the psychological heritage that they bring to marriage. One mate may manifest the indefinable resilience found in altruism while the other one may lean toward greater egocentricity.

There is, of course, no obvious polarity that husband and wife recognize in their life adaptation to each other. But it is predominantly one mate's efforts that cause the marriage to endure. This does not mean that husband and wife live in continuous and intolerable misery. It merely means that they do not achieve the full measure of happiness that their relationship could provide. As husband and wife grow in their capacity to adapt altruistically to each other, their happiness intensifies.

There are several general categories of "equally matched" mates between whom latent conflict can exist. The solution of the conflict will depend on the response of the mate whose emotional pattern prevails.

For instance, it is quite common in our society to find an altruistic woman married to an aggressive Mama's boy. Here is a woman with comfortable feelings of self-esteem developed in an emotional climate of benevolence, married to a man who shows every sign of a self-indulged childhood. This man may have many of the superficial traits associated with masculinity. He is aggressive, a leader in the community, physically virile, sophisticated in a shallow sense. During courtship none of these traits aroused feelings of suspicion or alarm in the altruistic woman.

Such a man exudes confidence and frequently has magnificent powers of verbal persuasion; he may be very successful in his business or professional life. If the woman he marries eventually comes to terms with his egocentric response to her and to life, the marriage can be an enduring one.

This does not mean that he is always egocentric or that she is perpetually altruistic. Within the large sphere of interaction required in order for each to experience the love-security necessary to function as husband and wife, many complex personality traits will be manifested.

In a crisis situation, however, the predominantly aggressive Mama's boy husband will tend to evaluate the problem from a unilateral point of view. He will unconsciously assess rewards or frustrations in terms of his own needs, particularly in his sexual life. Only gradually, aided by the benevolent flexibility of his altruistic wife, does he perceive that concern for the mate's needs and wishes can ultimately enhance his own happiness.

As a result, in the early years of marriage between an altruistic woman and an aggressive Mama's boy husband, cooperation is rare. A sequence of adjustment techniques must be utilized in this marriage. There is no true adjustment until the altruistic wife accepts the fact that her husband learned egocentricity as a boy in his relationship with Mama. At first quarreling and unresolved conflicts may characterize the relationship. After she has learned to accept Mama's boy as he is, the altruistic woman may employ another strategy. Surrender is astonishingly successful with a man who has been pampered as a boy. The love/power motif appeals to his ego.

In order for this to be an enduring marriage instead of a temporary one, the man must exhibit the capacity to grow toward his more altruistic wife, who is giving him the love-security he seeks. He must learn to accommodate himself to his wife by gradually accepting compromise in crisis situations.

As the self-indulged traits he learned from Mama imperceptibly but definitely dwindle, the husband will adjust to his wife on a much higher level of interaction, namely, cooperation. The need for feelings of superiority and love/power will diminish significantly as the husband discovers there is more profound joy in mutuality than in egocentricity.

When a passive-dependent Mama's boy marries an altruistic woman, certain emotional undercurrents he has retained from his childhood relationship may persist. A lack of initiative, feelings of inferiority, and intermittent depression are the passive-dependent Mama's boy's response to crisis.

There are complex ambivalent traits in his personality. Although he bears the scars of Mama's domination, he may emerge as a remarkably affable and congenial adult male. He always lets his wife have her own way because, unknown to her, he retains the indecisiveness and lack of self-reliance cultivated by Mama's egocentric authoritarianism.

If this marriage is to endure, the altruistic wife must discreetly accept the challenge of her mate's personality. She cannot realistically expect to transform her passive-dependent Mama's boy husband, but she can provide subtle opportunities for the development of traits such as personal responsibility, decisiveness and initiative.

The passive Mama's boy husband should be neither smothered nor coerced along a path of action and response that is beyond his emotional capacities. His childhood-learned responses should be redirected toward more affirmative and altruistic avenues of expression.

A woman married to a passive-dependent Mama's boy should thus restrain herself from making unilateral decisions for both of them, even though this is her husband's wish. He must realize that she believes he is capable of making decisions and taking the initiative. Her faith in his untapped abilities is her expression of altruism. Hence, she provides the emotional supportiveness her passive-dependent mate needs.

An enduring marriage must be based on the premise that the altruistic mate can and will continue to give of himself or herself, and the more egocentric mate will exhibit a willingness to redirect his or her destructive childhood patterns toward some measure of altruism. It is this fluidity of response, mingled with altruism, that is the essence of an abiding relationship. A marriage characterized by egocentricity and rigidity will eventually collapse, despite the constant efforts of the altruistic mate to bring into existence a more profound love-security relationship.

There is one other enduring marriage pattern: an altruistic husband and an egocentric wife. Our traditional male-dominated society has heretofore afforded the best disguise and protection for a woman still enthralled by an egocentric Daddy's girl relationship.

In this milieu it is the Daddy/husband who perceptively adjusts while his wife learns to cope with marital experiences in a creative and altruistic manner. This development, of course, is not a matter of weeks or months. It constitutes a continuous process of emotionally recycling the destructive egocentric patterns of childhood into "new" altruistic responses that enhance the love-security of each mate.

Women's liberation has exerted powerful oblique pressure on such women to change by expressing disapproval of any woman who manifests an infantile dependence on her husband. Not all Daddy's girl wives are passive, however. There are those who are aggressive, self-indulged and demanding because of the way they were emotionally exploited by Daddy in their childhood.

Learning to maneuver such a wife into appropriate nonexploitative emotional growth situations requires great sensitivity and restraint on the part of an altruistic husband. Because he is the more mature of the two, he is capable of providing her with the love-security she needs in order to develop an altruistic response to him. At the same time he can recognize that his own love-security needs must be held in abeyance until his wife's egocentricity has been modified.

The capacity of a couple to develop an enduring and happy marriage is limited only by the degree of motivation exhibited by the more egocentric husband or wife, who, in effect, can effectively checkmate the altruistic spouse. Failure to abandon the infantile Daddy's girl or Mama's boy mode of adjustment to the past where it belongs constitutes the greatest personal threat to an enduring relationship.

Traits of an Enduring Marriage

1.   **There is a psychological balance or harmony between the husband and wife.** The man and woman experience an ever-deepening love-security relationship with each other. One mate never threatens to deny love-security to the other. Love, therefore, is not conditional, nor is it based on any hidden contractual agreement that implies, "Only if you love me will I love you."

This harmony is the ultimate goal of marriage. It encompasses the total constellation of psychological, aesthetic and spiritual yearnings and values, including the psycho-sexual needs specific to the husband and wife.

2.   **The psychological balance is the proper one for that marriage.** The combination that provides love-security for one couple may not do so for another husband and wife. Such harmony is based on each partner's emotional reservoir, acquired from a benevolent childhood relationship with the parent of the opposite sex. The capacity of each individual personality for altruism determines the love-security potential of the relationship.

3.   **There is the transference of a value pattern.** The husband and wife hold similar values, values that were unconsciously transmitted during their Daddy's girl/Mama's boy relationships of childhood.

The enduring marriage relationship is, therefore, based on the integration of a religious/philosophical or cultural/humanistic heritage into the reality of daily life, with all of its frustrations, disappointments, and dilemmas.

4. **Marital interaction is based on cooperation, with its implicit recognition of equality and interdependence.** A pattern of dominance/submission, with its implicit power struggle, is characteristic of an egocentric and ultimately temporary marital relationship.

Admittedly, cooperation requires each individual to utilize the altruistic emotional resources learned in the childhood relationship with the parent of the opposite sex. It is thus contrary to independent open marriage, which is an infantile euphemism for sex with kitchen privileges and is the essence of egocentricity.

Cooperation affords infinite possibilities for creativity and productivity within the enduring marriage. Its consummate expression is in the creation and sustenance of new life.

5. **Husband and wife accept and cultivate a great creative role to which each makes a significant contribution.** Traditionally, the creative role of parenthood was the central task of the husband's and wife's lives. Their creative energies were directed not merely to biological reproduction, but to the more prolonged and imaginative life work implicit in the development of a child into an adult.

The existence of a common task, whose achievement lies outside of themselves, nurtures the sense of love-security of a husband and wife.

There is still another way in which creativity—in the sense of a contribution to humanity—can be expressed in marriage. The husband and wife who do not have children can direct their mutual efforts toward a task or series of tasks that will ultimately benefit mankind. Frequently the role of parenthood is combined with this non-biological creativity.

Such marriages reflect the most altruistic and abiding dedication of husband and wife to each other and to the common creative goal they share. For example, the Curies (Pierre and Marie), the Pasteurs (Louis and Marie), and the Schweitzers (Albert and Helene) gave to mankind as well as to each other the harvest of their altruistic relationships.

Creativity is essential to an enduring marriage. In whatever form it is expressed, it acts as a dynamic, cohesive force, promoting feelings of love-security between husband and wife.

6. **In marital interaction, each mate is willing to be as constructively altruistic as he/she is capable of being.** Each mate is sensitive to those situations or latent conflicts that may elicit adverse and destructive responses. This mutual desire of the partners to give to each other is the foundation of their deepening love-security fulfillment.

Portraits of the Enduring Marriage

The following portraits of two happy and enduring marriages depict two vastly different couples. Both, however, are examples of the complex meshing of human personalities based on the Daddy's girl/Mama's boy relationship of childhood.

That uniquely loving relationship which has transcended the crises, disappointments and anxieties inevitable in every human life has been re-created in their own words, from letters, diaries, and observations.

Written records of human experiences are particularly appropriate sources for an examination of abiding marriages. They enhance the validity of the psychological case history approach and emphasize the role of altruism as the essential trait in an enduring marriage.

Sean and Eileen O'Casey

Eileen Carey was a hopeful and stunning actress of twenty-three when she married Sean O'Casey, age forty-seven, a manual laborer who dreamed of writing a play for the Abbey Theatre. Their marriage lasted thirty-seven years, until Sean O'Casey's death in 1964 at the age of eighty-four.

Eileen Carey's attraction to a man substantially older than herself was directly related to her feelings about her absentee father. As a child she lived a hectic, insecure life with two parents who were unsuited to each other. After her father had gambled away their home, he left the family in London while he went to South Africa to try to make a living. After failing in his endeavors, he returned to London ill and depressed. When Eileen visited her father in the hospital just before he died, she recorded her feelings: "I had developed a romantic love for him; throughout life I would look for a father-figure rather than a husband."

Sean O'Casey was the perfect fulfillment of her yearnings.

They were married on September 23, 1927. The match distressed friends, who were skeptical of its success. Eileen's mother especially frowned on Sean O'Casey as a husband for her daughter, although he displayed the greatest patience and concern for the mother's well-being.

Like every other husband and wife, they learned to adapt to each other, deepening their understanding as they came to appreciate each other's idiosyncrasies.

Eileen had a penchant for hot baths, which were somewhat of a luxury with the uncertain plumbing in Dublin. On one occasion she asked Sean if he would get someone to repair the cold-water tap. She recalled his reply: "God, Eileen, these baths again. However often do you have to take one?" Despite his annoyance, he had the tap repaired and she had her hot bath.

Sean, on the other hand, lived contentedly in an incredible state of chaos, as far as his books and papers were concerned. Or so it seemed to Eileen.

She noted, "He was much happier with a table over which he could scatter his papers in what seemed to me, or to anybody else, utter untidiness. For Sean the pattern was clear enough: he could tell you at once where anything was. It was only when the table had been dusted that panic and chaos ruled for half an hour until he could put his papers into the perfect order which to the rest of us was perfect disorder."

More serious were the crises, which in their case strengthened their love for each other rather than weakening it, as would have occurred if one or both had responded egocentrically.

On the day before their first child was born, Eileen's mother came to visit her. Eileen always attempted to make gestures of peace toward the older woman, whom she was never on very friendly terms with because of the way she felt her mother had misunderstood her father. Eileen was shocked by her mother's revelation that day.

She wrote, "My mother, who was having tea with me that day, told me in her morbid style that I should prepare myself for the fact that my child might be mentally afflicted: my father had been unbalanced, and the child's father was an eccentric."

Unbeknown to Eileen, Sean was struggling with his play, *The Silver Tassie*. Not wishing to cause her anxiety, he had decided to wait until after the baby was born to tell her the news: the Abbey Theatre had rejected it. It was a severe disappointment, one of the innumerable setbacks that would plague them in the years ahead.

The next crisis Sean and Eileen had to face was the death of their son Niall. Throughout this fathomless tragedy each tried to lessen the agony of the other. Instead of driving husband and wife apart, as tragedy often does, the suffering brought Sean and Eileen closer together than ever.

Eileen recalled, "The Christmas of 1956 was the most awful I spent. Niall, arriving for his holiday, seemed to be ill. . . ." Later a specialist explained that Niall did not have long to live. He had leukemia.

Eileen stayed in the hospital room with Niall, who knew he was going to die. Her son Breon was with her. She remembered only Niall. ". . . in my mind now I see only Niall, Niall going from life. He said 'Goodbye.' I did kiss him, and from a corner of his eye a tear was trickling, the one sign of sorrow that his fight to live was over at the age of twenty years."

After Niall's death, Sean and Eileen tried to comfort each other in the bleak moments of desolation.

Eileen wrote:

On one fatal night Sean was keening softly in his room. After supper I tried to talk to him, but we seemed to have no way at all of helping each other. I kept taking an extra drink; it did not help. Then, suddenly, a wild impulse came over me to take all the sleeping pills I had and to end it there and then. I had no thought of Sean; I was just utterly selfish and self-pitying. What happened after I had taken the pills I do not know. Sean, it seems, came to my room to talk, found me unconscious, and was terrified. Immediately he telephoned the doctor who drove over at once.

I suppose an ambulance arrived to hurry me to the nursing home where the doctor did *what he must to save me. . . . Sean, who had come to the nursing home, had been nearly demented while he waited to hear if I had recovered.*

Next morning the doctor said to me simply, "You can go home, dear. Let us say no more about this. It is far best forgotten." . . . Nobody had seen me leave the flat or come back to it. Again Sean embraced me in deep emotion; not one word was said then, or ever after; we knew it was essential to carry on living instead of indulging in selfish grief. Sean threw himself into his work; I went on with my everyday life, and we got over the time somehow, as one must.

One memento of Sean O'Casey's enduring love for his wife Eileen is a letter he wrote to her shortly before his death. The letter, written from Torbay Clinic, was dated August 12, 1964.

Dearest and sweetest girl of my life; dear, dear Eileen,

. . . My whole being refuses to do away with my wish to be home, to be back again where you are.

That is my only home, has been so for many, many years—where you, my darling, are: where you get up in the morning, go to sleep o'nights: where you come and go, where we eat together and talk together, and walk the well-worn paths, still bordered with many bright flowers and many blossoming bushes.

. . . And so it has gone on for nigh on forty years, your hands alone moulding the life of the little household. . . .

All this time a good many years, you had to face the barrage of bills, with never enough money coming in to ever let you shake yourself free from them; they were the necklace always twisting round your lovely neck, for I had no gift whatever to write anything that would find a ready market. . . .

. . . Wherever you are, Eileen darling, is home to me. . . . You are, and have been indeed, the pulse of my heart, and this heart of mine loves you, and will love you unto the last. Oh, my darling girl.

Sean

As one goes on alone, the poignant love of a lifetime is remembered in the bittersweet nostalgia of everyday life in its simplicity, its ordinariness, its sharpening loneliness.

Wistfully Eileen recaptured the past:

When Sean was alive it was possible to go out with the knowledge that he would be at home waiting for me; now nobody, when I return, will listen to all I have done, share my moods of happiness or depression. I have had to adjust to a life without Sean; without having him to look after; without him to look after me; without our talk and our jokes; without anyone to admire me as he did; without anybody to whom I belong.

I dread the stillness I walk into; the solitude. Deeply now, and always, I miss opening the door and not hearing Sean's voice, warm and welcoming: "Is that you, Eileen?"

Charles and Emma Darwin

One of Charles Darwin's early memories of his father was an admonition that he would be a disgrace to himself and to his family.

Charles's father, Dr. Robert Darwin, was an impressive, brilliant, dictatorial man who could be unbelievably insensitive to the feelings of his children. Autocratic and pompous Dr. Darwin left a complex emotional heritage to his son Charles. Motherless at the age of eight, Charles was inescapably molded by his remaining parent and the absence of maternal love in his boyhood years.

Although he manifested no visible signs of emotional distress in his youth, it was significant that he should choose as his wife a woman who was the epitome of consolation, a woman who satisfied his profound unfulfilled yearnings for the love-security he had never had as a child. Emma Wedgewood, his cousin, proved to be the ideal wife for Charles Darwin.

Charles never externally rebelled against the oppressive domination of his father; instead, his emotions took an unexpected turn. All of the unexpressed, inarticulate feelings that Charles had so carefully hidden from his egocentric father became manifest in his lifelong hypochondria. He was constantly suffering from internal disturbances, headaches, and nervous tension.

This was Charles's way of rebelling against his father's egocentric tyranny. Since the Victorian child did not dare respond to Daddy, his emotions bellowed and whined and bubbled explosively in gastrointestinal disturbances. But Dr. Darwin only manipulated Charles further by utilizing his hypochondria as a means of making his son dependent on him.

Repudiation of an egocentric parent takes many forms. Charles reflected his aversion for his father's domineering egocentricity by becoming exactly the opposite kind of parent himself. Charles rarely reproached his children. He was physically affectionate, sensitive to their feelings, and never imposed his convictions on them.

Where would such a timid young man find a loving wife, one who would always take tender loving care of him and honestly enjoy providing the love-security he so urgently needed? Where, of course, but among his cousins, with whom he had shared childhood moments of joy and lighthearted gaiety.

His cousins were the Wedgewoods, and Emma was one of the "dovelies" of that large and happy household. Contemporary friends described Emma as "a rock to lean on," a young woman who could always be depended on in any circumstances.

Meticulously, and with scientific objectivity, Charles Darwin weighed the advantages and disadvantages of marriage. He noted some advantages first: "children, if it please God, a constant companion, charms of music, female chitchat." Then he listed the disadvantages: "terrible loss of time, if many children forced to gain one's bread, fighting about not going out in society."

His conclusions: "My God, it is intolerable to think of spending one's whole life like a neuter bee, working, working, and nothing after all. No, no, won't do. . . . Imagine living all one's days solitarily in smoky dirty London. . . . Only picture to yourself a nice soft wife on a sofa, with a good fire and books and music perhaps."

Decidedly he wrote: "Marry, marry, marry."

The wedding of Charles Darwin and Emma Wedgewood took place on January 29, 1839. They lived together happily until his death on April 19, 1882.

How could a marriage survive between a retiring, hypochondriacal Mama's boy and a vital young woman who did not have the slightest interest in or knowledge of her husband's complex theories on evolution, insect-eating plants, and cross-fertilization?

Emma would have been considered a remarkable woman in any age; altruism is a timeless quality. Her need to give exactly what Charles yearned for created the perfect love-security environment and was fulfilling to both of them.

Charles did not require her to share in the complex facets of scientific research that occupied his life. They shared countless moments of life intimately and deeply. The intense humanness of their relationship and the pleasure they took in each other's companionship is revealed in minuscule glimpses of their life together.

Charles and Emma had a game of backgammon after dinner each evening. They were avid but friendly competitors. Charles noted to one of his friends that his poor dear wife had won only 2,490 games, while he had won 2,795 games.

One of the more sobering aspects of their life was the fact that three of their large family of ten children did not survive childhood.

Another problem was the violent storms of protest and indignation over his theory of evolution, which aroused much anxiety in Charles. It was Emma who shielded him against the debilitating attacks that his theory showered upon him. His perpetual illnesses were the perfect milieu for Emma's constantly developing altruistic nature.

Dr. Douglas Hubble, who made a study of Darwin's hypochondria in the *Lancet,* a British medical publication (December 26, 1953), should be credited with the most incisive and accurate analysis of exactly why this Mama's boy marriage flourished so beautifully.

He wrote, "Nursing was Emma Darwin's métier. . . . In the Wedgewood enjoyment of sickness lay the emollient influence that fixed irreversibly Charles Darwin's hypochondriacal habit. The perfect nurse had married the perfect patient."

Emma blossomed because of the constant attention Charles needed. Her day was planned so that she could be with him in all of his free hours. Solicitous, patient, sympathetic Emma removed from his world the clutter and distractions of an excessive social life. Unlike an egocentrically oriented woman, Emma derived her most profound joy from the knowledge that she was giving Charles the love-security he needed. His letters are filled with love for Emma.

To a future daughter-in-law, Sara Sedgewick, Charles Darwin wrote:

"Judging from my own experience life would be a most dreary blank without a dear wife to love with all one's soul."

He expressed this same abiding love for Emma in a letter to his daughter Henrietta. "Litchfield [Henrietta's husband] will in future years worship and not only love you, as I worship our dear old mother."

The grim Shrewsbury childhood was irrevocably etched in Charles's yearnings for love-security. To Emma he poured out his deepest, un-ashamed longings. "Without you when sick I feel most desolate. . . . I do long to be with you and under your protection for then I feel safe."

When the end of his life came, Charles offered Emma his ultimate tribute: "Remember what a good wife you have been to me."

6   The Mystery of Homosexuality

Although no parent deliberately rears a child to become a homosexual, either mother or father (or both), by expressing his or her unconscious ego needs, creates a milieu that predisposes a son/daughter to a future life of homosexuality. In the case history of a homosexual who seeks therapy there is almost invariably a pathological parent-child relationship. In many instances this pattern is not discerned until peer and societal influences on a son/daughter trigger overt homosexual activity. It is, of course, hypothetically possible for a young man or woman to gravitate toward the gay life without the preconditioning of a disordered parental relationship, but most case histories indicate a background of predisposing influences.

It is from within the early parent-child relationship that a son/daughter assimilates either an integrated or a distorted system of attitudes toward himself. It is within this parent-child milieu that a young person develops a propensity for homosexuality or heterosexuality. A personality distortion is narrowly defined by the individual himself on an unconscious level. When translated into overt behavior, it manifests itself in a sexual preference for a member of the same sex.

The complex psycho-sexual, peer and societal influences on a child will differ even within the same family. This is one of the reasons why, when two children grow up under ostensibly similar parental and societal influences, one may deviate while the other accepts heterosexuality. Although one can observe the emergence of certain characteristic traits, it is not possible to state that, because a son or daughter had a specific kind of relationship with a parent or parents, deviance is inevitable. An examination of such a disturbed parent-child relationship is central to an understanding of this behavior.

Deviation implies that a norm is recognized, not only in terms of biological development, but in terms of the societal impact of individual sexual activity. Heterosexuality expressed in an enduring monogamous marriage constitutes that norm; it best fulfills the sexual and human potential of an individual's personal and societal roles. Homosexuality is defined as a deviation from this norm because it does not provide for the fulfillment of these potentialities. The homosexual has abdicated normal marriage and family roles. However, there is a yearning for a permanent relationship that would assuage the characteristic pangs of insecurity and lack of self-esteem. The complex pattern of justification the homosexual offers to vindicate his/her life emphasizes the individual's inability to accept heterosexual life on a mature psychophysiological basis. As a consequence, the personality of the homosexual tends to be defined solely within the sphere of sexual proclivities, resulting in a stereotyped and inaccurate view of the distortions that initiated this life style.

In evaluations of homosexuals, emphasis is generally placed on the way he/she procures partners rather than on the parent-child relationship that distorted the son's or daughter's self-esteem, causing his or her subsequent vulnerability. Although homosexuals come from a variety of family situations, their early parent-child relationships with one or both parents are generally characterized by the absence of warmth and love-security, and by the presence of subtly or overtly masochistic or sadistic behavior on the part of either or both parents. Unconsciously, or sometimes deliberately, Daddy and/or Mama fosters deviance in a son or daughter by obstructing heterosexual development.

This occurs under multiple disguises. Basically, however, parental ego needs take precedence over the concern for the normal psycho-sexual development of the child. The sexual satisfactions of one or both parents determine the total emotional ambience of family life.

In the so-called normal intact family, the impediments to heterosexual development may be obscured by a façade of love. But beneath the façade there exists the same sadomasochistic pattern, with the same repercussions in deviant behavior. The parents may satisfy unconscious ego needs by expressing either extreme hostility or indulgence toward a specific child. They thereby establish a complex triangle in which the child is alternately exploited, indulged and ignored.

The impermanence of a family milieu consisting of a series of surrogate parents—either legal or informal—constitutes an indefinable shock to the child's self-esteem.

In the one-parent family, any serious sexual adaptation problems the parent may have will dominate the family life and adversely affect the parent-child relationship.

When a parent (or parents) within any of these family categories manifests deviant behavior, a pathologically disordered alliance is established in the son or daughter on an unconscious level, and this child will later emerge as a homosexual.

It must be emphasized that the child is, at this phase of life, searching in the parental relationship for a satisfying sense of love-security and self-esteem. If he experiences instead trauma, fear, rejection, hostility, inconsistency, parental sexual demands, or sadistic or masochistic behavior, he feels unloved and unacceptable to himself.

Thus begins the long unconscious flight from the sexual self that terminates in homosexuality.

The Gender Role

Homosexual behavior is both an unconscious and a conscious acceptance of sexual gratification in lieu of a normal heterosexual life adaptation. Biologically, the homosexual is a normal male or female. There is no genetic evidence to date to support a "fault" concept of hormonal imbalance in either the male or female.

Assumption of gender role is a complex cumulative process whereby the child acquires a systematized and integrated set of attitudes toward himself, based on his relationship with the parent of the opposite sex and his identification with the parent of the same sex. When the marital life of the parents is seriously troubled, the child's feeling for his/her gender role may be ambivalent, for he or she may receive contradictory and confusing messages. The child who is unwanted or unloved because he or she is of the "wrong" sex may experience this early threat to self-esteem.

In the Freudian, or classic, portrait of a homosexual, maternal responses to the son include domination, possessiveness and a subtle process of emasculization. However, in the majority of cases, there is a lessening or denigrating of the child's sexual self rather than an increasing process of masculinization or feminization.

This ambivalence in the child's perception of his/her gender role may grow through other experiences that lead the male or female child to conclude erroneously that it is not "good" to be masculine or feminine. The parent or parents, by their individual or collective responses to the child, convey to him the further notion that there is a "penalty" attached to a male or female life role.

The fact that a child has been rejected does not mean that he or she will later renounce heterosexual adaptation. However, it does increase vulnerability to homosexuality.

In acquiring his gender role the male assimilates, on an unconscious level, convictions, moods and feelings that will be stabilized later in life. If the mother is seductive, indulgent and excessively concerned about her son's well-being, she may interfere with normal gender identification by stifling or curtailing a relationship with the father. She may unwittingly stimulate gender confusion under the guise of love.

The female child establishes her gender identification in a continuously evolving process of unconscious acceptance or rejection of her mother. The mother-daughter relationship, even in childhood, may be characterized by fear, hatred and a sense of yearning by the daughter for love that the mother, because of her own disturbed personality, withholds.

Many of the distorted attitudes that the female assimilates are transmitted to her by a maternal parent who may be revolted by the physiological processes related to sex, marriage and childbearing. Lesbians, even the "feminine" partners in adult relationships, were usually unintentionally conditioned in childhood to fear and abhor heterosexuality, for it leads to pregnancy, childbirth and, possibly, venereal disease.

A young girl's guilt feelings about her gender role may not be recognized in the preadolescent years. The female child may believe that she will become a sexual serf. These distorted attitudes are reinforced in an adverse relationship with the paternal parent.

Because the parental relationship is either overtly disordered, temporary or characterized by sadomasochistic behavior, the female child develops feelings of fear, hatred, revulsion or disgust toward her father. Whatever his unconscious ego needs are, they involve a sense of alienation from the mother, which further confuses the daughter's gender identification.

The damage done to a male or female child by such gender distortion is rarely perceptible in childhood. Only as adolescence approaches are there glimmerings of the emergence of an altered personality.

Occasionally a series of sex-related traumatizing experiences will occur during childhood. These will further destroy the male's or female's already diminished sense of his or her sexual self. It is not unusual for a homosexual to report in therapy incidents of exhibitionism, attempted seduction, masturbation by a parent in the child's presence, or other frightening behavior.

The cumulative impact of these adverse events is to foster distorted perceptions of the sexual self. A tendency to drift toward the homosexual life is created by an eroded gender concept.

Taboo Against Heterosexual Interests

Although we have examined each of the factors contributing to vulnerability toward homosexuality individually, each emerging trait actually develops within a cluster of other traits, all of which exert profound pressure in this direction.

Gender role confusion continues to have a negative impact on the psycho-sexual development of the child as he grows into preadolescence and adolescence. However, in these impressionable years it is the taboo against heterosexual interests that decisively reinforces the antipathy toward the sexual self.

Prolonged emphasis by one or both parents on the idea that normal intercourse is evil, dirty or disgusting adversely conditions the male or female child during these sensitive years. A father or mother may protestingly explain that such a strategy was employed to inhibit sexual experimentation. Out of immaturity and confusion, the adolescent son or daughter misconstrues this information and is further alienated. The idea of heterosexual adaptation becomes uncertain, for it is surrounded by formidable obstacles created by one or both parents.

The taboo may also be fostered by a total parental denial of heterosexuality as a genuinely significant facet of marriage and family life. When a father or mother resorts to this strategy, a son or daughter may remain completely ignorant of the most elementary sexual information. He or she is then forced to seek sexual facts from the peer group. Meanwhile the dangers of heterosexuality are thrust on the male or female adolescent at every opportunity by the parent. A thoroughly negative conditioning occurs over a period of years, during which the distortions of the sexual self deepen.

Also, the parental marriage may undergo radical alterations, or a divorce may occur and the paternal parent may be designated as the villain. From the female adolescent's point of view, the psychological rift in her relationship with her father becomes a chasm. As a consequence, she may have neither father nor boyfriend with whom she can enjoy a relationship that takes cognizance of her emerging sexuality.

The stifling process, or establishment of obstacles, may involve nothing more than a parental unwillingness to provide a son or daughter with social opportunities where heterosexual interests could be developed under optimum conditions. There is a wide range of ways in which parents foster a taboo attitude against heterosexual interests.

The cultivation of heterosexual interests is a crucial phase in the normal transition from childhood to adolescence to adulthood. Because there are a considerable number of overt and covert obstacles in the adolescent's path, the future homosexual may adapt by withdrawing into a pattern of isolation. It is in these years that the unconscious distaste for heterosexuality is manifested by a revulsion toward the adolescent's contemporaries in general. The tendency to become a loner then further increases the adolescent's vulnerability to recruitment by an adult homosexual. If a loner pattern is established in adolescence and neither the mother nor the father expresses concern, this absence of concern generates a further predilection toward a homosexual adaptation.

Parental efforts to discourage heterosexual interests encourage the adolescent son or daughter to search for love-security and esteem through essentially destructive experiences. Feelings of fear and competitiveness intensify as normal heterosexual interests become remote or even vanish from the adolescent's life pattern.

There are two ways to fill this void. The adolescent may confirm the parental indoctrination against heterosexual development by becoming a loner, defining for himself a mode of adaptation characterized by withdrawal. Or he or she may begin to make tentative friendships of a non-sexual nature with members of his or her own sex that will ultimately lead to active homosexuality.

It is vital to understand that at this critical juncture in his life the adolescent's ego strengths have been almost totally obliterated. He is at the crossroads, and his emerging erotic needs are now pathologically oriented, although he may not yet have participated actively in homosexual activities. The heterosexual alternative appears to him, on an unconscious level, to be out of the question; his life experiences force him to reject it and seek substitute sexual gratification.

Friendships with Members of the Same Sex as a Prelude to Homosexual Activity

By the time the male or female child reaches adolescence, he or she is crucially sensitized. The child is particularly susceptible to any experiences or interactions that might promote further homosexual leanings.

The adolescent's relationship with his or her parents is characteristically nebulous and uneasy, filled with conflict and aggressiveness and devoid of love-security and esteem. As a consequence, the adolescent searches for reassurance in affectionate, but still non-sexual, friendships with members of the same sex. He or she may still retain the loner's sense of isolation and self-estrangement.

Several other powerful influences tend to divert the male or female adolescent from entering into the heterosexual arena. Because of the anti-heterosexual conditioning of one or both parents, there is a gradual unconscious surrender of expectation that the adolescent will be accept-able or desirable in an enduring relationship with a member of the opposite sex. The stress and suffering these perceptions arouse further predispose the adolescent to seek an affectionate friendship with a member of the same sex in order to ease his feelings.

On a conscious level, the adolescent may deny that he is opposed to heterosexual interests, but at the same time he has become almost totally oriented toward an acceptance of homosexual acts to provide an alterna-tive for his emerging sexual and emotional needs. Adolescents whose ego strengths have been particularly devitalized by this subtle process of conditioning and by a deteriorating relationship with a parent or parents are most susceptible to a homosexual experience.

A future lesbian is likely to have a very hostile relationship with her mother. Her father may, because of his own unconscious ego needs, engage in provocative or seductive behavior that arouses the female adolescent. Her father's attention to her may elicit anger and fury from the mother, which causes an increase in her anxiety because it indicates a deterioration of the marital relationship.

Or her father may be cold, brutal or domineering, and the daughter may seek a path of escape from this adverse relationship. It may appear only natural for the female adolescent to seek affection and love-security in feminine friendships. The adolescent may still not define her needs as specifically erotic.

The male is also ensnared in a similar pattern of anti-heterosexuality. The normal transitional phase—during which participation in friend-ships with members of the same sex serves as an expanding avenue of development toward heterosexual interests—becomes severely prolonged, and the normal development of heterosexual friendship through dating is inhibited.

Thus, when an adolescent male or female forms a close friendship with a member of the same sex, there is no objection, alarm or dismay on the part of either parent. For although these parents may have instilled adverse attitudes toward heterosexuality, they are not sensitive to the possibility of a homosexual relationship. The adolescent interprets a parent or parents' tacit acceptance of his friendship with a member of the same sex as explicit approval. The relationship appears to involve none of the dangers inherent in a heterosexual relationship.

An intimate, reassuring love-security relationship seems to be available to the adolescent only with a member of his or her own sex. Recruitment into the gay world is imminent, whether it is carried out by an experienced homosexual or by another adolescent who may have had occasional homosexual experiences.

The female adolescent probably will not define her needs as being solely erotic in the way the male adolescent will; rather, she will feel the need for affection in all its diverse manifestations, since it was critically absent in her relationship with the maternal parent.

When an adolescent cannot identify with the parent of the same sex, a decisive maladaptation takes place. The adult functions of male and female behavior are not achieved, because of the disordered parent-child relationship of the early years.

Obtaining Sexual Information

Parents transmit to a child a sexual value system based on their own unconscious ego needs. The system of behavior a parent prescribes is based primarily on the sexual adaptation of the individual; parents rarely make an objective and impartial transmission of sexual facts.

The male or female child in his or her earliest years assimilates sexual information informally. This indirect process constitutes a vastly more significant emotional experience than does any formal mode of sex education, because the child is inclined to accept the sexual norms the parents establish for him in the preadolescent years.

In the disordered parent-child relationship, sexual information, if it is imparted at all, is conveyed within a context of rigid, prohibitive or even evil insinuations. Negative connotations can be accompanied by physical abuse of the child for sexual experimentation. These constitute the principal forms of instruction. The young child may unconsciously perceive a complex range of negative parental emotions related to sex. He or she may also mislabel the genital parts of the body and/or confuse their functions with acts of excretion.

In a disordered relationship, the cumulative effect of the transmission of sexual information is to create irrational fear and revulsion responses in the child, rather than to promote future heterosexual adaptation. And the child's sexual value system will not be challenged by a comparable peer or societal influence in any serious way until he or she reaches adolescence.

Such a deleterious mode of instruction often leads to compulsive anxiety and preoccupation with sex. A total repression of sex and an absence of sexual instruction are frequently cited in the case histories of homosexuals. Exaggerating the secrecy surrounding intercourse can contribute to the curiosity and fear of a child. There are other pertinent parent-child responses that are less extreme than negative conditioning or a denial of sex. In the disturbed parent-child relationship, there is an absence of the vital "mothering" and "fathering" that each child needs in order to experience continuing love-security. Parents who are incapable of providing this sustained affection are inclined, because of individual personality problems, to represent sex to the child as an isolated experience. That is, such a parent may convey to the child the notion that sex as a function is not essentially integrated into the total human personality.

One of the crucial differences in background between the child who accepts heterosexuality and the child who does not seems to be in the manner in which sexual information was first conveyed to him/her in childhood. In the pathological parent-child relationship, negative and adverse sexual conditioning reveals a profound rejection of the child's sexual nature as male or female. Conversely, the child who will eventually accept heterosexuality learns sexual facts within a parental context of self-acceptance and flexibility. His parents convey to him a recognition of his sexual nature and its ultimate functions in marriage and family life.

Rivalry for "Love"?

A child's pathological orientation may be initiated by the parents' egotistic attempt to show love through indulgence. When the need of one or both parents for affection is not satisfied in the marital relationship, the parents may unconsciously direct these needs toward the child. Parents who are burdened with mutual recrimination tend to act out their unresolved hostility toward each other by competing for a child's love. The child emerges as the central figure in this complex triangle through which the parents are desirous of achieving ego satisfactions.

Typically this is the situation in the astonished intact family that is shocked when a son or daughter enters the homosexual world some time in late adolescence. One or both parents feel that they have been loving and lavish with the child.

If, for example, the mother offers the son love by indulgence, the male parent may become an adversary of the son, which will cause disturbed and guilty feelings in the male child. The male child cannot comprehend the controversy between his father and mother over their marital roles.

Only after he reaches adolescence, when there is an awakening of his sexuality, does he become aware of the hidden strife between his parents that has forced him into this distorted emotional alliance. The legitimate emotional needs of the child that have been thwarted and exploited by parents fester unobtrusively until crisis situations in adolescence force him to seek deviant sexual gratification.

One or both parents may find some relief from the turmoil within their marital lives by unconsciously making the son or daughter a substitute object of sexual satisfaction. However, the child seeking a durable sustaining love is thrust into alternatives.

The male child's normal need for maternal love and warmth will not be satisfied by a possessive, pampering and dominating response. Being his mother's favorite son is no longer gratifying when this intimate alliance arouses hostility in the male parent. The detached or antagonistic paternal response leads the vulnerable male child to seek alternatives. If the male parent is able to provide a son with a loving, sustaining relationship during childhood and adolescence, this affection will counteract the consequences of a distorted mother-son alliance. In effect, the sustaining altruistic love of the paternal parent allows the male child to identify with his father during adolescence. A rewarding relationship between father and son thus minimizes the susceptibility to homosexual adaptation.

Parental rivalry for the love of a female child has a somewhat different emphasis. The daughter's relationship with the paternal parent is rarely as intense as the mother-son pattern of the male homosexual. In therapy, a lesbian may recall a vague sense of estrangement and isolation, a feeling of inferiority based on the fact that she is a female.

Her father's behavior may range from explicit seduction to brutality, ineffectuality or even incidents of smothering protectiveness. There is not, however, the all-pervasive passionate substitution of paternalism for sexual gratification that appears in the mother-son relationship of the future male homosexual. There is not a comparable psychological trauma in the female child's attempt to divest herself of the male parent's domination.

Rather, there is a repetitive pattern of lovelessness in her relationship with the male parent. This creates a devastating void which arouses in the female child an intense need for love and self-esteem. These feelings are further exaggerated by the maternal parent, who conveys to the child the notion that as a female she has automatically been assigned an inferior or degrading life role.

The female child does not necessarily reject or denounce her male parent, but at an early age she develops ambivalent feelings toward him which are reinforced by the mother's inability to express warmth and affection. As she reaches puberty, she becomes acutely aware of mixed feelings of revulsion, and has no pronounced need to emulate the maternal parent.

This conditioning can be minimized when there is a very favorable relationship with the maternal parent. The adverse repercussions of the father-daughter relationship may be neutralized by a mother who provides her daughter with a sustaining warmth and affection. The daughter is then capable of acknowledging the fact that, although she may not love her father, these feelings do not preclude the possibility of eventual heterosexual adaptation.

There is yet another factor that may determine whether a female child will eventually develop an inclination toward heterosexuality or homosexuality. Should a baby girl be a Daddy's girl and enjoy all the love, affection, attention and caring she craves, and then gradually come to perceive the mother's display of open affection to her husband as a threat to her love-security, the child could conceivably harbor feelings of jealousy and resentment.

This love-security might also be threatened by the birth of a brother who usurps a major portion of the father's attention and love. Either or both of these possibilities, if felt deeply enough by a female child, might produce a powerful sense of rejection. These feelings can then contribute to her unconscious preference for a lesbian partner in later life.

The varied and complex reasons why parents become rivals for the love of a male or female child provide a breeding ground for all kinds of destructive life experiences. As we have seen, an extenuating factor that can conceivably alter the predisposition toward deviation is the relationship of the parent of the same sex with his/her child. If only one parent is truly maladjusted in the marital role, and that parent is of the opposite sex, the child is motivated to identify with the normal parent. This increases the possibility of eventual heterosexual adaptation, as it strengthens gender identification, despite the other adverse relationship. Above all else, the male or female child needs to have transmitted to him/her the concept that it is "good" to be a man or a woman.

Peer and Societal Influences

A child who has been preconditioned at home is most susceptible to the intricate peer and societal pressures that will be inflicted on him during his struggle through adolescence.

These transitional adolescent years are focused on the individual's growing opportunities for sexual experimentation and on a challenge of the sexual value system of the parents, whether or not it is anti-heterosexual. A heightened perception of the sexual self (including the maze of contradictions assimilated from the prepuberal years) combined with peer pressure may precipitate the adolescent's introduction into the homosexual world.

Societal and peer pressures tend to be inextricably meshed, so that the male or female adolescent who is vacillating between homosexual alternatives and heterosexual commitments is inclined to shuttle back and forth during the early adolescent years. During late adolescence, he may surrender to homosexual recruitment despite his reservations.

From non-sexual friendships within the peer group, he may quite easily drift into an erotic relationship that defines him as a homosexual. As a consequence, he may proceed unconsciously to justify his adaptation by adhering to the peer and societal influences that tend to vindicate his activity.

Within the last generation, society's definitions of male and female roles have changed dramatically. Biological, social, economic and educational definitions of the function of the male and the female have been transformed. The shift in emphasis has not been merely to a more pliable male and female life integration, but rather to a condition of normlessness in the relationship of the sexes to each other, thus aiding and abetting deviation as a mode of sexual adaptation.

The adolescent, who is already confused and disturbed by his emerging sexual self, discovers that his anxieties regarding heterosexual adaptation are groundless. Society has produced an elaborate rationalization that seems to resolve the adolescent's dilemma by offering as solutions homosexual alternatives which have now been defined as acceptable or even superior to heterosexual adaptation. Thus the drift toward unisexuality and normlessness.

The adolescent is, however, more profoundly confused by society's acceptance of homosexuality than he would have been by its non-acceptance. Although in the evolving normless society no one is socially ostracized, there are still consequences, most notably the deepening psychological and moral conflicts within the adolescent. The absence of norms for the regulation of his sexual conduct perplexes him. Should he or should he not experiment? The adolescent tends to remain cautious until unfavorable emotional conditions swamp him, at which time he succumbs to a homosexual excursion.

What are some of these conditions that arouse such turmoil in the adolescent?

The struggle for sexual identification intensifies during the adolescent, or transitional, years. The potentially homosexual male or female has developed a complex network of fear and/or hatred responses to the parent of the same sex. At the same time he or she is overwhelmed by his/her inability to make a successful heterosexual adaptation in the peer group. Such an adolescent is most likely to be influenced by society's tacit endorsement of experimentation.

The adolescent's quest for love-security and self-esteem narrows as his inner frustrations, doubts and hostility increase. If he is uncomfortable or rejected in heterosexual peer activities, he may join alternative social groups where he is accepted.

The female adolescent may be seeking surrogate maternal warmth rather than specifically sexual gratification. Frustrated by a chronic pattern of struggle with her natural mother—and hence perhaps an unsuccessful adaptation to peer society—she may yield to the warmth of an older, more sophisticated lesbian.

As the adolescent perceives the evolving normlessness of society, which now appears to encourage the coexistence of homosexuality and heterosexuality, he also becomes aware of other social forces that suggest that heterosexual adaptation may be ultimately eclipsed by homosexual adaptation. Attempts by older homosexuals to attract the adolescent to the gay world gradually become more appealing to him and to those of his peers who are preoccupied with grave self-doubts.

The adolescent may be aware of the growing body of proposed legislation that would permit various homosexual acts between consenting adults. The uninitiated discovers that the experienced homosexual may make a plea within the context of a political minority group, which is likely to evoke sympathy from a naive and gullible adolescent.

The adolescent tentatively accepts this world because it enables him to accept himself. During these years he subconsciously comprehends that there is some nebulous relationship between his discomfort in heterosexual peer society and his lack of expectation of successful adaptation to the group. An affiliation with the homosexual world offers him some of the warmth and self-acceptance for which he yearns.

Within this maze of personal and societal contradictions, the adolescent finds still another form of persuasion: pornography.

Explicit homosexual activity is recorded in films and books, enabling the adolescent to participate vicariously in the sensual satisfactions he needs to compensate for his disordered childhood. Pornography is one additional societal stress inflicted on the developing adolescent groping for sexual adaptation. Pornography, because of its vast audience, obliquely invites the tortured adolescent to join the subculture. The unique sexual inclinations of the group become, for the confused adolescent, a means of gaining satisfaction.

Peer and societal influences thus converge adversely on the adolescent who is already unconsciously prepared to seek alternatives. The cumulative process initiated in infancy continues unabated under a mask of tolerable parent-child adjustments until adolescence. At this critical juncture the adolescent is besieged by formidable external stresses that may definitely dissuade him from heterosexual adaptation.

In order to avoid homosexuality, the adolescent must have the strength to resist the combination of stresses acting on him. Otherwise, as he perceives his increasing difficulties in the sphere of heterosexual adaptation, his marginal adjustment torments him, and he yields to the tolerable haven of the gay world.

Attributes of the Homosexual Personality

Once the older adolescent or young adult accepts his homosexual adaptation, he rarely struggles to participate in heterosexual activities. However, like the male or female who successfully integrates his/her heterosexual adaptation into his/her life pattern by means of marriage and family, the homosexual yearns for an enduring relationship that will provide love-security and self-esteem. Herein lies the critical problem in terms of life adaptation.

The homosexual personality is riddled with paradoxes. Although he may feel a sense of security in belonging to a definable subculture, he also feels profound isolation and estrangement. He wanders from one partner to another in casual promiscuity. He may abhor and berate himself for these excursions because they are contrary to his goals of self-acceptance within a continuing relationship.

Moreover, during these years a distinct breach between himself and one or both parents may occur. Since it is unlikely that either parent will recognize his or her contribution to the homosexual orientation of a son or daughter, a serious and final rupture in the parent—adult child relationship is a definite possibility. The consequence is a deepening sense of rejection, succeeded by the child's acceptance of a complex system of justification for his/her life adaptation.

A combination of emerging character traits proves an additional obstacle to the establishment of a continuing relationship. The homosexual's low self-esteem is subtly eroded by a predictable succession of partners who seek only sexual gratification and ignore his total human personality. This fragmentation becomes intolerable to him, for his overall human needs are being casually dismissed. He is inclined, with the passing of time, to come to view himself primarily as a sexual commodity. His sense of worthlessness is a constant reminder that the possibility of an enduring relationship is remote.

His need for anonymity drives him further from contacts with the heterosexual world, and his sexual orientation exaggerates interpersonal difficulties. He is bereft of love-security, self-esteem, and understanding. Although he may gain a sense of acceptance from the larger homosexual or lesbian world, in a one-to-one relationship he is circumscribed by the essential transiency of all his sexual encounters.

A sense of extreme dependency on his temporary partner—coupled with an awareness of the futility of his situation—aggravates him. Eventually the turbulent anguish caused by the predatory nature of his or her impermanent relationships may motivate the homosexual to seek therapy.

Is the Homosexual Personality Modifiable?

Stress reaches its climax when a liaison between two homosexuals has run its course and one of the partners moves on to a new encounter, leaving the other with a deep sense of rejection, rage and despondency. It is at this juncture that a homosexual may be motivated to seek counseling, in order to obtain relief from the intolerable collection of emotions with which he is threatened.

The homosexual tends to carry on an incessant and angry war with himself, due to his jealousy, suspiciousness and inability to sustain any enduring relationship, even non-sexual friendships. There is generally a predictable pattern of casual, superficial and unsatisfactory human relationships. As a consequence, the homosexual who has recently been abandoned by a homosexual partner rarely has any other deep human attachment to sustain him during this critical experience.

Despite their unhappiness, these individuals may denounce therapy. They wish to remain as they are even though they understand that continuing with their life style will probably cause further stress. Therefore therapy will attract only certain homosexuals. By far the greater number of homosexuals have come to believe, because of their system of justification, that their life adaptation is natural for them. These people usually live an active life, and they are most resistant to personality modification through therapy of any kind. Moreover, with the gradual evolution of a normless society, this group clings tenaciously to the notion of a non-threatening, coexistent homosexual and heterosexual culture of the future. There is little realistic expectation that these people will seek out therapeutic assistance.

In order for the homosexual personality to be modified, the complex network of fears and hatred unconsciously cultivated through the disordered parent-child relationship must be diminished or at least partly neutralized, and the erotic drive must be redirected.

Those individuals who reluctantly enter into therapy because they are overwhelmed by the pain of rejection (rather than because of a desire to change) have a difficult and extensive therapeutic journey ahead of them. If a homosexual remains in therapy for a sufficient amount of time, he or she will be capable of determining a goal for himself/herself. That is, he will either become more powerfully motivated to change, or he will express a wish to remain in the homosexual world, in which case he will then merely need to modify his inner conflicts so that he becomes better able to cope with the pain of rejection by a homosexual partner.

A number of homosexuals eventually return to the haven of the homosexual world; others gradually become capable of entering into heterosexual life and marriage. There are some who make the shift to a heterosexual adaptation but are unable to sustain the relationship; they eventually return to their former world.

The homosexual most capable of personality modification is the individual who is voluntarily motivated to change. An individual who can express to his or her therapist a desire for a heterosexual adaptation and its inherent love-security and self-esteem is capable of making a shift in his or her self-conceptualization.

An alteration in the sexual value system of the individual is possible only when the person is not totally committed to homosexual adaptation. Realistically, from the therapist's point of view, this means that only those who are completely disillusioned with the homosexual world—as well as male and female teenagers who have had only isolated experiences—are generally susceptible to personality alteration.

It must be emphasized that it is the individual himself, not the therapist, who establishes the goal of heterosexual adaptation. In order to reorient erotic needs toward a capacity to enjoy heterosexual intercourse, marriage and family life, a positive conditioning process must be initiated and sustained. Ideally, such therapy would involve one or both parents and the male or female adolescent. A lessening of any anti-heterosexual feelings of either parent would help to reduce the self-devaluation that can lead to homosexuality. Counseling the family as a unit, as well as counseling the individual, may produce optimum results.

The therapist necessarily deals with the total personality of the individual, and not merely the sexual self. Hence, he or she will attempt to guide the adolescent and the parent or parents toward a reduction in the chronic tensions and conflicts that characterize their disordered relationship. The therapist will seek to improve parent-adolescent interaction so that a positive identification can be established with the parent of the same sex. At the same time, the adolescent's gradual acceptance of heterosexuality will tend to improve his or her relationship with the parent of the opposite sex.

The potential for personality modification is greatest when societal influences reinforce the desirability of heterosexual adaptation. As long as the normless society exploits the disordered parent-child relationship by presenting homosexual adaptation as a superior life pattern, then the outlook for the committed homosexual remains significantly unchanged. The contradiction between personal and societal rewards must be settled before the committed homosexual might be motivated to seek personality alteration through therapy.

As the male or female adolescent's self-esteem is enhanced by success in heterosexual friendships, a gradual transformation in self-image occurs. The individual begins to believe himself capable of entering into and sustaining heterosexual relationships. Moreover, as he or she experiences warmth and reciprocal love-security, he or she depends less and less on the homosexual world for assurance and acceptance.

7 Marital Case Histories

The question each person must answer is to what degree he or she is a Daddy's girl or a Mama's boy, rather than whether or not he or she is one at all. We may deny it vehemently or admit it with the greatest reluctance. Nevertheless, our relationships with our Daddies and Mamas have a profound impact on our adult lives.

In eighteen years of clinical practice, we have seen literally thousands of Daddy's girls and Mama's boys. Happily, most of their tangled problems have been worked out with the assistance of a counselor. Certain cases have taken many months to resolve; at times, a man or woman has needed several years of intensive counseling in order to gain sufficient insight into the problem to improve his/her patterns of behavior. Sometimes, however, the psychopathology of a Daddy's girl or a Mama's boy is so complex and irrevocable that the problem is never resolved.

Here are some typical cases in which the husband and wife were motivated to modify their behavior by the desire to continue an enduring marriage and to lead a happier adult life.

Beauty and the Beast

Wife	Husband
Denise Cloy	Herbert Cloy
Age 24	Age 35
Married at 18	Married at 29
Housewife and mother	Bank guard

It was a sultry midsummer day when Denise Cloy came into my office.

She was a stunning young woman. There was a subdued voluptuousness about her. Her long auburn hair was fashionably groomed, and her makeup, although simple, enhanced her beautiful skin.

Mrs. Cloy sat down gracefully in an upholstered chair opposite me. She seemed very rigid as she began to tell her story.

"I don't want Herbert to touch me anymore. As a matter of fact, I am revolted by him. I cringe when he comes near me. Sometimes," she admitted, "it's almost like being raped. I don't know what's the matter. Our sex life has skidded downhill ever since Jeanine's birth eleven months ago.

"We have three children. Bob is four, John is three, and our daughter is the baby in the family.

"After Jeanine's birth, when Herbert and I resumed our sex life, everything was different. When we were first married I was wild about Herbert. We made love every night. I was in seventh heaven. Then after Bob and John were born, our sex life changed. We were not so close. But I still didn't have the terrible feeling I have now about Herbert. It's a kind of physical revulsion."

Mrs. Cloy went on. "I came from a rather religious family. We grew up in Georgia on a farm, and there wasn't much money, but we were happy. Daddy was the center of our lives. Of course, I loved Mama, but I never felt close to her. She was always so busy with the chores. She did all the cooking, ironing, sewing, canning, gardening, housework, and she even wrote music that would occasionally be played in the church.

"Daddy worked hard, too. At one time he had three jobs. He worked the farm with my two brothers, and he helped a neighbor who had a small place about a mile down the road from us. Then on Sunday Daddy used to help the preacher with the collection and the maintenance of the church building. We were all proud of Daddy. He was like a port in a storm. I knew I could always depend on him. I can still remember Daddy kissing us good-bye after the church services while he stayed behind to help the preacher.

"In spite of all the work he had to do, Daddy was the one who used to sit and read to us, and we'd have long talks together. I remember snuggling close to him on his lap and leaning my head against his chest, feeling that everything was right with the world. On one of these occasions Daddy explained the facts of life to me. He did it in such a beautiful way that it didn't upset me. I felt good all over. After Daddy told me where babies come from, and the relationship between a man and wife, he kissed me on my forehead and I slid off his lap. Then he went out to work with my brothers."

Mrs. Cloy interrupted her tearful recitation to blot her eyes.

"I don't usually cry in front of strangers," she said.

"Well, to tell you the truth, I don't know what Daddy has to do with this trouble between Herbert and me. When I'm depressed I think of Daddy because he seemed to be able to make things come right again. Do you know what I mean?"

Mrs. Cloy frowned. "I know it's not going to be right again—that is, our sex life—until someone or something changes.

"You know, only last week when Herbert and I went to a symphony concert I had this same horrible cringing sensation when he touched my knee in the car. I felt as if some enormous beast was pawing me and I couldn't escape.

"When Herbert and I got home and went to bed I moved as far away from him as I could. I couldn't escape. He was all over me, pawing me. He's my husband, and I hate myself for describing him as a beast. He ignored my protests and went on making love to me. I shouted, 'You're a beast, Herbert, a beast.' "

I was startled by Herbert's appearance when he came to my office later that evening for an appointment. Although he was only in his thirties, he had a gaunt look about him. His hair was already gray, and his humped back caused him to shuffle down the corridor in awkward lumbering steps, somewhat like an orangutan suddenly forced to conform to the ways of civilization.

He had a very dark beard and a widow's peak, both of which emphasized the overall hairy effect of his appearance. His head was slightly deformed so that, although it was not exactly pointed, there was a well-defined, rounded protrusion at the back of his skull.

Mr. Cloy sat down and began to speak in a sad voice which contrasted sharply with his appearance.

"How come a gorgeous girl like Denise married a guy like me, you're asking yourself? Look at me, and look at her. You know, she is the most beautiful woman in the world."

For a moment he was lost in grief and lapsed into silence.

"I love Denise very much," Herbert said, his voice still pensive. "I would do anything in the world for her and the children. The truth is that she doesn't seem to know I exist. Sex has become a nightmare. I've turned into some kind of monster in her eyes. If you could only see the way she looks at me when I try to touch her. I used to think a man and his wife could have intercourse maybe up to sixty or even seventy, but we've come to a dead end. Denise probably told you about our last episode in bed. I couldn't help myself. I had to make love to her. After it was over, she cried and cried. I felt like a beast. I hated myself, and I hated her. At the same time I love her, and I don't understand why she avoids me."

Mr. Cloy proceeded to lean back in the chair and relax. He said, "I'm a bank guard. It doesn't pay much, but at least it's an honest living. I try to make the money go as far as I can. I love to buy beautiful clothes for Denise. She could be a model, she's so good-looking. She could have a bunch of guys running after her, but she settled for me." He said it reflectively, as if he could not imagine why he should have been chosen above other more handsome men.

"Denise and I love our children. We don't have any problems in that department. Bob is very close to his mother. John takes after me. And Jeanine is our little doll." He smiled for the first time, with what appeared to be a great deal of inner satisfaction.

"We're buying our house, and I'm painting it. You'll have to pardon me. I guess I still have some of the paint on my hands. I think I'm getting more on myself than on the house."

Suddenly Mr. Cloy veered in another direction.

"Isn't it natural for a husband and wife to enjoy their sexual relationship? Today everything is so open. You can get all the 'how-to' information in a paperback or a public library. As a matter of fact, I went to the library last week and found a book by a well-known doctor. I wanted to find out if I was doing anything wrong. Apparently not, but I've lost my touch," he admitted wryly.

"I put the book on the nightstand in the bedroom, and I suggested to Denise that she might want to read it. She just shrugged her shoulders and walked out of the room.

"Sometimes when I want to make love to her and she calls me a beast, I want to hit her. I could smash that lovely unforgettable face so that Denise would never be beautiful again. Then I think, 'Denise is right. I am a beast.' But I want her to love me the way I love her."

The Counselor's Comment
Like a collection of jigsaw-puzzle pieces that did not fit together, their stories lacked something, some pertinent piece of information that would point the way toward a resolution of the Cloys' marital difficulties.

Denise and Herbert were counseled individually for six or seven conferences. Then they were seen jointly for another dozen sessions. Each was given a battery of personality tests. An exhaustive case history of each side of the family, including a thorough sexual history, was prepared.

It was apparent that Denise was still influenced by a romanticized image of her father. He was bigger than life, with all of his human imperfections erased. In her memories Denise had preserved the image of a man who could only be described in superlatives.

During the initial counseling sessions, Herbert indicated that although he knew Denise loved her father, he was not aware that she cherished such a romanticized image of him. Denise was unconsciously comparing her husband with her father, and Herbert suffered in her evaluation. That she could not admit this to herself was part of her problem.

One day after nearly six months of counseling Denise impulsively pulled out a collection of plastic-covered photos of her children. They were indeed handsome and lively youngsters. Then, as she was about to place the photos back in her purse, she said, "Here is Daddy, the dearest man in the world, even though he's gone now." She blinked back the tears and handed the photo to me. This was the missing piece of the jigsaw puzzle. Here was the "beast" to whom Denise had referred repeatedly in counseling sessions.

Her father was an older version of Herbert. That Denise had never consciously admitted the startling physical similarity of the two men was the key to her problem. The fact that Herbert had not recognized this physical likeness only compounded their sexual difficulties.

How was this marked similarity of Denise's father to her husband related to the couple's sexual difficulties? Denise had revealed in earlier sessions that their sexual relationship had been satisfying before the birth of the first two children. She stated that a gradual change had taken place in her attitude after John was born. Because the two children were close in age, Denise and Herbert waited an additional year before the third child was conceived. After the birth of Jeanine, their sex life was dramatically different.

Originally sex was a happy experience for Denise because she wanted children. Every caress and word of love, including the actual act of intercourse, had a glow about it that would have been pleasing to Daddy. If Daddy said foreplay, intercourse, conception and childbirth were exciting, Denise was a willing participant. Psychologically she felt fulfilled. She believed that she was living out a promise to Daddy to be a good wife.

However, Denise gradually lost interest in sexual relations when conception did not follow, for she had learned from Daddy that the two were inextricably bound together. Herbert enjoyed sex and closeness with Denise, and he did not share her attitude that intercourse must result in conception. As a consequence, Denise found herself rejecting even the most casual caress, since it was a cue that Herbert wanted to make love. That would not be Daddy's wish.

Since Denise did not want any more children, she unconsciously did not want a sexual relationship with Herbert. He became, in her mind's eye, a lecherous beast intent on his own selfish desires. Repeatedly she had said, "I don't want Herbert to touch me. I am revolted by him. It's almost like being raped."

Herbert had indicated to Denise that they could not afford any further additions to the family. He planned to have a vasectomy.

With continued counseling Denise was able to admit to herself that she was a Daddy's girl, and that her memory and imagination were perpetuating an image that obstructed the cultivation of a positive sexual relationship with Herbert.

Gradually, with the help of this strategic insight into her feelings about her father, Denise was able to move once again toward an acceptance of Herbert as husband and lover, and her feelings of loyalty and intimacy returned. She was eventually capable of objectively accepting the knowledge that, while she loved her father, it was immature to attach sexual significance to that love and, most importantly, it was inappropriate to let it interfere with her sexual life with her husband. Herbert was now seen not as a "beast" but as a loving husband who did in fact resemble her cherished father.

Stop It, Neville

Wife	Husband
Mary Virginia Pate	Thomas C. Pate
Age 33	Age 33
Married at 23	Married at 23
Housewife and mother	Office manager

Tom Pate was a slight man with a receding hairline and an unexpected booming voice which issued forth from his reedy frame. He wore an unkempt business suit and had dirty fingernails. Mary Virginia Pate was a rather dowdy-looking young woman. Her clothes seemed to hang on her, and she wore her hair combed starkly back from her gleaming, unpowdered face. She was visibly uncomfortable and fidgety.

At our opening conference she seemed to feel a need to pout in order to divert attention from her husband when he was speaking. Finally, after Tom Pate laughed loudly, Mary Virginia's angry voice burst forth to command center stage. "I haven't slept with Tom for months," she began.

"I don't think he's sure of his manhood, his financial status, his sexuality as a husband, or his position as a father. I think he masturbates because he certainly doesn't have sex very often with me. You would think he would ask me to come back and sleep with him," she said moodily.

Mary Virginia swallowed hard. "Tom always wants his own way. He was the baby in his family. There were seven children, and they are all characters and problems. He refuses to talk about his childhood. Instead he says he can't remember any of it. My family lived about fifty miles away from his family in Oklahoma. His parents were not very happy. His mother is dead now. So much for family," she said flatly.

"Tom has no ambition. He doesn't make very much money, although he has fourteen people whom he supervises. As a matter of fact, he earns only about one hundred dollars a month more than two of the men who are under him.

"Tom has some sort of respiratory ailment which he denies. I can't stand to sleep with him because of this. He tells me I am mistaken and he refuses to go to see a doctor. We never seem to find friends that both of us like. I don't like his friends and I don't like his office parties. At one of these recent parties Tom had to prove to everybody that he was ping-pong champion. He made a perfect ass of himself. Tom ignored the hostess who announced dinner and went on playing a game with a young man. When he finally came to dinner, everyone had already begun to eat. I was so embarrassed."

Tom Pate stared morosely at the floor while his wife continued.

"He has absolutely no leadership qualities. He is a bungler of the worst sort. When we returned from a recent excursion to Catalina, he forgot his key, so I had to help one of the boys climb in through the kitchen window to open the door for us. This is only one example. There are innumerable ones."

Mary Virginia took a deep breath. She avoided looking at her husband and riveted her attention on the painting on the wall behind him. "That reminds me," she said. "Tom wanted to buy a hideous landscape painting from a local artist on the island. I intervened just as he was about to squander our money. I forbade him to buy the painting.

"If you could only know how much responsibility I have had to assume because of him," Mary Virginia said. "He's not half the man my father is," she said, looking directly into the sober gaze of her husband.

Instantly Tom defended himself. "That's the root of our problem—her father," he said. "I am constantly being compared with her father. Ever since we've been married I have been reminded of my inferiority to this god who fathered her."

Mary Virginia's face reddened in embarrassment.

"Don't interrupt me now," Tom Pate warned, shaking a fist at his wife. "Every time she compares me with him, I'd like to punch her in the nose. In spite of her constant attacks, I still love her, but I loathe being called a homosexual. She isn't telling you the truth about our sexual relationship. All of a sudden she tells me she doesn't want to have anything to do with me. Well, it all goes back to her father. Mary Virginia was very close to him as a child. He taught her how to do cabinetry and build a lot of things just as if she were a boy.

"Then when she was about nine, a baby sister was born, and her father shifted his affections to her instead. Mary Virginia denies this, but to this day the two of them don't have much to do with each other.

"Her family, meaning her father, sends Mary Virginia money every year for a vacation to go back to Oklahoma with the boys. Do you know, she doesn't even invite me? She takes this solo trip with the boys and ignores me. I tell her we should have family vacations, but it doesn't change her plans one whit."

Tom Pate still had his fists clenched on the arms of his chair.

"Mary Virginia is a hypocrite, too. She doesn't want her family to know that she indulges in booze once in a while or cigarettes. When they came out here for a visit a few years ago, she hid everything. I think all she can think of is pleasing her father.

"She has this notion that he is going to leave her a lot of money because he told her that he won't leave it to her mother since she might go out and spend it all.

"Another thing," he said. "We have a problem with our oldest boy, Rob, who is seven and a half. Mind you, this goes back a few months, but let me start at the beginning. When Mary Virginia was still sleeping with me in the bedroom, Rob would come in the middle of the night and climb in bed between us. I used to blow up and tell him to go back to his own room. Mary Virginia would overrule me and tell him that he could stay. Now that she is sleeping in his room I think Rob has a lot of confused ideas about married life. Mary Virginia has given all three boys the wrong impression about a father's position in the home. Whenever they deserve a good swat on the rear, she defends them and refuses to let me discipline them. Instead she says that a word to the wise is sufficient.

"Speaking of the rear," Tom Pate said, "there's something else I want to tell you. It's peculiar, if you ask me. I used to come up to Mary Virginia and pat her on the fanny or maybe grab her in an affectionate way. Almost immediately and instinctively she would say, 'Stop it, Neville.' Now why would she do a thing like that? My name isn't Neville. That's the name of her father."

The Counselor's Comment

Mary Virginia was hypercritical of everything Tom did. According to her, he was a clumsy, incompetent bungler. She had projected an image of him that made him appear totally inept, and in his anxiety he seemed to live up to her expectations.

He wore slovenly clothes. He was one of the "before" pictures in a self-improvement advertisement. He drank too much and smoked too much. She didn't approve of or like his friends. He didn't have sufficient initiative. He should find a better job. She didn't like the way he made love. She didn't like his unusual voice. He slept late instead of going to church. The litany of Tom's faults was interminable. Hence, Tom was placed in a defensive position of constant preparedness for marital warfare.

After diagnostic testing and several conferences together, it was determined that in the best interests of the marriage Mary Virginia should commence a regular program of psychotherapy, while Tom would be counseled about twice a month.

In the early conferences Mary Virginia lamented her husband's multiple inadequacies and proceeded to demolish him, always contrasting him to the glowing image of her father which she embroidered with lavish reverential affection.

"Daddy was wonderful," she exclaimed.

Even as an adult woman Mary Virginia still referred to her father as "Daddy," although she called her maternal parent "Mother" in the customary adult fashion. She was unaware of the self-revelation implicit in this paternal term.

"Daddy bounced me on his knee," she said. "He told me fairy tales. He made a doll for me. We took long walks together. I adored him," she said. "When I grew older, he taught me how to use the tools in his workshop. I could build a cabinet as well as any man," she said proudly. "What's wrong with that? Women are not dolts, you know."

In the process of describing this intense childhood relationship, Mary Virginia was at every point comparing her husband to her father. Mary Virginia had exaggerated her father's abilities so that Tom always appeared at a disadvantage. She was, in fact, apologizing to herself for having chosen this man as a husband.

This ambivalence aroused considerable hostility which in turn was expressed in their sexual relationship. Mary Virginia unconsciously resented the reality of an active sex life with Tom, probably because she could not envision a sexual relationship with her father. She vented her ambivalent fury against her husband, who did not understand the complex conflict she was experiencing.

Mary Virginia's relationship with her mother acted as a further deterrent to a normal married life. The serious hostility she felt toward her mother plus the excessive adulation she lavished on her father caused Mary Virginia to marry a man like Tom, who did not have the kind of aggressive leadership qualities she believed she admired. Because Mary Virginia wanted to be like her father, rather than her mother, she unconsciously chose a husband she could dominate, despite the fact that this was bound to cause unhappiness. When she finally surrendered to these painful admissions about the past, Mary Virginia realized how powerfully her father had influenced her childhood. "I used to wait on Daddy hand and foot," she confided.

The counseling sessions enabled her to relieve herself of some of her unrealistic idolatry of her father. In fact, a plan was devised whereby Mary Virginia, without her children, was to go back to Oklahoma to visit her mother and father. She was to pay her own way. During the week's visit, she was to study carefully the behavior patterns of her father and her mother and record her observations in a diary. Upon her return, she read the following excerpt from her diary:

> When I first arrived on the farm mother met me at the door. She greeted me with what I perceived to be mixed emotions. She was glad to see me, but she must have sensed something different in me because she was not used to seeing me there alone. My mother could not understand why I had refused in correspondence with her the offer of my father to pay me back for the trip.
>
> Dad was [I noted that Mary Virginia referred to him as "Dad" for the first time since I had known her] seated in the front room, holding Freddie [her sister's little boy, age three] on his lap. When he heard my voice he almost pushed Freddie out of the way and bounded toward me. He kissed me on the mouth while hugging me and pulling me close to him. He had often kissed me on the mouth before, in fact, over the years, but this was the first time that it ever bothered me. I watched him closely over that week. The message came through that he was, as always, overwhelmed in seeing me and yet he paid less than usual attention to mother.
>
> As the week wore on and he did his usual thing of wanting to talk for hours with me, even sometimes after mother would grow tired and go to bed, I noticed that it took its toll on mother. She was preoccupied with other things and showed a kind of indifference to me. For the first time in my life I began to experience the reality of some of the things we discussed in counseling when you said to me, "Have you ever really quietly meditated upon the solicitousness of your Daddy?"
>
> These words rang in my ears during this week on the farm, and as I add the last notes in this diary on the plane returning to the Coast, the tears will not stop, and I hurt all over. For the first time in my life I feel I have shortchanged Tom.

Looking up from her diary with a pained expression, she continued, "He wasn't all that great, my dad. He can't be my husband because he's my father."

She had finally torn away the last Daddy's girl illusion from the hallowed shrine in her memory.

"I've got to think of Tom and the boys. They're my life."

Gradually Mary Virginia was able to perceive more realistic images of her father and of Tom. As her father's personality became more lifelike, so did Tom's. He was not the inept, bumbling incompetent Mary Virginia had made him out to be. She no longer felt the need to destroy his assets in order to ennoble her father.

Today she still loves her father very much, but the relationship has altered so that she is now able to understand him in terms of her hard-won maturity. Mary Virginia is still struggling to accept her mother.

Most significantly, she has completely changed her attitude toward Tom. She is gradually relinquishing the reins in the family and permitting Tom to take an increasingly active role of leadership. This has reduced the tension between them substantially, for it has enabled Mary Virginia to accept herself as a woman and Tom's sexual partner. The competition between them has decreased, and each is able to enjoy the other without fear of criticism.

Because Tom has taken the initiative in many areas of the marriage, he now sees his wife in different terms. She is no longer a formidable obstacle to his business success or his personal happiness. After an arduous struggle with their unresolved conflicts of childhood, they have at last learned to redirect them toward a warm and loving marital relationship.

The Modern Prodigal Son

Johnny Singleton
Age 29
Single
Television actor

Johnny Singleton was plainly a man in anguish. When I greeted him in the reception room he looked worried. He responded to my "hello" with a forced smile and an incongruous "hello there." His choice of clothes—slacks, sport shirt and a pullover sweater—and the way they hung on him indicated that appearance was just not his number-one priority. He wasn't especially overweight, but he was flabby. He bounded to his feet, and after we shook hands he swaggered into my office.

"You might as well know that I am here not so much on my own, but to please my parents," he said. "I am gay. I have this relationship with Chuck, who lives in an apartment below mine in the Hollywood Hills. We really have an understanding. We can share anything. We recently took a month off and just bummed around the entire country, visiting television stations and the network headquarters in New York. I am an actor and so is Chuck. I know this is probably not the average case you see in this clinic, but we're real people, too."

He then proceeded to explain his acting career. "I began my acting in high school and continued through college. I have worked in community theatre and several small production companies here in Hollywood. I haven't really been able to put it all together yet. I had a couple of small parts in television pilots, but so far they haven't sold. I draw my unemployment check, and that's how we make it."

I asked what he meant by "we," and he countered with, "Chuck also draws unemployment. He has been a little more successful than I have because he did a couple of commercials that bring in payments on a regular basis—at least as long as the commercials keep running. We get by. We often eat together, and this helps financially.

"I really love Chuck, and even though there are considerable pressures that others force upon us, we are quite open about letting people know that we do care for each other."

When I asked him how long he and Chuck had been lovers, he said, "We've made it about a year and a half. But if you're going to ask me how long it's going to last, I can't really deal with that now. All I can tell you is that I have very strong feelings for him and we love each other."

His face was bland. Looking down at the floor, he began uncomfortably, "I went with Sam before Chuck. In fact, we lived together for about six months in the Venice area. That was really an experience. We moved into an old house where a couple lived. There were also some single guys. I remember it was a Sunday, and my family helped me to move. I know they didn't understand what was happening. I think they were suspicious, but no one ever said anything.

"Before Sam I guess I've made it with three or four other guys, but there was no long, strung out, deep feeling involved. My first experience, believe it or not, came after college when I was working in a community theatre, and one of the guys knew I had the hots for him so he invited me to his apartment, and, to make a long story short, that was my first experience. Then I met this trumpet player who knocks about with local bands. We've gotten together a few times. He's really a tremendous artist. He goes on tours with some of the big orchestras from time to time, and he has even played in the Kennedy Music Center."

Johnny Singleton avoided looking directly at me. "Are you here to please your parents? Or is counseling something you want to do to help yourself?" He did not answer my question. When he did speak, it was about his family.

"My parents live in Tujunga," he said. "I have seven brothers and sisters. My mother is a homemaker and teacher. She works part-time at one of the schools in the Valley. She teaches English and Family Relationships. My father is a fireman."

He added soberly, "All this shakes my parents up. When I first told my mom that I am gay it was a bad scene. We had gone out to dinner, and she began questioning me about my life style. I just laid it on her. I told her I had had these feelings for several years, and that I saw nothing wrong with it. I hoped that she would accept it even though I knew she did not understand. The more I tried to explain things to her, the more she cried. It was hopeless. But it's just as well that she knows.

"Then she told my dad. He hasn't had too much to say about it. Incidentally, my father and I are not exactly buddies. He says he loves me, but he knows we have very little in common. I think the fact that I am gay has shocked him. I think he's falling apart because of my life style. I guess that's why I'm here."

The Counselor's Comment

Johnny Singleton really needed insight psychotherapy. He came to the clinic to satisfy his parents, who had agreed to pay a portion of the counseling fees. During counseling sessions Johnny Singleton was defensive and argumentative. He went into lengthy justifications of his homosexuality. Yet he was obviously unhappy and drifting. He knew that his relationship with Chuck was tenuous; their only common denominator was sex. Although he spoke glowingly of the sexual satisfaction he had from Chuck, it was apparent that he was torn between his life style and the respect of his parents, particularly his mother.

Mother was his favorite subject, but he was not sure that she loved him—at least as much as she ought. Johnny was the first child, and not exactly his father's favorite. It is often the case that a father will see his firstborn son as a competitor.

There is an ambivalence of feelings; there is love of a sort, but it is uncertain. The father feels incapable of dealing with his fear that he will not continue to be number one in the eyes of his wife. Johnny's father believed his wife loved him less after the birth of his son. True, the mother did spend a great deal of time with her new infant. The breast feeding, the changing of diapers, the cuddling, the playing, the soft, endearing words that seem natural for a mother can be misinterpreted by the young jealous father.

For two years Johnny was an imperious king around the house. When his sister was born, a dramatic change came over him. He was not willing to share the spotlight with this intruder, and he revolted. He cried, he fought going to bed, and he objected strongly when his mother attended to the new baby.

Johnny became suspicious of the affection his father gave to his mother. As the years passed it became apparent that Johnny was not going to be an athlete, nor was he going to follow in his father's footsteps; he refused even to learn how to work with tools. He showed a softness in his demeanor. He felt closer to his mother than to anyone else in the family, and he had little to do with his brothers or sisters. He became completely egocentric and self-seeking.

He did well in school and showed special ability in extracurricular activities, particularly those that involved verbalization and creative expression. While in high school and college he excelled in drama, speech and literature. Johnny showed almost no desire to change his life style.

Counseling was terminated after twelve sessions, and nothing more was heard from him for a year and a half.

Then one day a phone call came from Johnny. He indicated that he was seeing a psychiatrist, and he asked me to forward copies of his tests, as well as my opinion. I not only did this, but I called the doctor, for I was quite interested to learn what crisis had brought Johnny into therapy. The answer was exactly what I had predicted—Johnny had been jilted. Chuck had found another lover, and Johnny felt quite alone and despondent. In his depression he had confided in his mother. She had urged him to see a psychiatrist, but only if he truly wanted help.

The psychiatrist verified my observation that Johnny was a Mama's boy. The doctor believed Johnny would have stayed close to his mother had the new baby sister not arrived and usurped his kingdom. Because his father had unconsciously rejected Johnny, the boy found little to emulate in manhood. The influence of his mother and sisters affected his outlook on life. It made him soft and unusually sensitive. Since he lacked self-confidence, dates with girls did not come readily, which led him to believe he did not appeal to women. In a moment of weakness he gave in to the overtures of an older man. After that first encounter he continued on the path of homosexuality.

Another year passed before I heard from Johnny again. He told me that he had made some real progress. He was no longer involved in any homosexual activity. He reported that as he persevered in psychotherapy, he started moving into feelings of bisexuality. Months passed and finally he met a girl who liked him very much. They dated, and Johnny said that they had become intimate.

He was gradually gaining self-understanding and insight into the truth about his relationship with his family. He admitted that he was an egocentric person who had little love or concern for his brothers and sisters. He said that with time he hoped to grow closer to them. He also tried to make peace with his father and accept the reality of paternal love. His father, in turn, acknowledged that his jealousy and suspicions of young Johnny had been ill-founded. He knew now that his wife loved him, and that her motherly feelings for Johnny did not interfere with this love.

Finally Johnny faced his feelings about his mother. She told him that, although she loved him and wanted his happiness, she did not want to control his life. She admitted that pride at being a "super" mother had provided relief from her own frustrations early in the marriage. This made her realize that her husband might have misinterpreted the situation and felt hurt. She was eventually able to communicate her feelings to her husband, and the two had a tearful reunion.

Johnny Singleton felt trapped between his homosexual sprees and his bisexual yearnings. There were times when he was not sure whether he was male or female. However, during two years of counseling he was able to resolve his inner conflicts and come to terms with his mother, his father, his girlfriend and himself. He was at last a free man, for he had overcome one of the most difficult problems in society today—homosexuality.

Homesick on His Honeymoon

Wife	Husband
Gloria Sanchez	Newton Sanchez
Age 43	Age 42
Married at 43	Married at 42
Saleswoman in department store	Bus driver

Three people were sitting on the sofa in the reception area when I opened the door and requested Mrs. Sanchez. Instantly the younger of the two women jumped up.

"I'm Mrs. Sanchez," she said in a high-pitched, nervous voice.

"I'm Mrs. Sanchez," said the older woman as she moved slightly away from the younger man, who was blowing smoke rings at the ceiling.

The older Mrs. Sanchez cleared her throat dramatically. "This is my son," she said, gazing fondly at the middle-aged rotund man, who continued to blow smoke rings. "He is having problems with his wife."

The younger woman, her brown eyes flashing angrily, said, "I made the appointment. I am Gloria Sanchez." In my office Gloria Sanchez heaved a sigh of relief and then gritted her teeth as she said, "That woman!"

Gloria Sanchez was a slender woman with many nervous mannerisms. She drummed her fingers on the table next to her chair. She tapped her shiny black patent leather pumps against the floor as if she were listening to some urgent inner beat that had to be expressed. Her fire-engine red dress matched her smoldering emotions.

"It's none of her damned business," she declared. "That old snoop had to tag along today. Newton had to borrow his mother's car, and she insisted on coming with us for the ride, even though your office is clear across town from where we live.

"Newton and I have been married only six months," she said, waving her left hand, which had a minuscule diamond and a wedding ring on it. She caressed the rings gently.

"I have made up my mind that either we are going to have a marriage and a life of our own, or Newton can go home and live with his mama."

Gloria lighted a cigarette, inhaled, then continued, "Let me tell you about our courtship before I describe our marriage. I was living on the east side of town where I grew up, and I had a job working downtown in a department store. I met Newton on the bus. He used to drive the bus I would take to work.

"At first the whole thing seemed like a joke to me," she confided. "I'm no spring chicken. To be honest with you, I had almost shelved the idea of marriage. Then I met Newton. He used to save a place for me on the bus directly behind the driver's cab. No matter how crowded the bus was, that seat was always empty when I got on. Several times there were grouchy faces looking down at me as I slipped into that seat. But Newton had a cheerful smile on his face whenever he saw me.

"Finally," Gloria said, "after six months of riding on his bus, Newton worked up enough courage to ask me for my phone number. We had our first date without his bus the following Sunday afternoon.

"And what did we do? Why, naturally we went to visit Newton's mother." Gloria almost spat out the words.

"I never understood that woman," she said. "She was pleasant enough to me on that first date, but ever since then I've had the feeling that she was nice to me only because of Newton.

"We dated for a year, during which there was some affection, but absolutely no sex. I think I might have been receptive if Newton had made any overtures. He was scared to death to touch me. He never even put his arm around me in public, only when we were alone."

She crushed out her cigarette and lighted another one.

"I remember one day we went on the bus to Disneyland for the whole day. I don't remember him touching me once. Then when he took me home he finally made advances. I told him good night.

"It isn't that I didn't want to get married. I did. I wanted to marry a man who would love me and protect me, a man who would enjoy being close to me physically. We're both probably too old to have children, but since the menopause has not yet come knocking at my door, I have some hope that we might even have a child.

"You know, Newton's a peculiar kind of guy in his way. He seldom took me anyplace on a date. He would just come over and hang around the house. He had money, but he couldn't seem to bring himself to spend it on me.

"And as you know, he's terribly devoted to his mother. He would often take her for a Sunday afternoon ride and out to dinner at least once a week.

"I'm not sure how he managed to propose to me. He was so damned noncommittal and evasive. At my age opportunity isn't going to knock too many more times.

"I had the distinct impression when he agreed to marry me that somehow his mother was going to have to give her consent, although he never admitted it in quite that way.

"We went to Las Vegas for our honeymoon," Gloria reminisced. "What a forgettable first night we had. Newton was exhausted, so there was absolutely no lovemaking. The second night was also a fiasco, and on the third night he tried again, but there was nothing. I was so disappointed. I refused to let him know how I felt. Instead I tried to comfort

him. He confessed that he had never before been so far away from his
mother and home. He told me he was lonely for her."

Gloria closed her eyes and grimaced in pain at the recollection.

"If our honeymoon was a disaster, it was only a preview of coming
attractions. When we returned home, we naturally had to move into the
third-floor apartment of his mother's home. Newton kept telling me that
he couldn't find a place that would be suitable for us. And I swallowed all
that jazz," Gloria said.

"I always felt Newton's mother was going to barge in on us at any time.
She definitely must have let herself into the apartment when we were at
work, because I used to find things moved around when I came home.

"Newton was a kind of married bachelor. He held on to his single
habits for dear life. Sunday was dedicated to Mama. He would take her
regularly for a ride in the afternoons exactly the way it was in the old
days. He was always talking about her, too. I was furious with him. He
couldn't seem to make any decisions without talking to her first.

"Finally, after three months, I gave him an ultimatum. I told him,
'Either we move out of your mother's home, or I'm going to leave you.' "

Gloria paused to catch her breath and take a sip of water.

"He was speechless. He didn't say a word to me. Then on the last day
of the month Newton came home from work and told me we were
moving in the morning."

Her staccato patter came to an abrupt end. I waited for her to go on
with her story.

"Guess where we moved? Next door. That old witch had such a
stranglehold on Newton that he moved next door. I knew I had married a
mouse instead of a man. Well, after I exploded, I packed our things, and I
moved out. I figured next door was better than being in her house under
constant surveillance."

Gloria tapped her foot impatiently and crossed her slender legs.

"Frankly, this is one hell of a poor marriage. Do you know, I still could
not get Newton out of his mama's clutches? Every day after work he
would visit her first, then come home to me. Every day"—she stressed
the word—"Newton would call her on the telephone. Now what kind of

a guy is that? I wish I'd never laid eyes on him and his damned bus."

"I should have bought a car," she concluded.

In contrast to Gloria, Newton was a man of few words. He was trapped between his mother on the one hand and Gloria on the other. He volunteered little information because he was used to letting his wife or Mama talk for him. Now he had to be encouraged to express himself.

Newton had an almost expressionless face. His emotions seemed to be carefully hidden behind his pendulous jowly face and his deep brown eyes. He had a low forehead and bristly dark eyebrows.

"I love Gloria. Even though we married late in life, I do want our marriage to last.

"Gloria doesn't understand that I have responsibilities to my mother. Before my father passed away he asked me, in those last moments, if I would take care of her as long as she lived. I made a deathbed promise to him. I can't go back on my word, even for Gloria.

"Like all women," he said, "she has her idiosyncrasies. She can't bear the thought that I should have any deep feelings for another woman. Gloria seems to think that just because I married her I'm supposed to forget about my mother.

"Gloria expects me to change the habits of a lifetime. Well, it's not so easy," Newton explained, somewhat chagrined.

"I'm an only child. My mother is all I have," he said. "What kind of a world would it be if a son abandoned his responsibilities? Besides, I love her. I'm not ashamed of that. I love my mother. Gloria hates her, so I try to make up to her for all the friction between the two of them.

"I don't want to lose Gloria, but I refuse to neglect my mother. She needs me," he said. "She can't get along without me."

Newton sighed. "I've dated a lot of girls in my time. I didn't want to get married until Gloria came along. And now she's ruining my relationship with my mother."

Newton was baffled. "I'll do anything to save our marriage," he declared.

The Counselor's Comment

Gloria and Newton were seen jointly over the next three months. Both were motivated to preserve the marriage. They always kept their appointments and were very punctual.

The key to Newton's personality was in his statement "My mother is all I have. She needs me. She can't get along without me."

All his life he had been a dedicated Mama's boy, inextricably bound to her by ties of love heavily mingled with his own dependence, which he did not recognize. His erroneous belief that his mother could not manage without him allowed him to retain his self-esteem. Actually it was the other way around: Newton had a very difficult time relinquishing his dependency on her.

However, because he truly loved Gloria, he made a sincere effort to be conciliatory and to wean himself away from his aging mother.

Newton began to see the value of adjusting and rearranging the priorities in his life. He learned that if he wanted to have a successful marriage, his first concern would have to be his wife. This did not necessarily mean that he should neglect his mother, but that he had to help the older woman accustom herself to a life away from him and Gloria.

Newton's declaration of independence was the establishment of a home of his and Gloria's own, about six miles away from his mother's. Once Newton was motivated to alter his intensely close relationship with his mother, Gloria found it easier to accept his daily phone calls to her. For even she admitted that Newton's concern for his elderly mother living alone in a large city was legitimate.

Once this adjustment was made, Gloria felt less threatened by the all-pervasive influence of Newton's mother in his life. She agreed to accompany him on occasional visits to his mother. Instead of the weekly schedule of visits, Gloria and Newton averaged about two visits each month.

In a typical Mama's boy marriage, it is almost impossible for the son/husband to interpret his emotions and actions objectively. He is too close to his mother and to his wife, and he is almost always deadlocked in a futile struggle to placate both women. Such a struggle can be complex and tumultuous, especially if one is without the assistance of a counselor who can view the situation objectively.

In such circumstances, a counselor will use patience and understanding to help a husband and wife see that the responsibilities of marriage constitute a profound pact between the two of them. Moreover, a counselor can point out to a husband and wife the fact that their relationship with each other has a preeminence over all others, including preexisting ones. When a couple is highly motivated, as were Gloria and Newton, the adaptation can take place.

In a Mama's boy relationship, the mother is usually more cognizant than the son of the fact that she has manipulated the relationship so as to have a continuing detrimental influence on the marriage. Newton's mother was no exception.

She appeared for several conferences. Even though the adjustment was painful, the elderly woman was willing to see that, with her in her advancing years, it was extremely important that her son develop a stronger relationship with Gloria.

Daddy's Girl Marries Mama's Boy

Wife	**Husband**
Marjorie Middleton	Steven Middleton
Married at 29	Married at 31
Housewife	Unemployed

Steven Middleton was undeniably good-looking—and very aware of it. He was quite tall, perhaps close to six feet four, and he was dressed in tennis whites that contrasted with his bronzed skin. He was smiling affably as he shook my hand and introduced his wife.

"Darling," he said, "this is our counselor."

Marjorie Middleton was also statuesque; she was at least five feet nine. With a soignée model's taste in clothes, she wore a white pants-suit which enhanced her slender figure. She extended to me a beringed and bejeweled hand and a devastating smile.

The Middletons' manner and bearing at first gave me the impression that they were very close. However, once the door to my office closed, they seemed more like a lion and lioness intent on devouring each other.

Steven began imperiously, "We're incompatible. Marjorie says she loves me, but I really can't say that I love her. We don't have any children because my wife has female problems. I don't know if there's any point in staying together. Recently we moved to California from New York City. I was fed up with the congestion and the dirt, and I informed Marjorie that I was going to the Coast. I had enough of the East. We were born and reared there. My wife was brought up in Washington, D.C., and I lived my childhood in Connecticut. I told her I thought it would be a good idea for us to separate for a while. As far as I'm concerned, we're incompatible."

Steven Middleton did not seem to notice his wife's smoldering eyes.

"We have two beautiful dogs," he went on. "When I arrived in California, I missed her"—Steven nodded in the direction of Marjorie—"but I especially missed those dogs. One is a fox terrier, and the other is a police dog. I felt foolish. I was very lonely when I came to the Coast, and to be honest with you, I think I missed the dogs more than my wife. In fact, I'll say it—I did cry over the dogs. I love the fox terrier. She is so attached to me. I wrote a letter telling Marjorie how much I loved the dogs and missed them. I think there are different degrees of love. We say we love a wife or our mother. We say we love our dogs, our furniture. I even love my Cadillac.

"Speaking of Cadillacs," he said, "you might wonder why I have a Cadillac, and I noted on the information sheet that I am unemployed. You might as well know everything," he exclaimed, somewhat red-faced, as if he had been caught with his hand in the cookie jar. "We were living in an expensive house in New York. I bought the Cadillac recently because I did not want to reduce my standard of living. I'll find the position I want here in California in good time. In the meanwhile, I want to keep up appearances.

"I've had asthma since I was a boy." Steven changed the subject abruptly. "It plagues me. I can't take dust. Marjorie is a lousy housekeeper. I've told her that if she continues to be so indifferent to my health problems we'll have to go our separate ways. Her idea of cleaning is to vacuum around a chair. She is too lazy to move it and vacuum underneath."

Suddenly he remembered something else. "Oh, that house we lived in in New York—I forgot to mention that we sold it. I deposited the money in my bank account in California. I feel the money truly belongs to me because the original money we used to buy the house was willed to me by my real father before he died. My mother and father were divorced when I was five. I was brought up by my stepmother until the age of sixteen, when she died. My real father was very irresponsible," he said; "a true cop-out."

Steven Middleton then returned to his problems with Marjorie. "The truth is that I grew intellectually in our marriage while my wife did not. When we were first married, she had absolutely no interests. I taught her all the important things. I taught her how to play golf, to play bridge, how to bowl and do crossword puzzles. I can do just about anything I put my mind to. I can understand complicated stock-market reports. I play chess. I am artistic and athletic.

"Oh, yes, I forgot to mention our sex life. I feel Marjorie should make some advances. It should be on a fifty-fifty basis. She can't seem to overcome her inhibitions. And since she won't try, I don't honor my fifty percent.

"She's too damned passive and lazy for me. I'm worn out trying to teach her all the things she should have known years ago. I obviously have more intelligence than she does in terms of all that I've done. I want to start a new life," Steven Middleton said with finality.

Marjorie Middleton spoke with assuredness and a touch of rancor. "I love Steven very much, and I want our marriage to work out. He is, however, a perfectionist. Ever since I've known him he has paid attention to the hole in the doughnut instead of the doughnut.

"I think there are many reasons why we are meant for each other. I know that I've been dependent on him. I do need him, but so many people have told us that we were made for each other.

"Steven is positively fussy. If you came to our home in Newport Beach, you would find it neat and orderly. When Steven examines the house, you'd think he was wearing white gloves and looking for dirt with a magnifying glass. He's always running his finger along a table top or bookshelf, or staring at the ceiling to find a cobweb. He doesn't hesitate to put a dirty coffee cup in the sink. It wouldn't occur to him to wash up after himself. I knew he was like this when I married him. But I thought this annoying habit would disappear afterwards. Instead, it's worse than ever.

"We are also at odds about the dogs. I love them, too, particularly the German shepherd, but Steven thinks the whole world revolves around that little fox terrier.

"He told you, of course, that he wanted me to be a fifty-fifty sex partner. I feel that Steven should make the advances, frankly. He is so damned proud of his ancestry. He seems to think he's a marvelous sexual athlete. Well, maybe he needs a nymphomaniac.

"Our sex problems began when we moved into Pop's house. It's rather complicated. Let me explain. Steven's father died and left the house in his brother's name. We call my husband's uncle 'Pop.'

"Well, Pop was quite old and wanted us to move in with him. I knew that he needed care and somebody to look after him. So I agreed to devote my time to his comfort in exchange for our being allowed to live in this beautiful home. I knew Pop didn't have long to live."

Marjorie glanced down at her ringed fingers.

"It was a mistake. I know now that Pop should have been put in a nursing home. The house, though, was situated on a golf course. It was like paradise on earth. Steven and I paid a heavy price for living there. Our sex life went down the drain.

"Pop used to wander all over the house, day or night. I felt I could hardly tell him what to do since it was really his house. Then there were the dogs. They were always in the bedroom. Our little voyeurs. When we were having intercourse, they were perched on the edge of the bed. I wanted them out, but Steven insisted that they be permitted to stay. Imagine thinking that much of your dogs, and nothing of your wife."

Marjorie flung a cold, hard look at Steven, who did not flinch.

"I wanted children," she said defensively, "but the doctor tells me it is impossible. So the dogs have become a substitute.

"When Steven walked out of the door of our home in New York to go to California, the last thing he said was, 'Good-bye, dogs. I'm going to get an annulment from Marjorie just as soon as I get to the Coast.' "

Steven flushed through his tan.

"My husband always said that my father was a tyrant and that everyone was afraid of him," said Marjorie, introducing another subject. "I want you to know that I liked my father far better than my mother. I'll always remember the time when he was sick in bed with pneumonia when we lived in Washington, D.C. I was a little girl then. Mother had to fly to Chicago for some important meeting, and I got to take care of my father for a whole week. He was really a great man.

"When he heard that Steven was going to leave me and go to California, he came over and laid down the law to Steven, who sat there like a mouse and didn't say a word."

Marjorie gloated over the moment of triumph.

"It was very inconvenient for my father to stop by and remind Steven of his responsibilities because he is not well. My father has always been fair. And he has told Steven that his selfish need to deposit the money from the sale of our house in New York to his own account is unfair."

Marjorie pointed out, "It was through my efforts and upkeep that the house was preserved over a four-year period of time. That should be worth something, although I don't honestly care about the money. It's the principle of the thing."

She asked, "Why is Steven constantly trying to please? Why is he relentlessly trying to achieve? What is it supposed to prove? It seems to me his only goal in life is to prove that he is better than everyone else."

Marjorie was puzzled. "I don't know which way to turn. He's determined to prove that we are incompatible, and I'm just as determined to prove that we're not. We have so many assets: good health, religion, financial security—providing Steven doesn't spend the money recklessly. Why can't he understand that his attitudes are going to wreck our marriage?"

The Counselor's Comment

There were many absurdities present in this marital situation that neither Marjorie nor Steven Middleton seemed to be aware of because of their closeness to the problem.

Here was a young man who was born into a comfortable, financially secure world. As an adult he still believed that the silver spoon of his childhood was present, never dreaming that privilege and responsibility go together. His self-centeredness was showing all over the counseling room.

Interestingly enough, his love for the female fox terrier was a clue to Steven's personality and his relationship with women. He had displaced his affection for his wife onto an appealing female fox terrier because all it could do was wag its tail in approval of his actions. It could never reprove him or admonish him as did his wife Marjorie, who reminded him that he was not the perfect male he imagined himself to be.

During subsequent weeks of counseling, Steven revealed the deep attachment he had had to his stepmother, who was the first love of his life. When she died of cancer in his mid-adolescent years, Steven could not bring himself to shed tears over her, but he was nonetheless deeply hurt. He missed her presence and secretly grieved her passing, holding in his imagination a portrait of this woman whom he felt personified perfection. All of his efforts were an attempt to achieve what he believed would have merited her approval had she lived. This memory of her was the ultimate against which Steven measured all other women who came into his life.

His perfectionistic tendencies were a direct result of her impact on his life. She had been a magnificent housekeeper. Therefore, of course, he would unconsciously evaluate Marjorie in an uncompromising and un-realistic way. Steven idolized his stepmother to such a degree that it was impossible for other women not to suffer by comparison. Marjorie fell short of the perfect memories he had retained from his youth.

When husband and wife took intelligence tests and Marjorie scored higher than her husband, this astounded Steven and revitalized Marjorie's sagging ego.

Steven further learned that his asthma was psychosomatic, or emo-tionally induced, and that he had perpetuated it during his childhood in order to continue an especially close relationship with his stepmother. He admitted that during early adolescence his asthmatic condition gave him the special privilege of sleeping in her room. He had persuaded her that he might have an attack at any time, thus assuring himself of her physical closeness and solicitous warmth.

With time and patience Steven began to understand why he behaved the way he did. The mother image, a remnant of his childhood years, was not being fulfilled by Marjorie. Hence, he felt the need to destroy their relationship and threaten separation.

As he learned to accept himself as a somewhat less than perfect male, he also became more expansive in his attitude toward Marjorie. He decided that she did not have to be perfect, and that she was, in her own way, a desirable wife.

Marjorie naturally had to accept the fact that Steven's need for a mother figure would never be totally extinguished. She would have to provide him with some maternal warmth if their marriage was to endure.

There were, of course, many inconsistencies and incongruities in Marjorie's personality that she had to discover for herself. She was most cooperative.

Her need to depend on Steven was based on a wish to perpetuate her childhood relationship with her father. When Marjorie married Steven, she was unconsciously looking for a man who would care for her, think for her, and make decisions for her, just as Daddy had done in the past. When she learned of her higher score on the intelligence tests, she remarked, "I can't believe I'm supposed to be more intelligent than Steven. I've accepted so much brainwashing from him."

Her newly discovered self-esteem gave her the confidence she needed to diminish her childish dependency on Steven. She became less fearful of making mistakes, and, as a consequence, she was willing to venture along unexplored paths of self-development without the approval or assistance of Steven.

When husband and wife are as intelligent and motivated as were Marjorie and Steven, there is usually an optimistic prognosis. Within a period of two months they had assimilated a tremendous bank of knowledge about their respective childhoods. This information aided them in deciphering the mysteries of their personality conflicts.

Their sex life was not really hopeless. It was just confusing with so many eyes in the bedroom. Once they were able to understand and accept the fact that Steven had been a Mama's boy and Marjorie had been a Daddy's girl, they stopped fighting the concept and began to grow toward a healthier and more mature adulthood.

When Marjorie made the prophetic remark "You'd think we were made for each other," she was unconsciously emphasizing the deep and profound relationship each mate had to the parent of the opposite sex.

As counseling enabled them to gain more self-understanding and to conquer the inconsistencies in their personalities, love indeed did shine forth, because the parents of the opposite sex had truly taught their children how to love.

8

The Child
in All of Us

Beneath its contemporary disguises, marriage has become an alarmingly competitive relationship. The women's liberation movement asserts vehemently that woman is man's equal. And this equality, by extension, has come to include the notion of competitiveness. Woman and man have become competitors in a frenzied "love battle" for sexual equality. The *raison d'être* of a relationship between a man and woman today is ostensibly meaningfulness. This meaningfulness is based primarily on sexual excitement and satisfaction. If the relationship is relevant sexually, then a "marriage," whether it is legalized or not, is valid.

The logical consequence of this type of thinking is a series of disenchanting and temporary erotic experiences that lack love-security, for a requisite of love-security is an enduring monogamous relationship between one man and one woman. Instead, these experiences produce tangled egocentric personality disturbances. An enduring marital relationship becomes more and more remote.

The price of serial relationships is more than most individuals have bargained for. At the demise of such a relationship, the instant joy is replaced by lingering egocentric distortions, which will worsen as time goes on unless the individual learns a new pattern of relating to the opposite sex.

Have the traditional reasons for marriage vanished?

Just because woman has become less dependent on man for economic survival, does this mean that a series of lovers with or without an occasional "love" child provides her with a cup of human happiness brimming over with unimagined and perpetual delights?

A man may shrewdly observe that women's liberation makes available to him in the name of sexual equality an almost infinite variety of women, catering to his egocentric exploitativeness. But does this mean that his need for love-security has vanished?

The need for love-security within the context of an enduring monogamous relationship remains essentially unchanged generation after generation, despite vast and complex external societal turmoil. Permanency, insofar as it is humanly possible (that is, "until death do us part"), creates the ideal milieu in which husband and wife can struggle to achieve an altruistic relationship.

For example, women's sexual and economic independence has placed children, one of the traditional reasons for marriage, into an expendable limbo. If a husband and wife decide to have children, the children can be reared in communes or day-care centers so that the wife, who is economically liberated, can pursue her own path of personal development. Thus the supportive, sustaining monogamous relationship appears to have been sneered out of existence.

As man's competitor and equal, woman is not his helpmate; nor is he her helpmate, for that might suggest a relationship of subservience or dependency. And dependency, after all, conveys the notion of assistance, support, helpfulness and sustenance on all levels.

The denial and repudiation of dependency as a legitimate adult need that can be filled through interdependency in marriage is one of the reasons why traditional marriage is floundering. Competitive independence is equated with strength and feminine equality. In the male, hostile aggressiveness, characterized by a "love them and leave them" attitude, masquerades as independence.

Dependency, conversely, is equated with weakness. It has become imperative in our "jungle" society that neither man nor woman appear to need anything but sex from his or her mate. For those who seek peripheral emotional responses of assurance, comfort, compassion and/or encouragement, for example, are dependent, and such vulnerability is a tacit admission of weakness.

This, in essence, is the dilemma facing contemporary men and women.

Notwithstanding the complex and constantly evolving external social forces that are modifying each generation, it is dependency that provides the crucial link between the parent-child relationship and its ultimate extension in marriage. Dependency—in the form of marital interdependency—creates the supportive and cooperative environment that is a requisite of an enduring marriage. It is Daddy's and Mama's attitudes toward dependency that guide the infant and child toward the cooperative or competitive pattern he will follow in all future relationships. The vast network of love-service traits involved in an altruistic monogamous relationship have their origin in dependency—and, by extension, in trust in the parent of the opposite sex.

Every husband and wife needs to be, at various times, the lover and the loved one, the protector and the protected, the one who is listened to and the listener. A man and a woman must be strong enough to admit their dependency on each other. When dependency and trust are learned in childhood, these traits become part of the individual's adult personality, enabling him or her to achieve marital happiness.

Approval is another key characteristic. The desire to please is an integral part of the cooperative interaction in a happy marriage. A lessening of this wish to please indicates some point of friction; a total lack shows unwillingness to care about the mate.

In the parent-child relationship, fidelity implies a continuing interest in all matters involving the child. Continuation is most significant, for it is here that the child first obtains some glimmering of what it means to have either an exclusive and abiding relationship with a parent of the opposite sex, or an episodic and apathetic relationship wherein the child is casually fitted into the parent's life only at the parent's convenience. Being loyal to a child in a haphazard fashion almost guarantees that in adulthood the child will be riddled with emotional disturbances.

Attitudes about sex and affection are also instilled subtly. Who has not known an adult man or woman who projected chronic dissatisfaction with his own personality onto his mate? It is his mate, he declares, who is frigid, or sexually demanding, or unexciting. This perpetual rebellion is characteristic of a person who has never known the stabilizing force of continuous affection from a parent of the opposite sex. One of the traits of such an individual is an accusatory nature; he or she spills out grievances against husband or wife in retaliation for the unsatisfactory relationship with a parent.

Dependency, trust, fidelity, approval and sexual-affectional satisfactions form the basis of human happiness. However, a relationship between husband and wife is not necessarily perfect simply because it possesses these attributes. Every marital relationship is in a constant state of flux. It is imperceptibly becoming better or worse as each individual either struggles toward greater altruism or surrenders to egocentricity.

The notion that a meaningful relationship is a superior vehicle by which one may discover the "perfect" husband or wife is extremely misleading. As each "imperfect" man or woman is discarded for a more "perfect" mate, the illusion of perfection dwindles.

Marriages can be categorized—in terms of gradations of altruism and egocentricity. Those marriages that are tottering on the brink of dissolution are in the narcissistic or egocentric range. The happy marriage is closer to the ideal of altruism, where sharing takes precedence over individuality.

A son or daughter who is accustomed to witnessing angry quarrels in which Daddy degrades or demeans Mama and she retreats into the role of housekeeper or even doormat tends to utilize a similar strategy in his or her own marriage. If Mama berates Daddy for repeated infidelities, his daughter unconsciously assumes that she will have the same experiences, and unwittingly she pursues an avenue of sexual expression guaranteed to elicit emotional turmoil.

The Daddy's Girl/Mama's Boy Syndrome

"After we have had sex, he always talks about his mother and father. He tells me how much he hates her because she ruined his father's life. And his father? He despises his father, too, for drinking himself to death. His mother then descended from riches to rags. It ruins sex for me. I can't bring myself to tell him I don't want to hear his sordid life story every time we have intercourse."

"She says she can iron his shirts better than I can. So I said, 'Go ahead.' She was speechless. So now I don't have to worry about a laundry woman. But he's mad at me."

"Oh, darling, now that you've made me so happy, don't look so sad."

"I don't make mistakes—ever. Maybe I don't have all the facts. Or maybe someone is breathing down my neck and I can't think clearly, but I don't make mistakes."

"I've had innumerable affairs. As a matter of fact, I can't remember the names or faces of the women I've taken to bed. I don't know why I can't get closer to marriage. I'm not going to be alone, though, in my old age, even if I have to marry someone to take care of me."

"My wife handles the money in our family. She gives me an allowance from each paycheck. I find this a very practical arrangement. I don't like to worry about money matters. Whenever my father handled money we were broke. When my mother took over we had more security."

"He's strictly a company man. He feels there's safety in numbers. He will never be a leader of anything—except the Boy Scout troops."

"I think I'll marry a nurse in case I get sick."

"He's such a darling boy. I just can't do enough for him. Why am I such a pushover for boyish types?"

"Men appreciate only what they pay for, believe me."

"I've sacrificed everything to put you through school. Now you want to quit practicing law and go off to Tahiti. Who do you think you are, Gauguin?"

"I am honestly in love with two men."

"For once let's have a little peace and quiet when your folks come to dinner. Let's try to remember it's our home even if they loaned us the down payment."

"He's a confirmed misogynist, but that doesn't stop him from marrying the same sort of woman over and over again."

"Darling, if I had it to do over again, I would."

Who are all of these men and women? Camouflaged Daddy's girls and Mama's boys. They espouse a broad spectrum of attitudes toward marriage, some of which assure conflict and some of which are conducive to happiness. Some are groping for love-security through the maze of their learned egocentricity, re-creating in marriage their childhood "solutions." Others have learned that childhood "solutions" point the way toward happy and enduring relationships.

The attitude of our current culture toward marriage encourages exploitation and egocentric fulfillment disguised as personal growth. These trends in turn perpetuate the delusion that there is little or no relationship between this marital credo and the emotional debris that clutters social agencies, courts, prisons, hospitals and the institutions that provide for the social rejects produced by this marital and family life style.

Freud has asserted that civilization is sustained by the difficult and arduous process of sacrificing instinctual pleasures for the common good and diverting these energies into creative efforts for the benefit of one's husband, wife, children and, ultimately, society. Sublimation of sexual energies has a valid function, and the more complex the society is, the more essential it is that sexuality be constructively channeled.

If our age appears to reflect the triumph of narcissism, we should remember that the Judaeo-Christian tradition has also attempted to contain and divert sexual energies into creative developments within the most intimate relationships of marriage and family life.

Prevailing interpretations of marriage have thrown out the baby with the bath water in a misdirected attempt to eliminate the limitations the traditional relationship seemed to place on personal growth. Reversal of parental roles in the name of individuality has further jeopardized the psycho-sexual development of children. For example, when the father stays home to care for the children while the mother assumes the function of breadwinner, there are all sorts of subtle changes and confusions in identity and esteem that affect both sons and daughters.

This does not mean that parental roles should be rigid, but rather that the primary maternal emphasis should be on the care and rearing of children—and this includes teaching a value system that will enable sons and daughters to establish distinct, mature adult lives for themselves. The paternal emphasis, although predominantly economic and supportive, should be complementary. The father should help to establish identity and esteem, which will facilitate the formation of altruistic traits in daughters and sons.

The evolving societal attitude is that traditional committed marriage is an obsolete encumbrance. This trend only adds to the insidious processes begun in egocentric Daddy's girl/Mama's boy relationships in childhood.

The substitution of sensual pleasure for the more comprehensive human achievement of an altruistic monogamous marriage is easily accepted. It requires little personal effort, and apparently offers something for nothing, which is irresistible to human nature. Individuals are more or less susceptible to this new life style, depending on their level of psycho-sexual development, which in turn depends on their relation to the parent of the opposite sex. Every man and woman has acquired learned responses from childhood that will tend to make a future marriage a success or failure.

An individual's personality may reveal certain combinations of egocentricity and altruism that will determine whether he/she will be capable of sustaining an enduring monogamous relationship or will proceed from one relationship to another.

The Ladykiller

What man has not secretly yearned to be completely persuasive and successful with women? This fantasy is the acme of the adolescent's dream of conquest. Literature and real life have an abundance of such anti-heroes, ranging from Bluebeard, who married and murdered one woman after another, to men who have acted out the same egocentric pattern in a series of liaisons or marriages because of a need for revenge against Mama.

The Mama of a ladykiller has certain egocentric characteristics that may propel her son toward, at the very least, a covert lifetime hatred of women, and, possibly, explicit deviant behavior.

Mama has, above all, psychologically abandoned her son. Her affection is meager and inconsistent, and is frequently interspersed with severe physical punishment and tongue lashings. She is derelict in a variety of ways. At an early age such a boy feels overwhelmed and frightened by women, whom his mother personifies. In his helpless rage he may vow to "get even" with her. He may not be exactly certain how or when he will retaliate, but unconsciously this desire to punish women will become the ruling passion of his life.

Should he maintain the semblance of social conformity, he may live a marginal life, adopting the veneer of respectability of a business or professional man. But intense inner conflict will arouse an attraction-repulsion pattern even if his yearning for love-security is directed toward a reasonably altruistic woman. In effect, his need to kill, whether literal or figurative, will obsess him and obliterate (or make very remote) the possibility of a truly loving and enduring relationship with one woman.

The Exploitative Sensual Male

From childhood days through young manhood, the exploitative sensual male lives and breathes in an atmosphere of sensuality created by his mother.

There may or may not be a father figure present, but there is a succession of males who attach themselves to his mother for varying periods of time. Her love life is the alpha and omega of her existence, and a son is incidental and extraneous. A son may not feel rejected, although he is being denied authentic maternal concern. His mother may acknowledge him as a sort of junior-grade lover by pampering him in between her own affairs and then casually ignoring him when she is occupied.

This Mama's boy has mingled feelings of awe and desperation. If his mother depends on sexuality for survival, her son may become cognizant that she is little more than a prostitute. However, if the economic environment is middle or upper class, the mother may be kept until her physical attractions deteriorate, and the son may not understand the real nature of her life. Occasionally he may be offered peripheral benefits by one of his mother's lovers, such as an opportunity for education that might not otherwise have been available to him.

Because his childhood is devoid of love-security, this young man does not know what he is missing in terms of emotional depth. By the time he has an opportunity to establish a marriage relationship, he may have yielded to a pattern of sensuality and shallow relationships that makes it virtually impossible to appreciate monogamy.

In addition to a pattern of constant change with respect to women, there is also a disorganized and aimless shifting from one set of adventures to another. Life becomes a matter of outwitting one's adversaries. Such a Mama's boy may be a gigolo one season, and the alimony-supported ex-husband of an older jet-setter or socialite the next year.

The lack of discrimination and restraint that Mama has exhibited in sexual matters boomerangs in her son's life. His feelings of worthlessness and self-destructiveness grow in proportion to his concentration on sex, and his other latent abilities remain undeveloped. Of all the Mama's boys, he is most incapable of altering the life pattern Mama has established for him.

The Exploitative Male
An individual does not change after marriage unless he is powerfully motivated to do so.

This is particularly true of the exploitative, egocentric, domineering male who has until now received society's tacit approval in the form of cultural conditioning. Such a male is the product of a Mama who insisted on making all—or most—major life decisions for him.

He has a need to escape from such a woman and an equally compelling need to assert his masculinity in a relationship that will give him reassurance.

Moreover, Mama has conveyed to him the notion that sex is evil, and has tended to frustrate opportunities to channel his aggressive energies in a constructive direction. In adult relationships he still suspects women of using him; he manages to take the initiative by egocentric domination, using women primarily as objects of sexual pleasure.

He is almost totally devoid of the ability to share because he has never known genuine kindness, sympathy or warmth, although indeed his Mama has "loved" him. He interprets any evidence of altruism as a form of compromise or even emasculation. He is a withholding, uneasy man and cannot give of himself in other facets of life either.

Frequently he feels uncomfortable and tense in the presence of children. He may refuse to have children because of his inability to go out of himself in order to enter into the lives of those who would be genuinely dependent upon him; this relationship would emphasize his essential insecurity.

His relationships with women are generally temporary interludes; they follow a pattern of sexual satiation, after which he expresses disappointment in the relationship. He then moves on with almost no insight into the nature of his problem.

Superficially he may appear to be a very self-assured individual. His commanding presence may appeal to an altruistic or passive-dominant woman. A compassionate woman who lacks emotional discernment is especially susceptible to the superficial charm of this insecure Mama's boy.

The Egocentric Passive-Dominant Male

The egocentric passive-dominant male appears in our society to be the "ideal" husband because he is so convincingly amiable and benevolent. He seems to have the most appropriate mixture of dominance (a woman will believe she can rely on him and yet not feel inferior to him) and flexibility (disguised passivity).

Such a man will usually have an affectionate relationship with his mother. He may even marry a woman who looks like her. Very definitely he will unconsciously search for the same traits that Mama had, and these will comfort him as he faces the discomforts of a realistic marriage. Although his mother dominated him, there was a substantial element of benevolence in her attitude toward him. Mama may have been abused by Daddy—not necessarily in their sexual life, but perhaps in some other aspect of marital life—and the son may decide he must compensate Mama for all she has endured.

He reveals distinctly ambivalent attitudes toward sex, and he is inclined to marry late, perhaps after his mother dies. Or he may insist that his aging mother, if she is a widow, live with him and his wife.

He is exploitative in the sense that he will employ a self-pitying attitude that he learned from Mama to realize his objectives with women.

He may lean heavily on his wife in a fairly immature way when he feels he cannot yield (i.e., cooperate) with her. He dominates in certain marital situations where he feels a marginal degree of self-esteem.

He transfers his ambivalence to his wife, and he may blame her for all the shortcomings of the marriage, particularly in passive moments. He wishes he could be a better husband, and perhaps he would try to be one if he did not already have some measure of love-security in his relationship with his wife.

The Exploitative Passive Male

The behavior of the exploitative passive male ranges from "spoiled child" behavior to the passive dependency of the "born loser," the loner or the alcoholic.

Typically, he is boyish, and thus elicits the "mother" in a woman. He is the man a woman wants to do things for because he is a charmer in a forlorn, wistful, dreamy way. He may have the shy, gangling charm of a movie hero. The qualities that first attract a woman to him are the same ones that later erode the marital relationship. The pity that draws a woman to such a man deteriorates after a while, and a reversal may occur in which the woman begins to pity herself rather than her husband, whom she now understands.

This male is not an obvious exploiter of women. He gets his way by evoking sympathy from his wife by improvising real and imagined cruelties the world or individuals have inflicted upon him. He is likely to have an erratic work record and to use varying strategies to persuade his wife to support him. He almost always maneuvers her into the role of decision-maker, then groans loudly that his masculine prerogatives are being usurped.

This Mama's boy may have had a childhood illness, such as asthma, that encouraged an exceptionally close, even stifling, mother-son relationship. The pampering and overprotective atmosphere of childhood lingers on in adult life. Inevitably such a man seeks a wife who will serve as his special nurse regardless of what form his passive exploitation takes. He yearns for and needs love-security, but because he was emotionally smothered by his mother in childhood, he may require twenty-four-hour-a-day care as proof of marital love. When his wife responds with solicitous understanding and even sexual advances, he may retreat into petulance and declare that his wife is demanding too much of him.

The exploitative passive male pursues his egocentric demands with a relentless stratagem of advance-retreat. If he becomes an alcoholic, it is because his wife expects too much of him. Obviously his mother did not. If he has a chaotic work record, it is because the jobs are dull or his health may collapse any moment. At any rate, eventually his passivity reveals the brutal fact that his wife's initial love for him was actually pity. His approach to marriage is essentially self-defeating.

The Altruistic Male

Altruism and egocentricity are intermingled in every human being. Their potential for increase or decrease depends on the learned responses of childhood and on the subsequent motivation of the individual to alter those responses.

The Mama's boy with a benign mother and father who accept, and do not reverse, parental roles is the most fortunate with respect to future marriage and love-security. From earliest childhood he has learned to develop the traits that will enable him to understand and accept a monogamous enduring marriage.

Rather than interpreting such a relationship as restrictive and alien to his sexual needs, he understands that instinctual pleasures can either enhance or detract from his total personality. Through this recognition and the consequent diversion of sexual energies into constructive societal achievements he is able to realize his optimum potential as a human being.

The boy who has a predominantly altruistic mother and a relatively egocentric father will grow into manhood with an entirely different attitude toward women than the boy who has a predominantly egocentric mother and an altruistic father.

The first young man will tend to develop a complex array of protective traits. He will be inclined toward greater adaptability to and identification with women. He may pursue a business or professional career in which he will have many female associates. He is not necessarily a latent homosexual because of this unconscious preferential identification. Unless the father's egocentricity is expressed in harsh and unloving responses to his son over a long period of time, the son will feel only detached respect—or even concern—for his father. When the father's behavior is extreme, emotional disturbances may arise, despite the maternal influence. A father's unloving ways by no means assure a pattern of homosexuality, but can be a contributing factor.

In marriage this man will attempt to compromise and cooperate because of the maturity he has learned in his relationship with his mother. Moreover, he will show traits such as tenderness, patience and kindness in his relationships with women.

If, however, the mother is the more egocentric parent and the father is predominantly altruistic, the son may enter marriage with feelings of antagonism toward women. This may be further complicated by the boy's interpretation of his father's benevolent nature as weakness. Misconstruing altruism as effeminacy, the boy is torn asunder by a conflicting image of what a man should be—not only in relation to a woman in marriage, but in terms of his own self-esteem (which is decidedly wobbly). Much depends on the respective degrees of egocentricity and altruism of Mama and Daddy and on the prevailing influence in the home.

The mother who usurps parental influence in a destructive way harms the child by giving him a pattern of self-imposed tyranny from which he will flee in his adult life through a series of sexual relationships. A genuinely loving mother who is capable of transmitting an affirmative sense of self-worth to her son provides him with the motive for creating a love-security relationship in an enduring marriage. That stable emotional foundation with which he is endowed permits him to perpetuate the convictions that his mother has lovingly bequeathed to him.

The Femme Fatale
Like her male counterpart, the ladykiller, the femme fatale harbors a deep resentment of men because of her early relationship with her father. There is a disguised pattern of vindictiveness and malice in her relationships with men. This woman flounders from one liaison to another,

deceived by the illusion that she is sexually irresistible. Almost always she requires from a man inordinate homage bordering on servility, and this eventually destroys the relationship.

Daddy, too, may have been a ladykiller. As a young girl his daughter became familiar with a pattern of vindictive sexuality, inevitable frustration and deepening cynicism. It does not occur to the femme fatale that there is any other way to live. Close relationships frighten her because they require some degree of altruism, which is almost totally alien to her character.

Femme fatales exhibit a wide variety of behavior ranging from overt prostitution to better disguised and more socially acceptable expressions of hatred of men. The suppressed rage from her childhood predisposes her to choose men who are reminiscent of Daddy. The femme fatale characteristically seduces, demands excessive homage, then thwarts the male to punish him, and eventually breaks off the relationship, saying that he could not fulfill her needs. This woman tends to drift aimlessly from one affair or marriage to another as long as her physical charms continue to attract males who will keep her. Then, usually in later life, she is forced to face the truth: that her hatred of men has influenced all of her relationships with them.

Logic should warn her that she must alter her behavior if she wants to enter into a lasting relationship with a man. But, unless such a woman gains insight through therapy and then is motivated to change, she is likely to end her days in some back-street liaison, all the while vociferously asserting that men are beasts.

The Exploitative Sensual Female

In our culture, inhibitions in the sexual sphere are lamented as a fate worse than death. The credo implicit in this philosophy is that unrestrained sexual stimulation is the ideal milieu in which to live.

The practical consequences can be frightening. This mass delusion tends to exaggerate what is already deviant in the exploitative sensual female. Reared in a home in which Daddy's sexual activities preempt all other aspects of family life, a daughter may develop a fixation that echoes her father's whims. Whether or not the father is present in the home as a permanent resident, his impact on his daughter's psycho-sexual development remains to haunt her in adult life.

There is a greater likelihood of incest in this relationship than in the other Daddy's girl relationships. Sexuality becomes the daughter's paramount concern at an early age. Although such a daughter is never loved by her emotionally disturbed father, she becomes psychologically enslaved by him. Over and over again in adult life she will search for a repetition of this relationship. She may refuse to speak of her father in adult life or may recall his name only in scathing recollection. The libertine life is all she understands, and she is in a rage to live.

The personality disorganization may take place subtly over many years; there may be a gradual breakdown in diverse areas of life. As she proceeds from one erotic escapade to another, her sense of self-worth diminishes and her feelings of self-hatred increase. Many of her capabilities remain undeveloped because of her total dedication to the sensual life.

She is forever searching for a love relationship that will re-create the feelings she experienced with Daddy. Her inner conflicts ultimately ravage whatever has remained of her personality, and her self-hatred becomes more apparent in acts of minor self-destruction—a series of automobile accidents, for example, or, ultimately, suicide. Without prolonged therapy, the exploitative sensual female squanders her life in a hopelessly self-defeating way. With therapy some modification of this personality is possible.

The Exploitative Female
In an effort to compensate for a childhood that was egocentrically dominated by her father, the exploitative female, in womanhood, reveals traits of initiative, leadership, self-assertiveness and rigidity. These traits are manifestations of inner fears that she might appear to be less than superhuman. She finds it necessary to dominate all male-female relationships.

Frequently, a girl whose father was egocentric and dominating will marry early in order to escape the family. But she may make a calculating evaluation of her husband's financial resources. She will tend to think in terms of exchange of her sexuality for an elegant and indolent life. She will attempt to escape into financial security in lieu of love-security, for she will consider that a worthy exchange.

Her personality traits will dominate the marriage. She may be moody, easily offended, impulsive. She may need constant monetary assurance of her worth. Her surroundings reveal her materialistic concerns, and her husband is merely the vehicle by which she achieves this ersatz security.

Fearful of being exploited by a male, as she was in her relationship with her father, this woman interprets expressions of compassion, patience, reassurance, tenderness or non-sexual love as indications of weakness in the male personality, and she discerningly takes advantage of the male so that he finds himself in a defensive position.

The exploitative female is necessarily on guard; she views her mate as a potential adversary. She must feel superior to him. There is little trust and less communication. The woman discovers that as the reasons for the existence of their relationship narrow, the man begins to tire of his captivity on her terms. This woman is unconsciously determined to "get" as much as she can; not surprisingly, she transmits an oppressive tension and insecurity to her husband.

Marriage may be entered into casually because there is no inner commitment or concern for permanence; nor is there any comprehension that love-security can be achieved by a modification of egocentric traits.

The rigidity of such a personality extends into relationships with children, should there be any in the marriage. Fearful of not "getting enough" out of marriage and family life, she may regard children as an impediment and an obstacle to her insatiable needs, which are a reflection of her distorted relationship with Daddy.

The Egocentric Passive-Dominant Female
An awareness of one's inner proclivities does much to increase the odds of having an enduring marriage relationship. The woman who is neither excessively passive nor dominant and who understands her inner nature may appeal to a wide range of men as a prospective wife. Such a woman

has enormous potential; her latent altruistic traits need only to be developed.

The passive-dominant female tends to consider Daddy her mentor and benefactor, and his relationship with her is characterized by a benign authoritarianism. He advised her in girlhood to proceed along certain paths of development because they were "good for her," and she trusted him implicitly. His domination may have been occasionally oppressive, but these experiences were compensated for by masculine sprees of pampering her little girl's ego.

The passive-dominant female very definitely looks for Daddy's stamp of approval on any marriage she may consider. She would be most reluctant to marry without his consent. In fact, the closer her husband resembles Daddy in personality traits, physical appearance and professional or business background, the happier the marriage relationship is likely to be.

Such a young woman will tend to prefer Daddy's companionship over Mama's, and although the parental marriage may be stable and satisfying, the passive-dominant female may interpret it as being somewhat unfair to Daddy. Perhaps she believes he works harder than Mama, or he does not receive the understanding or sexual affection that is his just due. At any rate, it is a factor in her choice of a husband.

This woman may exploit her husband by maneuvering him into a position where he hates himself if he does not give her what she wants. She may play the martyr, or little girl, or coquette, or use various strategies of evasion rather than direct confrontation as a means of exploiting her husband. There is ample vacillation and ambivalence in her learned pattern of response. If she exploits, she can also be exploited. But unlike her less fortunate sisters, she has, because of Daddy's benign domination, the potential to develop an altruistic response. She can be motivated to understand that in order to experience the deeper joys of marriage she must give of herself in cooperative responses.

The likelihood of developing a sustaining relationship in which the love-security needs of both husband and wife are realized is substantial.

Much depends on the motivation of the passive-dominant female. If she is satisfied with a minimal relationship, she may not cultivate her latent altruistic traits. On the other hand, if her marital situation requires some unusual effort on her part to sustain it, she may then renounce her lethargic modes of response and actively develop those traits that are conducive to love-security.

The Exploitative Passive Female

Males have an inordinately strong desire to protect the exploitative passive female. This charming, childlike woman seems to elicit all that is the epitome of masculine wisdom and strength. In her beguiling helplessness lies both her strength and the source of her marital problems. The traits that most appeal to the male during courtship are likely to destroy the marriage if she does not learn to modify her behavior.

Her overprotective relationship with Daddy provides the basis for future strategic exploitation of the male. Never will she demand. Rather, she will plead, cajole, whine, arouse, thwart and retreat in a turbulent and unhappy pattern, once the façade of her passivity has been penetrated. She tends to be a woman of many marriages. Once a man understands her rigid passivity and her unwillingness to alter her egocentric traits, she can no longer exploit him and the relationship may fall apart.

The passive female earnestly yearns for love-security, but when it is offered to her she is frightened by the need to react to it. Commitments, obligations and responsibilities—all of which are part and parcel of an enduring marriage—are carefully avoided by the passive female. Once the husband realizes the burdensomeness of this strategy, he may respond inappropriately with manipulative weapons of his own.

In her relationship with Daddy, the passive female dutifully reduced herself to a nonentity in order to receive "love" from him. As a frustrated adult, she unreasonably attaches herself to men who initially accept her difficult personality. By placing the male in an intolerable emotional position, she begs for love-security and for rejection at the same time. Sex is employed for manipulative purposes. She expects her husband to make her happy, and she employs interminable variations on the pout when he is less than perfect. The exploitative passive female is the product both of a Daddy's girl relationship and of a society that, by making the male preeminent, forced women with certain emotional propensities to adopt a hypocritical and inadequate life role.

The passive female may have unrealized altruistic capacities, but Daddy's overprotectiveness has forced her into a quandary which she will try to unravel for the rest of her life. Is it worth it to a woman, the exploitative passive female asks, to participate in a loving marriage when so much energy must be exerted?

The idea of attempting a personality transformation does not appeal to her, although intellectually she may be aware of its validity. The "triumph" of the self-defeating exploitative female is found in her belief that no one has ever loved her as she really is—not even Daddy.

The Altruistic Female

Probably the most astonishing and inadvertent contribution our male-dominated society has offered to the female is the opportunity to develop an altruistic pattern of behavior. Altruism suggests struggle because it is not innate. Because of their heretofore inferior position in society, women have had to develop those traits that would enable them to overcome such inequality.

The altruistic woman generally learned in her childhood relationship with Daddy to make the best of life as it really is. She is not inclined to think about what might be instead of what is. She has a common-sense approach to human relationships.

Her childhood is likely to have included some participation in the care of a parent or other relative who required physical care over a long period of time. Or there may have been adversity of other sorts: actual poverty or a sudden alteration in family life style because of the father's plummeting fortunes. The girl who develops an altruistic personality early in life accepts extraordinary responsibilities and triumphs over them by adaptation.

(There are many women, of course, who rebel or resent such responsibilities, and, as a consequence, their personality development is very different.)

A second characteristic of the altruistic woman is her acceptance of herself as a woman in terms of both sexuality and motherhood. She does not reject or deny her biological function and its place in her life. In contrast to those women who employ sexuality as a weapon against the male, the altruistic woman incorporates sexual satisfaction into the interaction between herself and men. She is neither obsessively preoccupied with its significance nor fearful or disdainful of sex.

In essence, she, like her masculine counterpart, maintains a constant awareness of and sensitivity to husband and children. She is genuinely motivated to provide for them an optimum love-security milieu. And what is most important, she is happy to accept the responsibilities and challenges that are an inextricable part of these relationships. This is merely another way of saying that the altruistic woman is committed to a permanent marital relationship with all of its unforeseeable hazards.

Finally, she is not enslaved by a desire for perfection in human relationships. The concept of sexual obsolescence (which suggests that a partner may move from one meaningful relationship to another that is more perfect because of novelty) is unacceptable to the altruistic woman.

The girl who matures into an altruistic woman has a father (and probably a mother) who transmitted to her a valid concept of self-worth and selflessness. Her father was neither a rakish lover/companion nor a pal. By channeling his sexual energies into a loving relationship with the wife/mother, he provided for his daughter an ideal training ground for the development of those traits that make up altruism.

Will Enduring Marriage and Parenthood Survive?

No human being fits neatly into a category. Not only is every man and woman unique, but there is considerable overlapping of traits, propensities, contradictions and exceptions in all of us.

Most normal men and women wish to avoid unhappiness. Unfortunately, the media have unrealistically and soothingly persuaded them that the only kind of marriage that is worthwhile is one in which there is a perpetual euphoria based on sexual ecstasy. This theme weaves its way in and out of soap operas and popular fiction. Its heroes and heroines are plastic people. The myth that they perpetuate is that of instant happiness.

Moreover, social scientists point out that monogamy is contrary to man's instincts. Therefore, a new system of contractual marriage is in order. Part of such an arrangement would be a provision for or against parenthood.

Antipathy toward parenthood has become more and more fashionable in the past decade. If there is any relationship between the current disdain for parenthood and the alarming increase in emotional disturbance among young people, it is being discreetly ignored.

Some social scientists have further postulated that the dissolution of marriage and the family can be a positive development. It is evident that within the past decade there has been an abrupt reversal and deterioration of attitudes that had previously bolstered marriage and family life. However, these reversals have been put forth as improvements in human relations based on the new needs and the new morality. This ostensible progress in human relationships encompasses "new goals" and "involvements" in lieu of enduring relationships, which have been interpreted as "unrealistic."

There is almost a total absence of aid to the marriage or family in distress. Instead, in its place is a bright "new" panacea for all marital and family ailments: discard the old and replace it with the "new." A "new" relationship, it is reasoned, offers a revitalized self-image, and that is the crux of the matter. Such thinking is an obvious deterrent to parenthood, because parenthood requires that Daddy and Mama have the ability to place the child's well-being ahead of their own. And this is less feasible within the presently fashionable context of meaningful relationships and self-indulgence.

Commitment to parenthood is a commitment to oneself and to one's husband or wife. It constitutes an act of faith in the abiding nature of the marital relationship. Almost all of this has been swept away because it does not fit into current definitions of marital happiness.

Will Daddy and Mama become anachronisms? Although society has whittled away their impact on the lives of their children, it is doubtful that their role will dwindle into nothingness. Continuing human relationships will persist. Marriage and parenthood fulfill man's primal needs in a way that no temporary relationships can.

Every marriage, depending on its duration, unfolds in a fairly predictable way externally. It is in the interior development of the self, however, that every man and woman meets or avoids the challenges of marriage. It is not realistically possible to avoid periods of unhappiness in marriage. Tensions, conflicts, unexpected crises and other unanticipated life experiences are all part of a full life. Rather, it is the manner in which husband and wife accept these marital problems that determines whether they will experience happiness and continuing love-security. In the childhood of each man and woman lie the seeds of his or her adult response to marital challenge. Each individual has a learned mode of responding that remains substantially unmodified unless unhappiness motivates him/her to alter his/her behavior.

Although no one fits exactly into any defined category, each wife and each husband has a little of Daddy and Mama in him, and this can be the basis of adult happiness or of tragedy.

9   Love-Security

The principal challenges to every marriage are to solve problems constructively, to meet and deal with crises realistically, and to acknowledge and identify negative emotions. Whether you, as an individual husband or wife, face these life experiences imaginatively or attempt to escape from them will be largely a reflection of responses learned in childhood. When the essential human need for self-esteem is inadequately met in childhood, a son/daughter is inclined to carry into marriage a number of self-defeating traits.

In every marriage there are predictable as well as unanticipated human experiences that require husband and wife to work together harmoniously if they are to preserve the relationship. How you respond to these unexpected conditions is indicative of how successful or self-defeating your marriage will be. Your responses to frustration, disappointment, illness, occasional sexual thwarting, economic setback, etc., are a critical factor in determining whether your marriage will be temporary or enduring.

A husband and wife can learn to be supportive of each other by learning to give. Each mate will discover that altruism is not a denial of individuality, but a positive participation in the creative awakening of another human being.

The more altruistic mate is inclined to be deeply sensitive to the discrepancies in the relationship, for he/she is aware of its unfulfilled potential. The innate capacity for altruism within the egocentric or exploitative mate can be developed, providing there is motivation to do so.

Happiness, or continuing love-security, is a positive state of well-being that encompasses the total personality of husband and wife. It requires an attempt by each mate to enhance the other's self-esteem. It is based on the cultivation of specific traits within the framework of a monogamous enduring marriage. Because, at one time or another, stress is inevitable in all intimate human relationships, you as a husband/wife must learn to divert negative energies and egocentric responses. This will enable you to strengthen and deepen your ties of loyalty and affection to your spouse.

The "new" marital goals society has inflicted on husband and wife have caused this concept to lose support. Today young men and women enter into marriage with the unconscious feeling that there is an escape hatch. This attitude constitutes a monumental psychological obstacle to the individual efforts of a husband or wife. Society provides each husband and wife with a self-defeating premise. If their marriage is to be enduring, they must recognize that thoughts of escape will only hamper their efforts to strengthen the bonds of their love.

Problem-Solving

Conflicts arise in a marriage when there is an imbalance between legitimate ego satisfactions and acceptance of responsibilities. Within the first few years of marriage certain techniques of problem-solving are established. When they are constructive, they tend to strengthen the intimacy and loyalty of husband and wife to each other.

Although husband and wife bring to marriage the problem-solving techniques they developed in childhood and youth, these attitudes and responses can be altered. Such changes within the personality of each partner may bring into alignment the delicate balance between ego satisfaction and acceptance of responsibility. Husband and wife will soon realize that through giving and receiving their relationship is strengthened, even if an individual mate is giving more than he is receiving in a specific problem-solving situation.

The everyday circumstances of life require husband and wife to deal with a myriad of external problem-solving situations. How much money shall we spend on a car? Where will we send the children to school? Should we save for a trip to Europe? These external considerations are only peripherally related to ego satisfactions; they cannot enhance or detract from the essential self-worth.

It is in the area of inner problem-solving that the real test between ego satisfaction and acceptance of responsibility lies. In this sphere, the altruistic mate is capable of delaying or denying himself/herself ego satisfaction if the circumstances warrant such a solution.

There are four major modes of problem-solving. These include a variety of aggressive and defensive techniques. Each method can be either constructive or destructive. A technique is effective only if husband and wife are aware of the strength implicit in each successful solution of a marital problem.

The first means of problem-solving is a direct and realistic confrontation of the facts. This does not mean that you should confront your wife and declare that she is a dowdy slob; it does mean that you might offer to pay for slimming treatments and keep her company on a diet so that both of you can reap the results.

Direct confrontation, like other modes of problem-solving, offers many options. When there is prolonged conflict, subtle assistance from the more altruistic mate may help the other to gain some objectivity. By exerting effort toward solving a problem, and perhaps delaying his/her own ego satisfaction, the more altruistic partner gives his/her mate an opportunity to realize that there are options if the mate is willing to accept greater responsibility in a given situation.

As husband and wife learn to utilize direct confrontation as a means of problem-solving, they are also learning to communicate candidly with each other. Their reservations dwindle as they find that they can help each other.

Every solution that a husband and wife arrive at mutually enhances individual ego satisfaction and assists the more egocentric mate to accept greater responsibility. By accepting responsibility he is moving toward a pattern of behavior that will enable him to like himself better. And for this subtle adaptation he receives the approval and encouragement of his mate. Only when a couple have not learned how to solve problems constructively does each individual conflict or difference between them assume distorted proportions.

Sometimes a husband or wife will try to solve a problem by taking a way around it. He or she will detour or adapt by way of compensation.

When a wife cannot return to school to complete work toward a degree, she may redirect her energies toward a satisfying goal in the home. She may begin a career as an interior decorator. Or she may study accounting and go on to establish a home-based business. In either case she has, in effect, taken a detour and found other compensatory ways of satisfying legitimate ego needs. This satisfaction in turn can generate deeper creative understanding between husband and wife.

Conversely, a husband who did not receive an anticipated promotion at the office may redirect his frustrated energies into a destructive pattern. He may turn to drinking or gambling to compensate for his feelings of inadequacy. Alternatively, he can compensate in a constructive manner. He may decide that he has reached a plateau in his company and is unlikely to receive any further promotions unless his immediate superior dies. He may then, with his wife's assistance and encouragement, proceed to find other companies that can offer him the career recognition he is seeking. His wife may see that he is impeccably dressed for job interviews. And when he does accept another position, his wife may reassure him that he has made a wise choice.

In this mode of problem-solving, imagination and a realistic assessment of solutions are part of the working-out process. A refusal by husband or wife to accept a compensatory solution tends to lead to destructive solutions. A person who irresponsibly blames his mate, company or coworker for a problem that is not of any of their making is taking valuable time away from constructive problem-solving. The measure of a mate's growing altruism is his or her ability to accept frustration or disappointment. At the same time, he or she will pursue an alternative solution that will reduce frustrations or tensions.

In the marriage of a passive individual and an exploitative partner, problem-solving usually consists of variations of withdrawal. Unable to cope with threatening life situations realistically, the passive individual may simply avoid recognizing their existence. A passive wife or husband may seem to be complacent while actually he or she is unobtrusively becoming more dependent in an immature way. This mate may surrender to whatever appears inevitable, particularly if the more exploitative mate employs destructive-aggressive solutions (temper tantrums or physical abuse). Whenever a husband or wife chooses to conceal his/her true feelings about a problem area of the marriage, he/she is inclined to believe that the situation will right itself. Adjusting to marital problems by pretending that they do not exist is an admission of defeat.

Variations of withdrawal or "standing still" are not always a reflection of poor adaptation. A husband and wife may solve a problem in this manner for a short period of time. The technique may be employed constructively in a combination crisis and problem-solving situation where time will eventually provide positive alternatives. For example, a wife may suddenly become ill, causing all sexual activities to be suspended for a defined period of time. In order to meet this experience creatively, husband and wife may employ a "standing still" solution. Generally, however, a "do nothing" or prolonged "wait and see" response implies indecision, which is a kind of decision in itself. It is a way of escaping from reality.

Unlike the husband or wife who attempts to solve marital problems by literally doing nothing, the individual who retreats may return to explicitly childish behavior to conceal his inadequacies. A wife may resort to crying when she is unable to have her way. This woman may remember that this ineffectual technique worked miracles with Daddy, who hated to see her cry. A husband may retreat into masturbation when his wife declines to have intercourse with him for some legitimate reason.

Occasionally retreat can be considered a constructive vehicle when it is employed to allow the couple to retrench and reevaluate the unsolved problem. After a reevaluation of the problem, retreat is no longer necessary. The pair can then admit that it was necessary to go back before a significant advance could be made. For example, a wife may retreat into withdrawal after she discovers that she has diabetes. After an interim period of denial, she will gradually accept the reality of her illness and, with her husband's help, gain some perspective on the future.

Effective problem-solving techniques relieve tensions and enable a husband and wife to face married life realistically. While a couple is exploring ways to meet and accept life's problems together, the individuals are developing a fundamental generosity of spirit.

Crisis Situations

The balance between satisfaction of legitimate ego needs and acceptance of responsibilities is particularly critical in crisis situations. It is at these times that egocentricity is most likely to emerge. There is an unconscious reliance on the learned responses of childhood; fear, anxiety or even panic can overtake a husband or wife at such a moment.

Each crisis situation may seem to be unique and to call forth a singular solution from a husband or wife. But the significance of a crisis can be determined only by seeing the experience in terms of the Daddy's girl/Mama's boy relationship of childhood.

Not every crisis, however, can be solved. A substantial number of these inescapable life experiences are simply endured. The husband or wife who succumbs to self-pity or unhappiness and attempts to escape from a crisis by ending the marriage and seeking happiness or love-security elsewhere will continue to re-create the same pattern of inadequacy until he or she learns to cope realistically with crisis.

There are several types of acute crises that are normally disguised or concealed. They are subtle, imperceptible revelations that all husbands and wives are confronted with in the innermost recesses of their beings, and with which they must learn to live. The hidden life crises are facing the problems of aging, the monotony of daily life, the need for sexual variety and revitalization within a monogamous marriage, and development of inner resources.

The more egocentric husband or wife will impulsively respond to these hidden crises with intense subjectivity and fear or panic. He or she will tend to resist facing such problems. The ability to respond to a crisis with objectivity is characteristic of the more altruistic mate.

The struggle toward altruism is most difficult in these intangible crisis areas. It is during these critical life experiences that the individual's inner turmoil and self-concern may lead him to believe that his mate has an unfavorable image of him.

Aging

The crisis of aging can be a smoldering and potentially explosive issue between husband and wife. A sweeping denunciation and denial of aging by the predominantly egocentric mate often leads to the dissolution of the marriage. The egocentric mate then selects a much younger partner in order to assure himself/herself that he/she is not really growing older. This erroneous affirmation is vital for an egocentric individual because he believes that aging is the death knell of his essential self, which he defines as his sexual self.

The tensions aroused by the aging process are complex and difficult to identify. Regardless of the degree of egocentricity or altruism present in a husband or wife, there is always the legitimate question, "What will become of me when I grow older?"

If the crisis reaches conflict proportions, a husband or wife may employ one of the problem-solving techniques to deal with this conflict within himself/herself. When this happens, the crisis becomes externalized and the mate is drawn into the quandary.

In addition to the interior pressures, there are the very real attitudes of society with respect to aging. Our society repudiates aging as something to be avoided or denied. Vast empires have been built on a denial of the reality of aging. The message is devastating: the aging man or woman is no longer desirable as a human being. He is, in effect, unwanted and worthless. In order to be loving, one must be physically attractive. According to this thesis it is only the external physical form of a man or woman that has value.

If they are to realize the benefits of an enduring marriage, a husband and wife must find a constructive way, bereft of disguises and illusions, to accept rather than resist the aging process.

Monotony

Despite the diversity of human experiences available in our society, husband and wife/father and mother are nevertheless circumscribed by a pattern of life activities. This gives them a sense of direction and at the same time a lingering sense of monotony. Their days are predictable, although neither can be certain of the specific events that will occur.

In the early years of marriage the intense sexual interest each mate has in the other generates enthusiasm and a willingness to participate in a variety of life experiences. It does not occur to husband or wife that the crisis of monotony is a gradual, nebulous process that will have to be realistically faced by the middle years of marriage, at the very latest.

When the problem arises, the couple may nostalgically choose the line of least resistance and unconsciously recall parental "solutions." Again, escape and diversity are the problem-solving techniques that occur to husband or wife baffled by this crisis.

The anxious and tense mate will be inclined to blame his spouse for this predicament. If I weren't married, thinks the egocentric husband, I wouldn't have all these bills to think about: mortgage and car payments, orthodontia for the children. I could go off to Tahiti or the Galapagos Islands and have an adventure instead of having to show up at eight-thirty every Monday morning at work. Clearly such a husband is ready to escape from the crisis of monotony. He believes that solutions are outside of himself, just as he believes that his wife constitutes an obstacle to the solution he has formulated.

Such a crisis calls for an acceptance of responsibility before ego satisfaction can be realized. The denial or delay of privileges and rewards for an indefinite period of time may arouse consternation in the egocentric husband or wife. The fact that monotony, or some predictable, even tedious path of action will result in long-range marital and family benefits appears obscure to the mate whose own interests come before the well-being of the family.

That monotony is a crisis should not be denied. However, constructive techniques should be utilized to reduce the tensions of this life experience. Husband and wife must work to discover imaginative variations to minimize monotony. With this cooperative approach, the legitimate ego satisfactions of husband and wife become the by-product of their acceptance of marital responsibility.

Adjustive techniques include not only the use of problem-solving methods but also the development of personality traits that lend themselves to supportive interaction in a crisis. Some of these traits are cheerfulness, courage, a reassuring manner and confidence. The husband and wife whose marriage will be enduring bring to each life experience, including crisis situations, positive attitudes and a conviction that their mutual efforts will sustain them in any circumstances.

The Need for Sexual Variety Within a Monogamous Marriage

A husband and wife who are secure in each other's love tend to accept the gradual changes in the physical intensity of their relationship that come about as a result of familiarity. There is less fear or anxiety that one or the other will search for new sexual thrills when their sexual compatibility is being reinforced by ego satisfactions in the emotional, psychological and spiritual spheres of their lives. Physical acrobatics, changes in position, dependence on "how to" marriage manuals do not contribute variety or inspiration to the husband and wife of many years, for their sexual satisfaction deepens only in relation to the unity they have achieved in other areas of marriage.

When there are many unresolved conflicts and substantial individual differences, sex is entered into with reservations. Under these circumstances, the unsatisfied and dissatisfied mate attributes the lack of sexual thrills to the familiarity of a husband's or wife's responses. This merely points out that such a husband and wife have taken to bed with them all of their unresolved resentments against each other.

Rather than focusing on the predictability of a mate's sexual response, the husband or wife who is growing in altruism will appreciate the fullness of his or her mate's personality. He will consider sexual relations not merely as the union of two bodies, but as an exalted completion, a manifestation of love's transcendence. Complaints about sexual variety are, in reality, accumulated grievances skillfully exaggerated and distorted by one or both mates in order to overemphasize the imperfections of the spouse.

A deepening sexual love is experienced only when the husband and wife accept a mutual responsibility for sexual satisfaction. Problems diminish or even vanish when each mate accepts the inevitable physical changes that are a part of life. This acceptance becomes a reflection of his or her altruistic adaptation.

The Development of Inner Resources

Sometimes an overt crisis, such as accident or illness, compels a husband and wife to make some major alterations in their life. An examination of the religious or philosophical meaning of life and human relationships becomes desirable. The sensitive husband and wife will want to look beyond the superficial consolation that "everything will be all right" to the "why" of married life's trials.

The husband or wife may realize that everything will not be all right. What then? If one mate makes a deliberate choice to make the best of married life as it is, what can he/she believe in to make this effort worthwhile?

How will a husband and wife adjust to a long, debilitating illness with its continuous emotional and financial anxieties? How will a husband or wife accept a disfiguring accident if he or she has not developed the inner resources that are related to a religious or philosophical interpretation of life? How will they, as parents, respond to the birth of a retarded child? What if a child becomes a drug addict or a delinquent? Where will they find the resources to deal with these inexplicable life conditions?

If neither mate has developed a religious or philosophical comprehension of life, the marriage is likely to flounder when crises occur. The predominantly egocentric mate is generally less accepting of this essential ingredient of a happy and enduring marriage—a religious/philosophical world view. He or she tends to be rigid and inflexible in his/her response to crises, and this may impede acceptance of a philosophical interpretation of the inevitable problems of married life.

The more altruistic mate can be supportive and encouraging in such a crisis. He or she will develop independent inner resources that set an example. At the same time he or she should not try to force the spouse to accept a similar philosophical orientation.

Gradually, as one mate adapts to deal with a crisis, the other may become less rigid and more desirous of accepting the problems of marriage. When husband and wife together develop inner resources or a religious/philosophical orientation, they are providing themselves with a unique cohesiveness which will enable them to face all of the trials of married life.

The Overt Crises

Overt crises are critical externalized life experiences that have a relatively temporary duration. They are emergency circumstances that require immediate decisions.

Sudden accidents, illness, childbirth, loss of job or status in the community—all these events alter a marital life pattern. In each crisis there is an explicit threat or challenge to the individual's ego.

When a woman, for example, is required to undergo a mastectomy, this may have profound psychological repercussions. How she and her husband respond to this crisis will alter the future course of their marriage. Once the alteration has been accepted, however, there is a rebuilding of ego strengths by husband and wife in order to sustain the self-esteem they need to continue life together.

In a marriage involving an egocentric mate, there is a more difficult struggle. Both husband and wife tend to panic. Each individual is concerned only with the survival of his or her own ego. An egocentric in this situation might eventually find reasons for leaving his wife and ending the marriage. His ego, he feels, is diminished by his now less than physically perfect wife. He cannot or will not alter his egocentricity in order to sustain his wife during this critical ordeal, and ultimately the marriage will collapse.

All crises, whether overt or hidden, require an acceptance of responsibility and a delay or denial of ego satisfactions during the critical period. These life circumstances undeniably call for sacrifice and fortitude.

The process of re-establishing and re-creating self-esteem once the crisis has passed requires constructive marital interaction. Husband and wife sustain each other; each has as his/her paramount concern the well-being of the mate.

Negative Emotions

The average husband and wife enter marriage without any clear understanding or appreciation of a mate's potential for expressing negative emotions.

Occasionally a husband or wife may exhibit moodiness, a temper tantrum, crankiness brought on by fatigue, or a need to be the center of attention. The concerned spouse usually does not look beyond the immediate circumstances that aroused these negative emotions. He or she is inclined to isolate these responses. Not only are they actually part of a continuing response to a mate, these negative responses are nullifying positive aspects of interaction between a couple.

Some couples employ negative emotions to solve all of their problems. They quarrel, blame the other mate, deny responsibility for individual actions, throw temper tantrums, withhold money or sex as part of their overall mode of marital adaptation. Their behavior is a reflection of psychological regression or arrested development due to a maladaptive parent-child relationship.

Rarely does it occur to such individuals that examples of negative behavior prevent them from enjoying a congenial and harmonious marriage. Only when a crisis situation compels them to make some extraordinary adaptation do they realize that alternatives are possible and desirable. Throughout life all human beings are confronted with thwarting or frustrating experiences that deny them immediate ego satisfaction. The resourcefulness that an individual displays in these circumstances is indicative of his or her social maturity and capacity to give.

The husband and wife who are determined to minimize self-indulgence in negative emotions and to channel their energy toward positive emotional interaction can do so. Getting along with a husband or wife is not some mysterious process that defies explanation. Generally speaking, the husband or wife who has desirable traits will find that he or she is successful in other social relationships as well. Conversely, the individual who reveals a bad temper, jealousy or selfishness will exhibit these traits in other relationships outside marriage.

Many negative emotions are, moreover, an indication of a deep-rooted sense of inferiority. A person who feels inferior is inclined to focus his attention and efforts on limiting and thwarting his mate in order to compensate for his own personality problems. This pattern is the ultimate consequence of negative emotions.

The ability to work patiently toward the eradication of negative emotions and the desire to replace these traits with positive emotions indicate an individual's growth from egocentricity toward altruism. As a couple learns to replace negative emotions with positive ones, individual self-esteem increases, and a balance is struck between ego satisfaction and acceptance of responsibility. The relationship loses its limiting and thwarting characteristics. There is a cooperation instead of resistance, freedom rather than domination, mutual support instead of calculated ego demolition.

In order to meet the challenges of married life, every husband and wife should be receptive to the concept of personality alteration. Marital relations will improve in proportion to the extent to which each partner is motivated toward and capable of personality changes.

Daddy's Girl/Mama's Boy Patterns to Avoid

Certain men and women will probably never be realistic candidates for an enduring marriage because of their early relationship with the parent of the opposite sex. These are the individuals who remain excessively egocentric, exploitative or narcissistic. They will enter into random erotic relationships and may even marry, but these men and women are not motivated to alter their behavior.

When these men and women marry, they become the instigators and generators of serious marital problems. The "victimized" mate will choose such an individual for a husband or wife because he or she does not or will not see the destructive pattern before marriage.

This disastrous combination can be prevented. The crucial factor in making a wise choice is to comprehend your future husband's or wife's relationship with the parent of the opposite sex.

How can you determine the degree of understanding or hostility that exists between your prospective mate and his/her parent? Realistically, the ideal approach is an examination of his/her family life on a comfortable day-to-day basis. Although this may appear to be obvious, our culture's dating system generally does not allow for such intimate perception. Our system is devised to disguise rather than clarify personality traits. Moreover, it tends to compel a man and woman to enter into immediate sexual intimacy before either one really knows the multiple and complex dimensions of the other's personality.

The exaggerated emphasis on sexual magnetism almost precludes the possibility of evaluating a prospective husband or wife in light of his/her relationship with the parent of the opposite sex. This concern confuses the basic issue, which is whether or not a specific man or woman has the capacity to sustain an enduring monogamous marriage. The dating experience is peripheral and incidental to the actual living process a prospective husband and wife will know in marriage, for it is, for the most part, oriented away from the home.

Patterns of family life observed in unguarded moments will allow you to decipher personality traits of a prospective mate that might otherwise be hidden. Is there an air of competitiveness and tension in the parental home? Does one individual dominate the family atmosphere? Are mealtimes a time of angry outbursts? How does your prospective mate respond to the emotional tenor of this family life?

You may discover that your date's family rarely sit down to dinner together. Perhaps they have family patterns of avoiding one another. Or maybe only one parent is present, and the other parent is consistently absent. A perceptive man or woman will be aware that this can indicate serious problems and possibly even a loveless future.

Perceiving the complex nuances of love, hate or fear that exist within the family of your prospective mate requires a continuing opportunity to participate in their lives.

Our culture places extraordinary emphasis on the one-to-one dating relationship as the essential means by which two people can evaluate each other as potential marriage partners. Society tends to ignore or even scoff at the significance of the far more relevant family pattern, which is a vital consideration in making a wise marital choice. Inter-family relationships harbor the seeds of almost all future marital conflict or love-security.

Attitudes that would not ordinarily be revealed in dating situations are spontaneously manifested in the family situation. Does your prospective mate disparage his/her parent of the opposite sex? Is he or she contemptuous? Or servile? Does Daddy or Mama clutch too tightly at his girl or boy even though he/she may be in his/her thirties or forties?

What if you have never met your prospective mate's family? Why does he/she refuse to invite you to the parental home? Obviously, as the individual moves out of adolescence into adulthood, there may be less reference to the family and more concern for the one-to-one dating relationship. Of course, your prospective mate's family may live in a different part of the country. In that case, it is imperative that you spend a reasonable period of time observing your prospective mate's behavior with close friends or relatives of the parental generation. This will offer clues that might never be revealed during dating.

There are several critical factors an individual should consider when determining whether or not a man or woman would be an appropriate partner.

Inability to Tolerate Frustration or Disappointment
The inability to tolerate frustration or disappointment is ominously significant in our sex-drenched society, particularly when a man or woman combines this attitude with the use of love as a vehicle of negotiation. For example, the exploitative man or woman whose only criterion is self-satisfaction may persistently demand a sexual relationship as a proof of love. A narcissistic female will need many conquests to pamper her insatiable ego.

The man or woman who explodes into outrage or destroys a relationship because he or she is not provided with immediate sexual gratification is reflecting an implacable personality that is not likely to be modified by marriage.

The perceptive man or woman will quickly understand that this inability to accept frustration or disappointment, especially in the sexual sphere, indicates a marital future of conflict.

Basic Attitudes and Beliefs

Before entering into an enduring monogamous marriage, a man or woman must objectively evaluate the values, habits, customs, education, religious/philosophical orientation, and goals of his/her prospective mate. He or she must understand that there may be great similarities or great differences between himself/herself and the prospective mate. Significant differences that cannot be reconciled by compromise or cooperation will affect a couple's future life together.

If a woman wishes to pursue a career at the expense of motherhood and a man is determined to have children, he is only deluding himself if he believes that he can change his future wife's attitude.

As more and more major differences are revealed, a subtle tension develops, because either the man or the woman will attempt to persuade the other that his/her attitude should prevail.

A dating relationship between such a couple may continue because of a powerful sexual attraction despite acknowledged differences. Each individual cannot or will not relinquish the other because of this sexual fascination. The result is a disastrous marital relationship.

There Is Only One Way to Do Things—MY Way

A person who is preoccupied with himself or herself will be an inflexible marital partner. Such a person will not adjust or accommodate, even though he may be in love, for according to his definition of love the man or woman who loves him should do all of the accommodating. The extent to which this trait can dominate a marriage cannot be perceived by the more flexible and altruistic mate. It is strangely inconceivable to him that under the influence of sexual love such a man or woman will not change.

The inflexible partner's harsh and uncompromising attitude may escape notice during courtship for a variety of reasons. The man may appear to be extremely self-assured, and he may have unconsciously chosen a timid or insecure woman who needs to lean heavily on him for psychological assurance. Before marriage, she may be only too happy to be agreeable. After marriage, however, she will eventually become disenchanted with her role as her mate's satellite. And the unyielding man will be incapable of tolerating any individuality on his mate's part. Resistance seeps into the relationship in the form of deception. A competitive pattern will smolder, only to explode eventually, when husband and wife no longer feel the need to make a good impression on each other.

This trait is especially prominent in the dominant-submissive relationship that evolves in many marriages. Neither partner examined beforehand how all-pervasive and destructive this characteristic can be as a source of continuing marital conflict.

Arguments, Quarrels and Belligerency

In every continuing human relationship, there are moments of maximum tension as well as moments of maximum intimacy. Chronic quarreling occurs when a relationship is burdened by stored-up, unresolved tensions. The state of tension is reinforced by every additional quarrel.

A man and woman in a courtship situation may be sexually magnetized to each other, even though almost everything else in their relationship is unsatisfactory to one or both of them. Unable to admit that they have no basis for an enduring monogamous marriage, they drift along in a relatively aimless pattern of quarreling and reconciliation. At least one of them soothes himself/herself with the fallacy that "the course of true love was never smooth," and he or she proceeds blithely toward a destructive marriage, in spite of his or her knowledge of the personality of the prospective mate.

A man or woman who is chronically contentious is revealing his/her need to be egocentric, exploitative or narcissistic in a clear and recognizable way. Quarreling not only indicates significant areas of disagreement, but, more profoundly, it reveals that at least one person learned to cope with dissatisfactions in this destructive manner in childhood.

The chronically contentious man or woman tends to compel his mate to employ this self-defeating pattern of problem-solving in marriage. In a dating or courtship situation this trait is often ignored or misinterpreted, and its consequences are realized only when the marriage begins to fall apart.

Sexual Braggadocio

In our orgasm-oriented society the number of sexual braggarts is increasing. Characteristically this man or woman pursues a pattern of conquest, satisfaction, discontent and change of partners. His proximate goals of gratification and ego satisfaction are attained at the price of emotional lacerations to his temporary partners. Such a man or woman is inclined to isolate sex from the total human personality of his/her mate or lover.

In a dating or courtship circumstance, this Daddy's girl or Mama's boy exhibits a kind of unrepentant charm and pseudosophistication, which has undeniable appeal in relationships where one partner is considerably younger than the other. It is possible for the sexual braggart to persuade not only a prospective husband or wife, but himself as well, that he is truly desirous of marriage. Nothing could be further from the truth.

Irrespective of age, this individual is devoid of the traits that are requisite to an enduring monogamous marriage. It would be impossible for him or her to explore and cultivate the total human personality of his/her partner, for he or she is incapable of relating to another man or woman except in the sexual sphere.

Usually the man or woman who falls prey to such a mate in marriage does so because he/she erroneously believes that his/her love will be so unique that it will transform a perennial philanderer into a faithful mate. The "victimized" husband or wife thus unconsciously chooses a mode of victimization that *could* be averted.

Are You Your Worst Self with Him/Her?

Understanding the deceptive personality—the man and woman who seem to be what they are not—is vital to making a wise marital choice. An individual must perceive that certain characteristic patterns of relatively unmodifiable behavior signal disaster for a forthcoming marriage.

In the social relationship that precedes marriage, a man and woman eventually discover whether they bring out the best or the worst in each other's character. Do you find, for example, that you feel obligated to lie or make excuses about your prospective mate's behavior? Are you persuaded to deny or repudiate values, customs or traditions that have meaning in your life? Do you feel that your present intense feelings cannot last into the future because of the way your date behaves? Does either one of you demand constant proof of love because in reality only one of you wishes to continue the relationship?

The troubled and disturbed Daddy's girl or Mama's boy tends to emphasize the importance of his/her own needs at the expense of a prospective mate's personality. This individual may be so cogently influential that he/she is able to persuade a mate to commit antisocial acts or to pursue a pattern of activity that is totally alien to his/her true personality. When such a situation occurs, the man or woman who is more adaptable becomes confused and bewildered. He or she knows that something is awry in the relationship, but may be unable to define this nebulous difficulty.

A dating relationship does not always deteriorate when this problem arises. Although one person may be remotely aware that he/she is not his/her best self with a prospective wife or husband, he/she does not terminate the relationship. A young woman may be desperately determined to marry despite the fact that she is vaguely disturbed about her fiance's personality. A man may be so sexually enamored that he does not understand that a particular personality trait of his marriage partner will probably lead to a temporary relationship.

The ability to discern unsuitable Daddy's girl or Mama's boy patterns of behavior requires self-understanding and honesty. Many temporary marriages should never have been entered into because of the predictably unmodifiable behavior pattern of at least one of the mates.

Altering the Daddy's Girl/Mama's Boy Pattern

The exclusivity of the marriage relationship depends largely on the self-control of husband and wife. When there is an abandonment of this commitment, or one mate seeks unequal ego satisfaction at the expense of marital responsibility, self-control is threatened.

A husband and wife may find themselves drifting apart for no other reason than that neither one has taken positive steps toward realignment of ego satisfactions and acceptance of responsibility. One or both mates need to alter their behavior in order to achieve such a balance. By modifying their behavior, husband and wife in effect give up certain traits that have aroused conflict and alter their response to each other so as to develop an abiding relationship.

In those marriages where there is a strong motivation to preserve the relationship, husband and wife can help each other to achieve the profound love-security each wishes to experience. How they can work toward this continuing experience depends on their resolution of conflict situations.

Almost all marital conflicts have one characteristic in common: each mate tends to blame the other for the unhappy circumstances that have arisen. A stalemate then occurs, because husband and wife have become defensive adversaries. This pattern must be altered in order to redirect the energies of each individual. The more altruistic mate must take the initiative by meeting his spouse's negative, critical or egocentric behavior with consideration. He must attempt to disarm his mate with a compassionate response. This response is crucial, because it enables the less responsible mate to save face and then redirect his behavior.

Probably the greatest challenge is dealing with the fact that one's mate has become an adversary. Some marriages continue for years in this state of limbo, because neither mate is sufficiently altruistic to respond to an ego attack with words and gestures of compassion and generosity. It is during this phase of behavior alteration that the more egocentric mate may permit the relationship to collapse because he falsely believes he can enter into another marriage where such conflicts will not occur. He reaches out toward a self-defeating pattern that he assumes is a solution to the problem.

In order to divert the self-defeating energies of the egocentric mate into constructive patterns of behavior, the more responsible mate must help him/her to control his/her destructive feelings. The more altruistic mate, by his/her sympathetic but non-judgmental attitude, can encourage his/her mate to gain some perspective on the irresponsible or inappropriate behavior that caused the conflict. By providing an emotional milieu of warmth and acceptance, the more responsible mate encourages his/her spouse to attempt to examine the conflict. In this way greater objectivity evolves.

Thus a husband or wife grows in self-understanding. This process affords him the opportunity to replace a poor self-image with better feelings about himself. As he comes to recognize and understand his irresponsible behavior, he can, with the aid of his mate, learn to achieve his ego satisfactions in a more responsible way. Because he recognizes that his behavior has contributed to or caused a conflict, he may decide that he no longer wishes to get drunk, or be unfaithful, or squander money. He learns that these activities are self-defeating. They arouse in him feelings of self-hatred, and they drive his mate further away from him. In reality, what he desires is a more intimate and secure relationship.

Gradually he comes to accept responsibility for his behavior. He has progressed to the point where, instead of blaming his mate, he can admit to himself that his own behavior has consequences or rewards. For example, a wife who unconsciously views her husband as another Daddy and blames him when she cannot have her way is able to reevaluate her behavior in terms of this new self-understanding. She therefore learns to grant her husband some of the ego satisfactions he needs in order to give her love—and to accept greater responsibility for her own actions. As husband and wife proceed toward a goal of responsible behavior, they grow in altruistic interaction, for each comes to value the love-security and mutuality of the relationship above all else.

The process of modification must be entirely voluntary; the essential difference between the enduring monogamous marriage and the temporary marriage is in the partners' willingness to adapt. In an enduring marriage, the relationship is always becoming more profound, for it is constantly being energized by a husband and wife who are alert to the delicate balance between ego satisfaction and acceptance of responsibility.

Committing oneself to marriage—that is, accepting responsibility for one's own behavior—carries with it an improved sense of self-esteem. The husband and wife who have dedicated all their personality resources to an enduring monogamous marriage can be certain of love-security.

The process of accepting responsibility is the crucial facet of adaptation in contemporary marriage. As a husband and wife alter the Daddy's girl and Mama's boy personality patterns they brought with them into marriage, they become more resilient, less inflexible, more objective, less egocentric or narcissistic. This character evolution enables them to consider the well-being of their mate before their own.

Major conflicts dwindle or vanish, because new techniques of adaptation have been accepted and put into practice. There is a reduction in areas of hostility and ambivalence. Husband and wife become more integrated and more at peace as they perceive the values inherent in an enduring marriage.

Of course, alteration of the Daddy's girl and Mama's boy patterns can be considered only within the context of the total personality, which includes hereditary characteristics and environmental influences. Modification of behavior does not mean that a husband or wife is so transformed in personality that he/she is unrecognizable as his/her former self.

The behavior patterns of a husband or wife are not infinitely modifiable; rather, they are malleable within the range of the individual's capacity to change. For example, a quick-tempered husband is unlikely to become a docile, even-tempered man on all occasions, but he may be able to alter his responses enough so that most of the time his outbursts do not precipitate major marital upheavals.

One mate may only be able to lessen the intensity of a negative trait, while another may be capable of adjusting his/her behavior to include some positive good. A wife may be able to progress from a reserved, withdrawn person to a spontaneous, affectionate woman. The greater the degree of behavior alteration, the more the relationship is improved.

When the balance between ego satisfaction and acceptance of responsibility is continuously, but subtly, shifting, the relationship is a milieu for optimum personality development. Husband and wife understand each other intimately. They know when one will give and the other will take, when one will surrender and the other will prevail. This indefinable meshing of personalities is the harvest of a loving relationship that transcends the limitations of all temporary difficulties.

Love-Security Can Be a Continuing Experience

To recognize our potential for more profound marital happiness is to admit that there is a discrepancy between the real and the ideal, which has not quite come into being.

Between the Daddy's girl or Mama's boy we once were and the husband or wife we may be, there is that dimensionless transition that links our desire to be loved with our capacity to love.

For some of us, the desire to be loved triumphs over our capacity to love, in which case we remain tangled in a maze of egocentric emotions which circumscribe our adult lives. For others, the journey from the narcissistic world of childhood toward adulthood is wracked with painful struggles to free the self. Still others achieve this transition from childhood to adulthood with comparative serenity because Daddy or Mama prepared them, by giving them the capacity to love, for an enduring and loving relationship of their own.

The struggle to expand our capacity to love requires all of our best efforts. We cannot pretend we are Daddy's girls or Mama's boys again when we experience marital problems or when we crave more intense ego satisfaction; we cannot delude ourselves into thinking that there are no marital responsibilities.

We must, if we wish to experience love-security, fortify ourselves with the inner resources that may have been lacking in childhood. We must shed the attitudes, feelings, responses and self-defeating decisions that have made our lives so devoid of love-security; and we must cultivate certain personality traits.

These traits are inextricably related to our capacity to love. Mutual dependence and trust provide that assurance of exclusivity which husband and wife need as the foundation for an abiding relationship. Fidelity and loyalty are essential not only in the narrowly defined interpretation of sexual faithfulness, but in the more comprehensive sphere of the primary concern of husband and wife for each other above all others. Approval satisfies the legitimate ego needs of husband and wife and reveals another vital characteristic, generosity of character. Sexual love and affection create and sustain that fundamental bond which is the keystone of the relationship between husband and wife.

An enduring monogamous marriage is the satisfying reward of a Daddy's girl and Mama's boy who have successfully transmuted the desire to be loved into the capacity to love.

10

A Gallery of Daddy's Girls and Mama's Boys

Does marital history repeat itself? Are marital decisions—to marry or not to marry—subtly woven into the day-to-day texture of life along with the pattern of love-security each individual will pursue in adulthood? The Daddy's girls and Mama's boys revealed here are diverse personalities from unique life circumstances.

The benign and devoted are here along with the egocentric. Their impact has been unjustifiably distorted by the current trend to look condescendingly on sentiment. Their efforts to contribute to the validity of marriage should be recognized.

Jacqueline Bouvier—Jack Bouvier

"Never reflect, never regret" might have been the credo of Jack Bouvier, whose life, from auspicious beginnings, plummeted into an abyss of loneliness in his last years. What happened to the dazzling moments when he was the great lover—when the assignation or conquest was everything?

Those were the reckless, exciting years when he was adored by everyone, especially his daughters Jacqueline and Lee. He taught them all there was to know about love and men.

Sloughing off marriage, Jack Bouvier came into his own once again to play the only role he knew in life. He dedicated his energies to the conquest of women who would idolize him and nourish his inexhaustible capacity for narcissism.

In his spare time he was incidentally Daddy. It seemed to be an ideal arrangement for a man of his temperament. How, though, did he appear to a sensitive adolescent girl on the brink of womanhood, who by now was familiar with the pattern of her father's life after divorce: his women, his parties, his clothes, his uncertain career, his sprees of indulgence and self-indulgence?

Would he always be exciting and flashy and persuasive, insinuating to her that she would follow in his footsteps and be a smashing success with men? His advice to her about men might haunt her in womanhood: play hard to get, be unapproachable; then when they succumb, go on to other triumphs.

Jack Bouvier had an apt pupil. Love-security in his daughter's world was measured by externals: houses, clothes, jewels, all the trappings of an elegant and opulent life. But in the midst of this splendor, there was the intangible feeling that Jack Bouvier surely transmitted to his little girl: that no one woman could ever satisfy him, because no one could love him as much as he loved himself. Would all of her relations with men be an escape from the perilous narcissism that Daddy bequeathed to her?

Diana Barrymore—John Barrymore

Intense self-destructive impulses and a confused repudiation of her father characterized Diana Barrymore's futile search for love-security, which ended in her despairing death.

Neglected by two narcissistic divorced parents, Diana began to idealize her absentee father at an early age when she learned that he was the idol of millions of women. The illusions were embellished by her vivid imagination, and not unexpectedly they collided with reality when, as a love-hungry adolescent, she met her movie-idol father, who visited her at a boarding school.

Introducing her to alcohol and ignoring her presence while he engaged in a session of amorous petting with a teenage classmate were two of John Barrymore's more casual contributions to his daughter's unconscious repudiation of him and her deepening pattern of self-destructiveness. Diana Barrymore was bewildered and confounded when she discovered her father's incredible capacity for egocentricity. When, as a young woman, she visited him in Hollywood, she was outraged to find him ordering her to get a call girl for him.

This revelation of the more sordid side of his life foreshadowed her own pattern of escape through alcohol and men. Her repudiation of him was complete. She was disgusted and angry with him because he had never really been a father to her.

But she loved him in her own way; wasn't that what a daughter was supposed to feel for her father? Because she could not reconcile these contradictions, she surrendered to self-pity. Diana Barrymore's narcissistic plea for love-security took two forms: a search for pseudo-love via theatrical and movie fame, and the choice of "wrong" men as husbands and lovers (a manifestation of her paternal repudiation).

In all of her marriages there was an unconscious plea: I am worthy of love. Don't you see I am worthy of love? Why don't you, Daddy, love me? You see, Bram loves me and Johnny loves me and Bob loves me. They all love me. Why don't you? This quintessential narcissistic plea for love-security was never fulfilled; Diana was estranged from her father at the time of his death.

Diana careened disturbingly from one marital disaster to another, frantically seeking a relationship that would offer her the love-security she had never known with her father. Her first marriage to Bramwell Fletcher, who was eighteen years her senior, was an act of rebellion and defiance. No one would tell her what to do. When Diana Barrymore attempted suicide shortly after she told her husband the marriage was over, did she recall the pattern of her father's life: the innumerable suicide threats, the heavier and heavier drinking, the women whose faces he could not and did not wish to remember? The desperate and deliberate retreat into his narcissistic self eventually narrowed his world down to a bedroom and then a hospital room.

After walking through a forgettable second marriage, Diana Barrymore met her third husband, whom she acknowledged meant more to her than anyone else except her father.

All the while, her theatrical career, which might have provided the compensatory love she could not find in human relationships, deteriorated because of her relentless drinking. Robert Wilcox, her third husband, was an unsuccessful actor and an alcoholic. He represented the collective miasma of her tormented relationship with her father.

Like other women who have repudiated the earlier paternal figure, Diana Barrymore, with full knowledge of his alcoholic problem, was drawn to a husband whose dependency on the bottle reflected one of her father's personality traits. What attracted her repelled her. She seemed to delight in the treacherous depths of alcoholism that she and Robert Wilcox shared. At the same time she hated herself when she thought of what she had once been and what she had become.

Was she, through her alcoholic haze, recalling her father's plea for a call girl when she sought to escape with yet another lover while still married to Robert Wilcox?

Was Diana Barrymore echoing her father's sentiments when she justified her actions to her husband by declaring that she was like a man about those things, that the episode meant nothing to her?

Finally, the yearnings of a lifetime flickered, and her agitated heart admitted that what she wanted most intensely from life was a strong man who would be both lover and father.

Svetlana Alliluyeva—Joseph Stalin

Embezzled moments of love have a way of festering in the unconscious. They may evolve into explicit acts of repudiation if the parent involved has seriously stifled normal psychological development of the child.

For Svetlana Alliluyeva, the daughter of Joseph Stalin, love for any other man constituted an overt act of betrayal. Patterns of ambivalence and repudiation were established early in life: her mother committed suicide, at which time her father declared his former wife to be his enemy. Svetlana Alliluyeva emerged as a reflection of this betrayal.

For Svetlana love always retained the taint of betrayal. Alexei Kapler, whom she loved in the winter of 1942–43 when she was seventeen and he was forty, was sent away by her father. Kapler was sentenced to two terms of five years each. The first term was spent in Northern Russia, and the second working in the mines in a prison camp.

Her first marriage to Grigory Morozov was an explicit act of revolt against a father who bound her too closely to him. Not unexpectedly, this relationship ended in divorce. Two years later Svetlana Alliluyeva married Yuri Zhdanov. It was a calculated marriage, a relationship of convenience. The cold and harsh man she married bore an undeniable resemblance to the father from whom she was trying to escape. Perhaps only she did not recognize the similarity. The marriage ended within a few years.

With the death of her father, the external shackles were loosened once and for all, and Svetlana Alliluyeva was at last free to follow her heart's desire. A period of loneliness only seemed to deepen the conviction within her that a love relationship somewhere, with some man, would give her life meaning.

Once again searching for love, Svetlana Alliluyeva entered into a relationship with a sophisticated Indian, Brijesh Singh, whom she met in a Moscow hospital in 1963. The relationship endured until his death in 1966. She was able to obtain permission to go to India to scatter Brijesh Singh's ashes. She was beginning the journey that would eventually take her to the United States.

Although her third husband, William Wesley Peters, a widower and a former son-in-law of Mrs. Frank Lloyd Wright, appeared to be a complete contrast to her previous husbands, the physical surroundings he brought to the marriage were hauntingly familiar. No impartial observer would compare Svetlana Alliluyeva's childhood in the Kremlin to her life at Taliesin West, where, until her separation and divorce, she resided with her third husband. In her imagination, though, the two became one. While her third husband, like her father, associated their home with security and a unique vision of life, for her such surroundings constituted a "prison." But didn't she choose this life, the third time around, of her own accord? The oppressive unresolved agonies of childhood were revived.

In her adult life she had unconsciously sought to duplicate what she had repudiated. Deprived of altruistic love by a father who could only offer love "at a price," Svetlana Alliluyeva evolved from a naive and trusting child into a determined adult, convinced of the validity of beginning again and again and again. In all charming simplicity, she believed that love was her due.

When the all-pervasive repudiation response clashes with an equally powerful need to love (indicated in Svetlana Alliluyeva's writings), it is difficult, and sometimes even impossible, to create an enduring love-security relationship in marriage. Such an individual can often sublimate her capacities for a marital love relationship, diverting them into some other form of emotional satisfaction. Svetlana Alliluyeva has apparently found love-security in her relationship with her young daughter by her third husband, and in her literary and religious/philosophical interests.

Her three marriages reveal an intense yearning for love and security, but each collapse and divorce was energetically followed by a process of rebuilding and re-creating. Trusting and effervescent, Svetlana Alliluyeva appears even now to be in the act of beginning again.

Elizabeth I—Henry VIII

"Crooked . . . carcass!" Essex had spewed in a passionate raving outburst against his queen.

Elizabeth I never forgot the words. As he sat in prison awaiting execution, Elizabeth tried to decide whether Essex deserved mercy or justice. The words badgered her. Did she perhaps pick up her mirror and recall the nursery rhyme

> *Mirror, mirror on the wall*
> *Who is fairest of them all?*

If at the age of sixty-seven she was not the fairest, she was certainly the most powerful woman alive.

Did Elizabeth, looking into the mirror, realize the truth about herself? Revolted by what she saw, did all of her whining vanity rivet itself on the moment when Essex's words had spelled his own doom?

He had dared to disagree with her, his queen, over the appointment of his uncle, Sir William Knollys. His temper had bubbled up and exploded; he had reached for his sword and defiantly shouted at her, "This is an outrage."

What was she to do? Vacillate? Forgive him as she had done again and again in the past, in those fervid gleaming days when he had fed her famished womanhood in a way that no other man had ever been able to do? What had Essex really done that was so heinous—offend an old lady? The truth, she realized as she gazed into the mirror, was that she was old and Essex, at thirty-four, was in the full vigor of his manhood. Was she not a fool to think of herself as a woman beneath the layer of dried and withered skin, beneath the red wig hiding her gray hair, beneath the "crooked carcass"?

Did he deserve to die? For as long as she could remember, Essex, above all the others, had provided an oasis in her barren life. For what other sort of memories of love did she have?

Could Elizabeth recall vaguely that day so long ago when her father had had her mother's head chopped off? She was not yet three at the time.

How unwanted she had been! Was her mother put to death because she, Elizabeth, was not a boy? Or was her mother rushed into eternity simply because her father was panting for his next wife?

One moment her father would revile her, declaring her to be illegitimate. In the next her licentious and shrewdly corrupt father would pamper her and pet her, calling her an heir to the throne of England. What did she know of love? In her childish mind, love was equated with her father's insatiable quest for a woman who would flatter the monumentally vain self-image his corrupt narcissism had allowed him to develop. Hadn't the four wives after her mother also failed to be what her father wanted? Not quite fifteen, Elizabeth was living with the last of them, Catherine Parr, when her father died.

Elizabeth grimaced at the memory of her stepmother's husband, who would have been a lecherous child seducer if he had had his way. But that memory only clarified the attitude toward love that her father had bequeathed her: a muddled repugnance toward sexuality.

Although she constantly tantalized all those who offered their hand out of love or desire for political power, she abstained most fastidiously from marriage. Deep within her welled a powerful revulsion against sexuality and all its implications. The whirlpool of indecision with respect to sexual matters remained with her all her life. And at its vortex was her father's reflection, taunting, remonstrating, cajoling, never allowing her to be her own woman. Why had he abandoned her and deliberately chosen all those other women?

And yet there was Essex, who had ignited her womanly and queenly array of talents magnificently. In those shining years, there had been no one else like him. There would never be anyone, ever again.

She was in a rage at herself, at Essex, at her father, whom she wished to forget but who was jeering at her now in her blighted memories of love. To be squeamish, to be womanly or sentimental at a time like this would be folly. Floundering in weariness and indecision, Elizabeth impulsively delayed the execution.

Why could she not forget her father at a time like this? Was she, after all, despite her protestations, her father's daughter? Had he not taught her the ultimate solution? Could she really look into the mirror and begin again as he had done so many times before her?

It would be so easy, she thought. He would be her mirror and perpetuate her insatiable vanities, for now that was all she had—the illusion that once she had been a woman. Beneath the withered skin, beneath the red wig, beneath the "crooked carcass," Elizabeth emptied herself of self-deception in one final terrible decision. Essex would die.

As her father had done, Elizabeth comforted herself with substantial realistic reasons for her decision. Conspiracy and treason justified this execution as adultery and the king's displeasure had justified others so many years ago. Out of the depths of muffled agony emerged an unyielding daughter who had the ability to demand revenge in an act that echoed her father's unhesitating condemnation of her mother.

Simone de Beauvoir—Georges Bertrand de Beauvoir

In a male-dominated society, a man who has no sons may fashion a daughter to his own likeness and image, even though he may be somewhat unsure of the mode by which he will effect this transfusion of personality, particularly in a society that is hostile to a woman whose intellectual abilities give her entrée into a male-oriented world of achievement and distinction.

From Papa, Simone de Beauvoir learned that there was only one way to escape the limitations of womanhood: by becoming an intellectual equal to the male, and, in effect, beating him at his own game by living like a male and renouncing marriage as an expression of conventional bourgeois hypocrisy.

Georges Bertrand de Beauvoir, a lawyer by profession and a dilettante actor on the side, used charm and persuasiveness, rather than tyranny, to guide his daughter into an esoteric world of philosophy and culture. His unchallenged position of preeminence in the home, where Mama always deferred to Papa's superior judgment, was not lost on Simone de Beauvoir. At an early age she became acutely sensitive to the differences between the male and female worlds. As she matured, the issue became clearer and clearer. The male definitely had more satisfactions in life, both intellectual and sensual. Simone de Beauvoir realized what Papa expected of her, and she had every intention of fulfilling his expectations.

The conflict between Mama's austere religious convictions and Papa's avowed skepticism left its mark on her. Mama gave her the distinct impression that sex was sinful, and Papa treated her as if she were simply a disembodied mind, with neither body nor soul. These contradictions are irreconcilable, as Simone de Beauvoir discovered in later life. Her repudiation of marriage was an outgrowth of the serious philosophical discrepancies between Papa's and Mama's attitudes.

Unwilling to accept a society that gave the male the privilege of enjoying a double standard and at the same time denigrated women with stereotyped categories of "respectable" and "loose," Simone de Beauvoir decided to direct her considerable intellectual talents toward rectifying this societal imbalance—she took up the cause of women's liberation.

In spite of her determination to diminish the inequities women suffer in marriage, she yielded to the blandishments of Jean-Paul Sartre and calmly accepted the bourgeois hypocrisies implicit in their long association.

Although the direct influence on her life of Papa, her first mentor, faded as she became an adult, it was primarily because she was reacting against his disembodied intellectuality that she found Sartre so acceptable to her. She believed that in this association she could escape from all the frustrating and circumscribed experiences of women, who were man's inferior in the society of her impressionable years.

Because of his antagonism toward Jean-Paul Sartre, Simone de Beauvoir gradually came to ignore Papa completely. She immersed herself in this new relationship. If she had qualms at first, they were quickly forgotten.

It was Sartre who now introduced her to equality. He taught her the essential rule she would have to learn in order to comprehend the male world: that although their relationship might constitute a fundamental love, each would be free to experience incidental love affairs. Only in this way, he explained to her, could the full gamut of love emotions be experienced. Her belief in the insignificance of marriage was totally confirmed.

If Papa was wretched because his protégée had denounced marriage as hypocrisy, he might have been mollified by the fact that his notion of her as a kind of disembodied mind, functioning apart from the frailties of flesh and blood femininity, was triumphant. For it is Simone de Beauvoir's conviction that the real physical conditions and experiences of human life are essentially of little consequence.

Eugene O'Neill—Ella Quinlan O'Neill

Repelled by the haphazard, transient life her husband's successful acting career imposed on her, Ella O'Neill surrendered to a state of perpetual atonement when her baby son, Edmund, died of measles while she was on tour with James O'Neill. The backstage life heightened her sense of loneliness and insecurity, and now she had only herself to blame for her son's death.

Eugene O'Neill was born to replace Edmund, whose death was mourned by his mother for a quarter-century. Only reluctantly did Ella accept her husband's suggestion that she become pregnant again. She did not believe anyone could take the place of her dead son. Caressing her grief and punishing herself, she unwillingly became pregnant. She hoped for a daughter; instead, Eugene was born.

In order to ease labor pains, Ella was given morphine. After the birth of her son, her personality seemed to change gradually, and James O'Neill at first simply attributed it to postpartum depression. Amidst the turmoil that followed, Ella accused her husband of obtaining the services of a cheap quack who had initiated her into the use of drugs. He denied it vehemently, but in the years ahead Jamie, the elder son, and Eugene began to echo their mother's convictions.

For almost twenty-five years Ella's drug addiction and James O'Neill's heavy drinking established the mood of this wracked household. As a child Eugene O'Neill felt compelled to "take sides" against his father so as to protect his victimized mother. Perhaps out of a desire to expiate her own guilt over Edmund's death and her addiction, Ella declared that she wanted Eugene to become a priest. He was revolted by the prayers and more prayers his mother uttered requesting that she be delivered from this baffling, unnameable affliction that Eugene saw but was too naive to identify. In his anguish he repudiated her and her religion, Catholicism. He grew to despise her mumbling supplications, and in the process he came to be filled with self-loathing.

When Ella attempted to commit suicide, Eugene's father and his brother Jamie abruptly revealed the nature of Ella's problem to fifteen-year-old Eugene. Only after twenty-five years of addiction did Ella O'Neill at last wrench herself free of drugs. By then it was too late for her son.

Eugene O'Neill's misshapen relationship with his mother, caused by this catastrophe emanating from his birth, is reiterated in almost endless variations on themes of guilt, punishment, pity, self-pity and self-destruction. At the heart of his agitation is his plea, which might be expressed as, "Forgive me for being born. Look what a mess I've made of your life. And mine, too."

Eugene O'Neill emerged from one excess only to dive into another: prostitutes, drinking sprees, attempted suicide, one marriage after another. No woman could satisfy the haunted craving he had for maternal love, and he could only inflict punishment on other women in retaliation for what he believed his mother had done to him.

O'Neill found solace only in his creativity. His life dwindled into a long, rambling, wounded, writhing maze in which prostitutes alternated with wives in a frenzied effort to re-create the tormented relationship of his boyhood.

Andrew Carnegie—Margaret Carnegie

Andrew Carnegie idolized his overburdened and authoritative mother from his boyhood days until she died. His hero worship was so intense that he promised her he would never marry and that he would make her rich in order to compensate for his father's inability to support the family.

The fact that a mother is forced into a role of dominance in marriage because of the father's lack of success as a breadwinner does not always doom a son. Much depends on the traits each parent elicits in the other and in the child. Fortunately, Andrew Carnegie's mother was benevolent, self-sacrificing and generous; she hadn't a trace of narcissistic self-pity.

Andrew's father was not destroyed by the poverty his family had to endure. He acknowledged his wife's talents at mending shoes and making do with what they had while he sold woven tablecloths from door to door. Andrew Carnegie's youthful love and respect for his father continued until the day he died, and his feelings in no way conflicted with his all-consuming desire to repay his mother for the poverty of their early days in Scotland and the United States. He never thought their poverty was due to some flaw in his father's character; rather, he considered it to be a result of external economic conditions.

What sustained Andrew Carnegie during the bleak years of his youthful poverty was his mother's gentle prodding, which he transformed into a compulsion to achieve wealth. He wanted to erase forever the memory of the toil-ridden years during which she lacked the security of having a man to provide for her.

Any deviations from this goal appear to have been judiciously managed by his mother. Although Andrew Carnegie had promised never to marry, he did enjoy feminine companionship, which undoubtedly caused her some alarm. She would say, "No woman is good enough for my Andra"—and she meant it. Any longings he may have had for love and marriage were discreetly hidden from his mother.

After his father's death, Andrew Carnegie, who was five years older than his brother Tom, unobtrusively slipped into the role of the man of the house. At last his darling mother had a manly shoulder on which to rest her weary head. And he was genuinely happy that he could give her some of the security she had been denied for so long. He, his mother and his brother were inseparable until their deaths.

In cases where a mother must assume some of the breadwinning responsibilities in the home, detrimental marital or parental responses can gradually erode family relationships. A son may unconsciously feel anger or contempt for a father who is unable to fulfill the traditional function in family life. His feelings may be reinforced by the mother's antagonism if she resents the additional responsibility with which she is burdened.

Brisk, loving and resilient in her wifely and maternal roles, Margaret Carnegie was the epitome of the helpmate. No manifest or subtle change in the marital relationship occurred. Andrew Carnegie was aware only of the fact that his mother was a resourceful woman. She did not nag, humiliate or demean her husband, and thereby permitted an atmosphere of optimum love-security to flourish despite the problems of poverty. Only as she came to depend more on her son did Margaret Carnegie reveal the possessiveness that might be construed as less than benign authoritarianism.

Andrew Carnegie respected his promise not to marry during his mother's lifetime. At the age of forty-four, he met Louise Whitfield, a much younger woman, but he did not marry her until after his mother died. He was then fifty-two.

Never did love for or dedication to his mother wane because of this self-imposed restriction. His ultimate tribute to her was to christen his daughter after her.

Moreover, the idolization of his mother was transferred to his wife. After twenty years of marriage, Andrew Carnegie said of Louise Whitfield Carnegie, "My life has been made so happy by her that I cannot imagine myself being without her guardianship."

Charles Joseph Whitman—Margaret Whitman

A normal mother-son relationship is partially dependent on the father's ability to sustain a loving relationship with the mother. It is impossible to isolate the interpersonal responses of a mother and son during his developmental years as if this relationship existed in a vacuum without a paternal influence.

When a man acts out a pattern of tyrannical egocentricity in his role as husband and father, he creates a formidable obstacle to the normal development of the mother-son relationship. Although both wife/mother and son may respond to husband and father with cringing subservience, beneath the face of such an intolerable relationship lies a tangle of hidden, explosive emotions: fear, anger, rage, contempt, hatred and self-hatred.

In 1966 Charles Joseph Whitman went on a shooting spree at the University of Texas, killing fifteen people and wounding thirty-one. It was no accident that he began this orgy of rage by murdering first his wife and then his mother.

From childhood Charles Joseph Whitman lived in a family world dominated by a passionately angry and violent father, who extracted submissive obedience from mother and son through threat of physical punishment. A son, living in constant fear and suppressed rage but unable to manifest these emotions, tends to look to the other parent to free him from the bondage from which he wishes to escape.

What did Charles Joseph Whitman find? His mother was equally frightened and paralyzed into indecision. Unable to shield her son or herself from random assaults, she seemed to be accepting more and more physical brutality from her husband. This deepened the cleavage between the façade of normalcy they maintained and the more ominous need to repudiate through revenge. Gradually the son's emotional perception of his mother underwent serious alteration. In a family situation where the father arbitrarily and cruelly controls the life of each person to a substantial degree, the son may react to his mother in a compensatory manner. That is, he may attempt to make up to her for all the unhappiness, lack of love or physical indignities she has experienced. However, as the son leaves childhood behind and becomes an adolescent, he may assimilate some of the traits of the hated father. Gradually Charles Joseph Whitman became aware that what he despised most in his father was beginning to surface in his own personality. Physical bullying, intimidation and a wily and cunning contempt for those who feared him became part of his emotional arsenal.

He now looked at his mother with different eyes. Charles Joseph Whitman acknowledged to himself the futility of trying to make up to his mother for all the suffering his father had caused her. If his mother had really loved him, he reasoned, she would have found some way out of the nightmare. Perhaps she had deserved what she got. Of course, he hated himself for thinking such thoughts, but if it weren't for her he would be free of this tortuous hatred of his father. Although he would have vehemently denied it, he looked on his mother with contempt. And he would certainly have denied that his wife-beating was reminiscent of his father's abhorrent behavior.

Superficially, then, the façade of normalcy was maintained. He was a young man who loved his wife and mother, and it was regrettable that he did not care for his father. Everyone pretended that the more intense feelings that were perpetually churning within him did not exist or that they were not a matter for serious concern. Over the years, however, the need for revenge became more distorted and more urgent in his mind. If he could not get even with his father because he was still so quiveringly afraid of him, he would punish his mother and his wife. They had victimized him too, in their way. In his relationships with them, he acted out what he hated most: the despised, bullying, sneering, ineffectual father from whom he could never seem to escape.

If he could destroy them—his wife and mother—he might destroy his raging hatred. Then his father would fear him. In this way their deaths would be the ultimate compensation. Neither mother nor wife would ever suffer again. They would never feel anything. He would extinguish their human lives in one swift stroke and at the same time quench his thirst for revenge. However, his hatred did not end with their deaths. He went on to murder thirteen other people, and finally to turn the trigger on himself.

Douglas MacArthur—Mary MacArthur

It used to be that when a woman exhibited decision-making abilities in her maternal role, she was suspected of taking over a traditional masculine function in marriage. It then followed that the son of such a mother was considered likely to become the worst kind of effeminate Mama's boy.

In reality, a maternal influence based on altruistic dedication has a positive effect on emotional maturation. It cannot be emphasized too strongly that a bond of devotion between mother and son even in adult life does not necessarily indicate that the paternal influence is negligible.

In narcissistic power-struggle marriages, where a disappointed wife seeks to arrest the psychological development of her son for her own emotional satisfaction, the mother-son relationship may deteriorate. The son may then manifest serious psycho-sexual problems in marriage or a series of marriages.

Mary MacArthur, the mother of Douglas MacArthur, was an assiduous and methodical woman who was determined that her son would have as glorious a military career as his father had had. She was the one predictable human being young Douglas MacArthur could depend on as the family moved from one military post to another because of his father's changing assignments. Even when his father was stationed relatively nearby, Douglas lived with his mother, and she was his primary source of inspiration, guidance and emotional security. Another factor that contributed to their close and abiding relationship was the death of his brother Malcolm in infancy. He and his older brother Arthur were tutored by their mother in preparation for distinguished military futures. His brother received an appointment to Annapolis, and he was accepted at West Point.

Douglas MacArthur had to face many barbs and insinuations during his training at West Point because of his mother's proximity to the military academy. Instead of walking with a girlfriend on Flirtation Walk, as was the custom, he strolled along with his mother. Undaunted by offensive references, he cultivated his mother's companionship without regard for the criticism of his fellow plebes.

In the meantime, his father's military career took him to Washington, Texas and the Philippines. He rose from captain, his rank at the time of Douglas MacArthur's birth, to major general. By the time his son was graduated from West Point, he had become military governor of the Philippine Islands.

Characteristically, a son with a satisfying and secure emotional relationship with his mother tends to marry somewhat later in life, particularly when he believes himself to be his mother's sole masculine protector. This unconscious decision to remain unmarried can be justified on the basis of external circumstances. For example, if the father dies, one of the sons may tacitly accept the protector role. When Douglas MacArthur's father died, he left his widow bereft of any masculine emotional sustenance other than that proffered by his son. As a consequence, Douglas MacArthur deferred to his mother's wishes when it came to a consideration of military assignments. His life revolved around her, and it was such a satisfying and deep relationship that he did not marry until he was forty-two.

Despite an auspicious relationship with Mary MacArthur, his first marriage was not a success, and he waited until the age of fifty-seven to marry a second time. His mother had, in fact, met the second young woman on shipboard and knew that she would be the perfect wife for her son. Indeed, Douglas MacArthur's marriage to Jean Marie Faircloth provided him with all of the emotional sustenance he needed. It was, like his parents' marriage, an abiding and loving union, because to an astonishing degree his wife reflected the personality traits of his now deceased mother.

This complex transference of emotional satisfaction is a remarkably predictable pattern when the mother-son relationship is altruistic in nature and the influence motivates the son toward distinguished achievement. We must replace the derogatory image mother-son relationships have had over the past decades with a more realistic assessment of their impact on the male in marriage.

Your Workbook

How do you rate as a Daddy's girl or a Mama's boy? Using this workbook, you can examine and evaluate your personality and the relationships around you. This evaluation will take time and patience and will be an ongoing process of self-discovery.

Identify those areas of behavior that are causing problems for you. The traits you uncover may be self-limiting, they may be imposing limitations on others, or they may be exploitative in nature.

Keep a daily notebook and jot down instances of problem behavior. For example, "I 'got even' with my husband because . . . ." Or, "I discourage my adolescent daughter from losing weight because then she will be going out on dates, and I won't know where she is."

Ask yourself how you can contribute positively to an interpersonal relationship so that tension can be minimized and satisfaction enhanced. Encourage the other person in a one-to-one relationship to grow, and you, too, will achieve greater inner strength and self-direction.

Consider this record a journey into your inner life. Know what you are seeking and what efforts you must put forth to achieve character and personality changes. Above all, persevere. You will find that as you rely less and less on the use of destructive traits to impede the growth of others and more and more on constructive behavior, you will generate an attitude of self-worth which will invite an altered response from others.

Once a week, evaluate your progress. Use your daily notebook to determine how often you have indulged in destructive patterns of behavior and how many times you were able to redirect your energies into constructive traits that strengthened your personal relationships and your sense of self-direction. As the balance shifts toward predominantly affirmative traits, you will enjoy an awareness of your own capacity to determine your future and provide love-security for those nearest and dearest to you.

Are You a Daddy's Girl?

To answer this question, circle the number that best expresses your reaction to each of the statements that follow. Try to determine what you honestly feel.

> Key   5 = Definitely YES
> 4 = Possibly YES
> 3 = Definitely UNDECIDED
> 2 = Possibly NOT
> 1 = Definitely NO

Once you have completed the questionnaire, add all the numbers you circled. The scale at the end will tell you to what extent you are a Daddy's girl.

In Childhood:

Daddy tried to make you feel like "his girl" so that you would make him happy.

1. He gave you dolls, expensive games and toys, clothes, anything your heart desired.   5 4 3 2 1
2. He painted grand visions of all that he could do or buy for you.   5 4 3 2 1
3. He gave you the feeling that he was omnipotent, that he could solve all of your problems.   5 4 3 2 1

4. He never permitted you to experience frustration.   5 4 3 2 1
5. He never disciplined you, but left that up to your "witchy" mother.   5 4 3 2 1
6. He chose all of your friends so subtly that if you liked someone he did not favor, you never knew why the friendship was terminated.   5 4 3 2 1
7. He hinted that no boy could possibly be good enough for you, even in childhood friendships.   5 4 3 2 1
8. He discouraged you from learning to make independent decisions. He persuasively insisted that all matters, regardless of their insignificance, be referred to him for final approval.   5 4 3 2 1
9. He conveyed to you the feeling that you were "two against the world."   5 4 3 2 1
10. He made you feel that you were a princess and he was a prince and you would live together "happily ever after" in the vague future.   5 4 3 2 1

Your unconscious learned responses:
1. to be totally dependent.   5 4 3 2 1
2. to expect things to be done for you.   5 4 3 2 1
3. to expect that a man could and should give you everything you want.   5 4 3 2 1
4. to believe that a man can "make you happy."   5 4 3 2 1
5. never to trust your own decisions.   5 4 3 2 1

Daddy manacled you to him in a subtly devastating network of possessiveness.
1. He seemed to be omnipotent, and his power over you made you fearful.   5 4 3 2 1
2. He doled out physical punishment on an erratic basis. 5 4 3 2 1
3. He demanded physical affection from you, and he did not seem to care about or notice your fears or anxieties.   5 4 3 2 1
4. He made you feel that he was entitled to fondle and caress you in a way that was disturbing to you. He conveyed to you the feeling that you had to submit to him physically because he had the power of life and death over you.   5 4 3 2 1

5. He told you repeatedly that you owed him your very life, that you would not be here on earth if it were not for his decision. 5 4 3 2 1

6. He let you know in a variety of ways that your legitimate needs, such as an education, adequate living conditions, food, clothing, and medical and dental care, constituted a tremendous burden on him.   5 4 3 2 1

7. He displayed feelings of contempt for human relationships.   5 4 3 2 1

8. He built a vast cocoon of self-pity for himself, and he expected you to protect his wounded ego by feeling sympathy for him. 5 4 3 2 1

9. He discouraged you from learning to make independent decisions.   5 4 3 2 1

10. He repeatedly conveyed to you the notion that your future belonged to him as payment for all the sacrifices he had made for you.   5 4 3 2 1

Your unconscious learned responses:

1. to have seriously ambivalent feelings about men in general.   5 4 3 2 1

2. to avoid relationships with men, and at the same time to seek out men like your father so that the pattern of childhood could be repeated.   5 4 3 2 1

3. to believe that, although sex can be thrilling, more often it is repugnant and fraught with danger because a man might harm you if you do not give him what he wants.   5 4 3 2 1

4. to have profound feelings of worthlessness.   5 4 3 2 1

5. to fear your own ability to make value judgments about men and your relationships with them.   5 4 3 2 1

In Adolescence:

Daddy's charm permeates your awakening sexual and maternal instincts.

1. He lets you in on a secret you already know—that he is very disenchanted with his marital relationship.   5 4 3 2 1

2. He encourages you to do more "wifely" things for him: to cook his favorite foods, to reflect his sexual or political prejudices, to listen to and agree with his every word, to be a vast reservoir of balm to his weary ego.   5 4 3 2 1

3. He in some way draws you into a dating relationship with him. He may try to pass you off as a girlfriend if your parents are divorced. He may insist on taking you to the high school prom. There is a flirtatious, mutedly sexual aura about your adolescent relationship with him.   5 4 3 2 1

4. He discourages you from dating boys your own age. Either he criticizes them for their callowness, bad manners and sloppy dress, or he is secretly enraged by their sexual overtures to you. He wants you for himself.   5 4 3 2 1

5. He is aware of your growing uneasiness, and he reassures you with extravagant gifts. He is very conscious of the fact that his gifts bind you to him because you feel indebted, but you do not know how to escape without hurting his feelings.   5 4 3 2 1

Your unconscious learned responses:

1. to believe that all men are like Daddy.   5 4 3 2 1

2. to think that if you can make Daddy happy, you can make any other man happy by employing the strategy Daddy has taught you.
                                                       5 4 3 2 1

3. to be almost completely unaware that there is any other way of responding to a man.   5 4 3 2 1

4. to develop a deepening psychological need to play "little girl" in all encounters with men.   5 4 3 2 1

5. never to recognize the need to share that is vital to a normal marital relationship.   5 4 3 2 1

Daddy has established a pattern of control that makes you desirous of escaping from him.

1. He employs physical threats and verbal abuse if there is any indication of rebellion.   5 4 3 2 1

2. He refuses to allow you to date, or else he pushes you into dating prematurely. In the latter instance, he may supply you with contraceptives and a fear of pregnancy. Implicit in his actions is the non-verbalized attitude "Men are no good."   5 4 3 2 1

3. He confuses you still further with his determination to prevent you from making independent decisions, particularly in the sphere of relationships with young men.   5 4 3 2 1

4. He is shocked when he discovers your sexual attachment to a girlfriend or an older woman.   5 4 3 2 1

Your unconscious learned responses:

1. to want to escape from Daddy's domination.   5 4 3 2 1

2. to seek a love relationship that will provide some degree of emotional satisfaction.   5 4 3 2 1

3. to be attracted to girls or women because of a deepening fear of male sexuality as exemplified by Daddy.   5 4 3 2 1

4. to be attracted to young or older men who are social rejects, school dropouts, have a police record, or are definitely emotionally unstable and lack well-defined life goals.   5 4 3 2 1

5. to feel that "no worthwhile man could love me."   5 4 3 2 1

In Courtship:

There is a gradual shift in emphasis of the relationship between Daddy and his little girl.

1. He balks at the notion that you are sexually attracted to another man (a prospective husband).   5 4 3 2 1

2. He does everything in his power short of absolutely disowning you to sabotage the relationship.   5 4 3 2 1

3. He plants seeds of guilt in you so that, although you may feel traitorous toward him, you also feel an urgent need to establish another relationship, even a poor one.   5 4 3 2 1

4. No matter whom you choose as a husband, he will cause you to feel uncertain as to the wisdom of your choice.   5 4 3 2 1
5. Shortly before your marriage, he will make it clear to you that you can always come home to Daddy and he will take care of everything for you.   5 4 3 2 1

Your conscious learned responses:
1. to seek escape from Daddy by entering into a marriage relationship with another man whose character may be a reflection of Daddy's.   5 4 3 2 1
2. to return the love-security of Daddy, either literally or figuratively, should you become disillusioned with your marriage partner.   5 4 3 2 1

By now, Daddy's domination of your life is so all-encompassing that your need to escape into another love-security relationship may amount to an obsession.
1. Daddy has made it clear to you through the years that all you can expect from marriage is ultimate disappointment and misery.   5 4 3 2 1
2. He has conveyed to you the notion that sexual satisfaction is a very temporary sensation at best, and that it can best be experienced by changing partners. Therefore, he has subtly indoctrinated you with the idea that marriage is essentially an impermanent relationship.   5 4 3 2 1
3. He has instilled in you profound feelings of suppressed antagonism toward men.   5 4 3 2 1
4. He has conveyed to you the feeling that without him you will be a failure in all emotional relationships.   5 4 3 2 1

Your unconscious learned responses:
1. to form temporary sexual liaisons, thereby assuring yourself of deepening frustration and bitterness.   5 4 3 2 1
2. to experiment with lesbian relationships.   5 4 3 2 1

3. to reject motherhood.   5 4 3 2 1
4. to maintain an ambivalent tendency to repudiate all love-security relationships and at the same time search for a permanent emotional relationship that will belie Daddy's devastating indoctrination.   5 4 3 2 1

In Marriage:

Your attitude toward your husband:

1. You expect him to take up where Daddy left off.   5 4 3 2 1
2. You are partially or totally unequipped to cope with the sexual realities and responsibilities of marriage.   5 4 3 2 1
3. You are excessively dependent on him, especially in the sphere of decision-making and marital finances.   5 4 3 2 1
4. Your dissatisfaction in the marriage increases in proportion to the extent to which your husband demands that you "grow up."   5 4 3 2 1
5. You experience deep and serious conflict in proportion to the extent to which your husband cannot fulfill the Daddy image for you.   5 4 3 2 1
6. From the beginning of marriage you encounter many areas of conflict. You act out with your husband the unresolved residual conflicts from your relationship with Daddy.   5 4 3 2 1
7. Your sexual relationship may range from aversion to abstinence to frigidity, with only occasional experiences of pleasure and release from tension. You blame your mate for your sexual unhappiness.   5 4 3 2 1
8. You seek relief from your own unresolved conflicts in affairs, lesbian relationships, or a series of marriages and divorces.   5 4 3 2 1
9. You refuse to have children, or agree to have one only because of a husband's wishes. If you do have a child, you reject the responsibilities of motherhood.   5 4 3 2 1

10. Every time you enter into a new relationship, you expectantly believe it to be the "perfect" solution to your yearning for love-security. With the end of each relationship, your unresolved conflicts deepen. They manifest themselves in a variety of emotional problems, most of which have underlying traces of dependency.   5 4 3 2 1

If you scored:	You are:
150 or above	DEFINITELY A DADDY'S GIRL
125—150	POSSIBLY A DADDY'S GIRL
100—125	UNDECIDED
50—100	POSSIBLY NOT A DADDY'S GIRL
0—50	DEFINITELY NOT A DADDY'S GIRL

Are You a Mama's Boy?

To answer this question, circle the number that best expresses your reaction to each of the statements that follow. Try to determine what you honestly feel.

> Key 5 = Definitely YES
>   4 = Possibly YES
>   3 = Definitely UNDECIDED
>   2 = Possibly NOT
>   1 = Definitely NO

Once you have completed the questionnaire, add all the numbers you circled. The scale at the end will tell you to what extent you are a Mama's boy.

In Childhood:

Mama tried to make you feel that only you could make her happy, thus burdening you as a boy with an awesome responsibility.

1. She conveyed to you the feeling that you were the consolation prize for all the vague and unnamed marital misery she had to endure in life.   5 4 3 2 1
2. She smothered you with praise and admiration.   5 4 3 2 1

3. She filled you with the notion that when you became a man you would accomplish great and wonderful deeds for her. 5 4 3 2 1

4. She never permitted you to experience frustration.   5 4 3 2 1

5. She led you to believe that all other human beings would submit to your wishes because you would make some outstanding contribution to the world.   5 4 3 2 1

6. She discouraged you from making independent decisions. She persuasively insisted that all matters, regardless of their insignificance, be referred to her for final approval.   5 4 3 2 1

7. She taught you to believe that your every wish was her command.   5 4 3 2 1

8. She led you to believe that since you were going to accomplish "great things" in life you could not possibly be interested in girls.   5 4 3 2 1

9. She never punished you physically. She expressed disapproval, alarm, dismay or anger in subtle ways.   5 4 3 2 1

10. She painted a nebulous vision of the future in which somehow you would always be together.   5 4 3 2 1

Your unconscious learned responses:

1. to be totally dependent.   5 4 3 2 1

2. to expect that things would be done for you.   5 4 3 2 1

3. to expect that a woman could and should give you everything you want.   5 4 3 2 1

4. to believe that a woman can "make you happy."   5 4 3 2 1

5. never to trust your own decisions.   5 4 3 2 1

6. to need to conquer in order to bring the prize back to Mama or a female image.   5 4 3 2 1

Mama seemed to be omnipotent, and her power over you made you fearful.

1. She doled out physical punishment on an erratic basis. 5 4 3 2 1

2. She sometimes demanded physical affection from you and at other times neglected you. She did not seem to care about or notice your fears or anxieties.   5 4 3 2 1

3. She led you to believe that she had the power of life and death over you.   5 4 3 2 1

4. She told you repeatedly that you owed her your very life, that you would not be here on earth if it were not for her decision.   5 4 3 2 1

5. She let you know in a variety of ways that your legitimate needs, such as an education, adequate living conditions, food, clothing, and medical and dental care, constituted a tremendous burden for her.   5 4 3 2 1

6. She displayed contempt, hatred or fear of close human relationships.   5 4 3 2 1

7. She built a vast cocoon of martyrdom for herself, and she expected you to feel sympathy for her in order to protect her wounded ego.   5 4 3 2 1

8. She discouraged you from learning to make independent decisions.   5 4 3 2 1

9. She repeatedly conveyed to you the notion that your future belonged to her as payment for all the sacrifices she had made for you.   5 4 3 2 1

Your unconscious learned responses:

1. to have seriously ambivalent feelings about women in general.   5 4 3 2 1

2. to avoid relationships with women, and at the same time to seek out women like your mother so that the pattern of childhood could be repeated.   5 4 3 2 1

3. to believe that women are to be conquered and subdued, and at the same time to fear them.   5 4 3 2 1

4. to have profound feelings of worthlessness.   5 4 3 2 1

5. to doubt your own ability to make value judgments about women and your relationships with them.   5 4 3 2 1

In Adolescence:

Mama lets you in on a secret you already know—she is very disenchanted with her marital relationship.

1. She encourages you to do more "husbandly" things for her: to help her with repairs around the house, to drive her to and from social

engagements, to reflect her cultural or sexual prejudices, to listen to and agree with her every word, to be a vast reservoir of balm to her weary ego.   5 4 3 2 1

2. If she is divorced, she may wear a beguiling negligee in your presence and make muted sexual advances. She will be alarmed if you respond to her.   5 4 3 2 1

3. She discourages you from dating girls your own age. Either she criticizes them or she warns you that there is no girl good enough for you. She implies that she wants you for herself.   5 4 3 2 1

4. She is aware of your anxiety and occasional acts of rebellion. However, she reassures you with extravagant gifts, or she oppresses you with the feeling that she would be unable to endure her intolerable life without you.   5 4 3 2 1

Your unconscious learned responses:

1. to believe that all women are like Mama.   5 4 3 2 1

2. to think that if you can make Mama happy, you can make any other woman happy by employing the strategy Mama has taught you.   5 4 3 2 1

3. to be almost completely unaware that there is any other way of responding to a woman.   5 4 3 2 1

4. to develop a deepening psychological need to play "Mama's boy" in all encounters with women.   5 4 3 2 1

5. never to recognize the need to share that is vital to a normal marital relationship.   5 4 3 2 1

Mama has created a pattern of domination that arouses tangled feelings of love, hatred and/or guilt.

1. She discourages you from dating by insinuating that all efforts not directed toward great accomplishments are so much wasted time. Or, if you have become a passive-aggressive personality, she hints that a girl could make a fool of you in a variety of ways. 5 4 3 2 1

2. She attempts to destroy your interest in young women by verbally demolishing them. She conveys to you the idea that "women are no

good." Concealed beneath this attitude is her protective declaration: "Stay with me and I will protect you from all those wicked women."   5 4 3 2 1

3. She is shocked when she discovers that you no longer have or never did have an interest in girls, but instead are interested only in men. She wonders what she has done to deserve this behavior from you.   5 4 3 2 1

Your unconscious learned responses:

1. to want to escape from Mama's domination.   5 4 3 2 1
2. to seek a love relationship that will provide some degree of emotional security.   5 4 3 2 1
3. to be attracted to boys and men because of a deepening attitude of fear, anger and hatred toward women.   5 4 3 2 1
4. to be attracted to women who are social rejects, manifest serious antisocial behavior, are emotionally unstable, or reject their own sexuality.   5 4 3 2 1
5. to feel that "no worthwhile woman could love me." 5 4 3 2 1

In Courtship:

Mama conveys to you the idea that you would be betraying her if you were sexually attracted to a young woman (a prospective wife).

1. She does everything in her power short of absolutely disowning you to sabotage any promising relationships, because she is afraid of losing you.   5 4 3 2 1
2. She plants seeds of guilt in you so that, although you may feel like a traitor, you also feel an urgent need to establish another relationship, even a poor one.   5 4 3 2 1
3. No matter whom you choose as a wife, Mama will cause you to feel uncertain as to the wisdom of your choice.   5 4 3 2 1

4. Shortly before your marriage, she will make it clear that your bride will never be able to iron your shirts and cook as well as she can. She will make it known to you that you can always come home to her.   5 4 3 2 1

Your unconscious learned responses:

1. to seek escape from Mama by entering into a marriage relationship with another woman whose character may be a reflection of Mama's.   5 4 3 2 1
2. to return to the love-security of Mama, either literally or figuratively, should you become disillusioned with your marriage partner.   5 4 3 2 1

By now, Mama's domination of your life is so all-encompassing that your need to escape into another love-security relationship may amount to an obsession.

1. Mama has made it clear to you through the years that all you can expect from marriage is ultimate disappointment and misery.   5 4 3 2 1
2. She has conveyed to you an attitude of hate/fear/anger toward women which leads you to treat women primarily as objects of sexual passion. Therefore, she has subtly indoctrinated you with the idea that marriage is impermanent or intolerable.   5 4 3 2 1
3. She has instilled in you profound feelings of suppressed rage toward women so that your search for a love-security relationship may cause you to seek a homosexual attachment or one with a woman who is much older or younger than you are. Or you may completely repudiate all human relationships.   5 4 3 2 1
4. She has conveyed to you the feeling that without her at your side you will be a failure in all emotional relationships.   5 4 3 2 1

Your unconscious learned responses:

1. to establish a suppressed attitude of hate/fear/anger toward all women.   5 4 3 2 1

2. to form temporary sexual liaisons, thereby assuring yourself of deepening frustration and bitterness. 5 4 3 2 1

3. to experiment with homosexual relationships, form an attachment to a much younger or older woman, or repudiate all human relationships. 5 4 3 2 1

4. to reject fatherhood as a natural outcome of a normal sexual relationship in marriage. 5 4 3 2 1

5. to maintain an ambivalent tendency to repudiate all love-security relationships and at the same time to search for a permanent emotional relationship that will belie Mama's devastating indoctrination. 5 4 3 2 1

In Marriage:

Your attitude toward your wife:

1. You need to conquer her over and over again, not only in a sexual sense but by totally subduing her. Your unconscious fear of women compels you to act as a benevolent dictator. 5 4 3 2 1

2. You expect her to function as a joyous receptacle of your sexual passion, while at the same time you deny her any profound sexual happiness because you unconsciously wish to avenge the indignities you suffered in your relationship with Mama. 5 4 3 2 1

3. You compel her to play Mama by abdicating or refusing to fulfill your masculine responsibilities in marriage. 5 4 3 2 1

4. Your dissatisfaction in marriage increases in proportion to the extent to which your wife refuses to "baby" you and demands that you "grow up." 5 4 3 2 1

5. You experience deep and serious conflict in proportion to the extent to which your wife cannot fulfill the Mama image for you. 5 4 3 2 1

6. From the beginning of marriage you encounter many areas of conflict. You act out with your wife the unresolved residual conflicts from your relationship with Mama. 5 4 3 2 1

7. Your sexual relationship may range from impotence to perversion, with rare occurrences of mutual satisfaction and release from tension. You blame your sexual unhappiness on your wife's frigidity or excessive demands.   5 4 3 2 1

8. You seek relief from your own unresolved conflicts in affairs, homosexual relationships, or a series of marriages and divorces.   5 4 3 2 1

9. You refuse to have children, or reluctantly agree to have one only because of your wife's pleadings. You reject the responsibilities of fatherhood if you have fathered a child.   5 4 3 2 1

10. Every time you enter into a new relationship, you expectantly believe it to be the "perfect" solution to your yearning for love-security. With the end of each relationship, your unresolved conflicts deepen. They manifest themselves in a variety of emotional problems, most of which have underlying traces of dependency.   5 4 3 2 1

If you scored:	You are:
150 or above	DEFINITELY A MAMA'S BOY
125—150	POSSIBLY A MAMA'S BOY
100—125	UNDECIDED
50—100	POSSIBLY NOT A MAMA'S BOY
0—50	DEFINITELY NOT A MAMA'S BOY

Learn to Understand Yourself

If you are at this moment seriously unhappy in any of your relationships, be assured that you are capable of making profound character changes that can alter the course of your life. These personality alterations are not merely superficial cosmetic changes, but deep and authentic changes that require effort on your part.

Such a transformation is necessarily gradual and requires patience. We do not abandon our "old" personalities; instead, we learn by sustained effort to achieve character changes that will enable us to have more effective interpersonal relationships. Personal happiness and contentment are by-products of our creative adaptation.

Faith is an essential ingredient in this character transformation. We know that man/woman has the capacity to re-create and reconstruct life even out of the most unpromising circumstances. No one is doomed to a life of perpetual unhappiness, except by his own inner choice. Every great religion of the East and West offers human beings the promise of a better tomorrow, based on one's willingness to put forth that effort which brings about growth.

In order to be content, you must align your inner feelings with an objective religious/philosophical code of behavior. Your subjective attitudes (what is "good" for you and what makes you happy) must reflect a code of behavior that transcends your specific individuality and embraces what is good for humanity.

Within one generation we have veered from a philosophy of repudiating abnormal feelings of guilt to one in which there is a total absence of feelings of guilt in the sense of integrity and responsibility, particularly in relationships. This has been due to a general abandonment of an objective religious/philosophical ethic. This is, we believe, the most powerful and destructive societal force pervading personal human relationships today. Its impact, coupled with the existence of an increasing number of negative and immature Daddy's girl/Mama's boy relationships, has led to massive societal confusion. As a consequence, we live in a world in which the concept of human obsolescence prevails—if a partner is not satisfactory, replace him or her with a new model.

One basic contradiction affects all of us: we have a right to personal happiness, but we also have a responsibility to sustain those intimate relationships that offer man/woman the most profound love-security.

Unhappiness should not be considered a signal to terminate a relationship. By forcing us to confront a problem, it offers us the opportunity to change our life direction by changing our personality responses. By strengthening marital, parental and human relations, we can achieve inner contentment.

How do we go about this process of personality transformation? Do positive thoughts in themselves solve our problems? Certainly not. You become capable of transforming your life only through a process of conscious awareness and perception. It involves a realization that unconscious negative behavior patterns can be redirected. You and only you can be in charge of the redirection process that leads to love-security.

This personality alteration does not constitute a state of human perfection, but rather an optimum life condition (a "being" and "becoming" process) in which you consciously appreciate your capacity to accept myriad varieties of frustration, disappointment and human imperfection. Simultaneously, you deliberately choose interpersonal responses that sustain and strengthen crucial life-affirming relationships.

It should be understood, above all else, that this character change which you desire is a lifelong endeavor, not a "crash course" in personality modification. Your personal happiness in human relationships will depend primarily on three factors: (1) your conscious awareness that unconscious destructive behavior patterns can be redirected into positive interpersonal responses, (2) the depth of your motivations and your efforts to make these "new" responses a part of your inner life, and (3) your sensitivity to and acceptance of your inner subjective feelings (how "good" and "comfortable" a human relationship is), measured in terms of an objective religious/philosophical standard which takes into account the human dignity of all mankind/womankind.

As your character transformation proceeds, you will discover that, although external circumstances and interpersonal relationships will not change suddenly, you as an individual will make gradual progress toward a more mature and profound understanding of what it means to contribute to the happiness and well-being of another person.

As you learn to relinquish those traits and responses which demean husband/wife, son/daughter, friends, co-workers or strangers, you will recognize that the characteristics that diminish another individual's humanity also diminish your own. You do not feel "good" about yourself, although you may not consciously know why.

When you respond with supportive, genuinely caring and altruistic traits, you add to the dimension of another human being. By this process of giving, you also enhance your own sense of self-worth. You feel "good" about yourself. You find more profound satisfaction in a relationship, and this interdependence serves as the foundation for reciprocal love-security.

Learning to understand yourself begins with self-examination of the troublesome areas in your own life: the collection of attitudes, habits and egocentric responses that have dogged your footsteps throughout life and have become unconscious obstacles to your happiness. Almost all conflict-ridden relationships involve one or more of the following destructive attitudes. You can begin your personal evaluation by examining them in relation to yourself as an individual, a husband/wife, a Daddy/Mama. There is usually considerable overlapping. Rarely does one or a series of destructive habits exist in one relationship without spilling over into others.

As you evaluate these destructive modes of interaction, you begin to formulate a composite image of yourself. The identification of personality problems and the development of motivation to change become a simultaneous process. This should not be regarded as a discovery experience in which you punish yourself for not being the "right" sort of person. Instead, you should develop greater self-understanding and a desire to redirect your efforts toward responses that will dramatically alter your personal relationships. Your personality changes will eventually come from within.

Destructive Attitudes Are Self-Limiting

Hatred

No marriage begins with obvious hatred; however, incipient hatred may be lurking under a façade of agreeability.

Invariably one or both mates will have low self-esteem, which can masquerade as arrogant superiority or as self-effacing inferiority. The behavior of a husband/wife who lacks a sense of self-worth may veer from one extreme to another, and he/she generally responds to a mate in the same way that Daddy or Mama responded to him/her. Often one partner is escaping from a stifling Daddy or Mama and hopes that marriage will solve his/her personality problems. This mate may unconsciously see marriage as a kind of halfway house or rehabilitation center with the partner as therapist.

If these expectations are not realized, which is particularly likely to happen if the other mate has similar expectations, the eroding impact of hatred manifests itself in a wide variety of destructive habits, and the partners eventually lose respect for each other. Discovery of this kind of response usually leads to confrontation, repudiation and a breakdown of the relationship. Yet a substantial number of the men and women in this situation never separate or divorce. They need to hate each other, because they have never learned any other response from Daddy or Mama. The most serious problems may surface in these relationships: alcoholism, flagrant and aimless promiscuity, or psychopathic behavior.

Such a husband and wife do not know how to live any other way, and many of them could not live apart from each other. The possibility that counseling could help does not occur to either mate, because each is certain that the relationship is hopeless and that the other individual is responsible.

Revenge: The Vendetta Syndrome

The need to "get even," by far one of the most common and destructive marital patterns, occurs especially in those relationships where one individual considers his feelings the sole criterion for his interpersonal responses. This pattern of behavior may merely cause delay, inconvenience or other similar minor frustrations. But in its most intense expression it may range from threats to acts of bodily harm.

A vindictive marital partner or parent is revealing a serious inability to cope with life in general and especially with intimate relationships, where a certain degree of misunderstanding and routine frustration is inevitable.

Such an individual does not use an objective religious/philosophical value system as a criterion for appreciating individual differences. If queried by a counselor regarding retaliatory activities, this individual is likely to say, "That's the way I am. That's the way I feel." Occasionally there are glimmerings of remorse over some particularly vindictive act, but the man/woman smothers any uncomfortable feelings by rationalization, telling a counselor, "Look what he/she *did* to me."

Sexual Exploitation

Sexual exploitation, both explicit and implicit, has become one of the commonplace tragedies of our time. The great irony is that although there is now considerable information on sexual sensitivity, there is also greater callousness, due to an emerging societal attitude that sex is a "commodity." It has been isolated from the total human personality and an objective religious/philosophical ethic. The premise is that "better sex" is readily available. The increase in the number of divorces is a reflection of sexual exploitation as well as sexual dysfunction. It is particularly in this narrow sphere that the idea of human obsolescence becomes evident. There is a prevailing attitude that "if sex isn't terrific with him/her, I'll just get a new partner, and then sex will be marvelous."

This idea that more diverse and intense sexual improvisations are the essence of human happiness is most damaging to the human personality. It causes varying degrees of disintegration, leaving a man/woman less and less capable of recognizing and achieving love-security. Moreover, sexual exploitation as a means of adaptation suggests a conqueror-conquered relationship with the participants as adversaries. It can never be an expression of deep unity or love, because the exploitative individual is generally fearful of making a total commitment of his/her personality to the other human being. Instead, there is a deliberate and primarily unconscious "refusal" to relate to the non-sexual humanness of the sexual partner. The personality frustrations that result when this occurs are characterized most succinctly by the term "used" or "had." One feels genuinely victimized by the other. Depression is an early symptom of a sexually exploitative relationship.

In the parent-child relationship, such exploitation may range from actual incestuous relationships to the use of abuse and other obstacles calculated to prevent a young adult son/daughter from entering into a heterosexual relationship independent of Daddy or Mama. The majority of the strategies used to frustrate the latent capabilities of a mate or a son/daughter to realize happiness in a relationship can be classified as implicit exploitation.

Whether sexual frustration and disappointments create a hate re-sponse or whether a husband/wife is motivated by hate (for other unconscious reasons) to punish via sex, this destructive habit can be devastating. One of the most frequent "solutions" is the extramarital liaison, which superficially serves to diminish sexual tensions. However, although it may alleviate frustrations, this sort of sexual relief only complicates marital and parental relationships. Occasionally the pattern of sexual exploitation is pursued by the male as an expected symbol of manhood, and by the female as her "equal right" to fulfillment with a series of partners. This destructive pattern may be resorted to in instances where sex as a performance ritual is related to a precarious sense of self-esteem.

Possessiveness ("Belonging")

A counselor often hears an irate husband declare about his wife, "She *belongs* to me." This statement is then followed by an avalanche of recriminations based on the assumption that she is his "possession." Or an adult son/daughter may pour out a litany of restrictions enforced by a parent who demands that the child serve as Daddy's or Mama's alter ego.

Interpersonal relationships in which an individual is treated as a possession can be agonizing. Each person in the relationship loses respect for the other individual.

Phrases such as "He's my man" or "She's mine" are all too familiar. The need to have someone belong to you constitutes an unconscious search for emotional satisfaction based on infantile demands. It represents a reversal and distortion of that unity felt early in marriage, when sexual intimacy is the primary means of communication between a husband and wife. Then they are delighted to belong to each other. Later in the marriage, when some balance between individuality and unity must be established for normal human satisfaction, the sense of belonging alters to fit the unconscious destructive needs of the one who must possess.

The possessive husband or wife may develop a domineering and demanding response which reflects a pattern learned earlier in the Daddy's girl/Mama's boy relationship.

A husband rarely openly feels that he belongs to his wife. However, because of illness, money or even extraordinary beauty, she may "call the signals" in their relationship, and he may be unable to perceive that he is gradually suffocating. All he knows is that he is unhappy. This sort of long-suffering admirable husband may be the "perfect husband" in the eyes of other women. To his wife, who considers him merely a possession, he is someone to manipulate according to her whims. A marital relationship held together by this burdensome sense of belonging is a source of mutual antagonism and self-destructiveness. Because of infantile needs, neither mate tries to extricate himself/herself from the relationship.

The problem with this kind of relationship is that although the façade may allow the relationship to appear successful to others for a time, the camouflage is only temporary. The husband or wife may break through the chains of possessiveness with an act of physical violence.

A similar pattern is visible in Daddy's girl or Mama's boy. A young adult son/daughter who is weighted down by destructive parental possessiveness does not venture out into the world to establish his/her own individuality and life satisfactions.

Dominance-Submission Power Struggle

Sooner or later there is a power struggle in every marriage and every parent-child relationship. Whether it is resolved in a mature manner or a destructive manner depends on the inner resources of each individual and his/her willingness to reconcile differences on the basis of an objective religious/philosophical value system.

When one partner or parent inflicts intolerable pressure on a mate or child in the name of dominance (superiority), maximum tension occurs. Even after the conflict seems to have been resolved, with one declared victor and the other victim, both participants experience inner defeat.

When one individual denies a mate or child respect by using force and/or threat to set up a dominant-submissive relationship, destructive behavior eventually ensues, even though the relationship may appear to have remained intact. When Daddy wields power over an adolescent daughter, she becomes negatively programmed. Although she may resent the demeaning relationship, she grows accustomed to it. There is a danger that she may unconsciously transfer these learned destructive needs to her own marriage later on.

In an intimate relationship, any attempt to regard one human being as decidedly submissive (inferior) to the other will result in hostile behavior.

An individual who seeks power over another will never find any authentic love-security in the relationship. He/she will become totally immersed in the power struggle. The satisfactions are vicarious and destructive. The dominance (superiority) will be reluctantly acknowledged by the submissive (inferior) mate or child, but the seeds of hatred and resentment will have been sown.

When intimidation, threats and humiliation are utilized as a means of interaction, insecurity and instability will shape the personality of the victim. The victor, too, is trapped in a self-defeating pattern; he eventually finds that his ostensible dominance (superiority) does not yield the anticipated love-security. The relationship is one of frustration and unhappiness.

Inability to Accept and Enjoy Non-Sexual Intimacy

One indication of maturity in a husband/wife, Daddy/Mama is the capacity and desire to share non-sexual areas of human life—to appreciate the genuine uniqueness of each person.

A considerable number of men and women find this aspect of human interaction to be very difficult to master. It is not unusual today for a husband and wife to claim that their sex life is intensely satisfying, but that they have nothing else in common.

In a parent-child relationship, this problem may be camouflaged by the busyness of the parent. He/she does not have enough time to watch a son/daughter perform on the swim team or debate team, for example. Because of their sophisticated excuses, Daddy and Mama may not be aware of their unconscious attitudes. A parent may tell a counselor that an adolescent son/daughter is capable of fending for himself/herself. This is the parental rationalization for an inability to enjoy intimacy with a son/daughter.

A similar situation can arise in friendships outside of the family circle. An individual who refers to his/her "tennis friends," "office pals" or "bridge partners" may unconsciously be isolating and categorizing individuals so as to know only one narrow facet of their personalities. In this way one can avoid the potential risks and rewards of a deepening relationship which depends on continuing sharing and discovery.

This destructive trait is characterized by the absence rather than the presence of powerful negative emotions. When a mate or a son/daughter becomes resigned to loneliness or to a lack of enthusiasm from a spouse or parent, the relationship can erode.

Lack of Supportiveness

Individuals with low self-esteem are fearful of giving of themselves in human relationships. Because they dare not support a mate or child, they maneuver the relationship so that the other individual is doing all the giving and they are receiving.

Sometimes loving traits such as encouragement, consolation, reassurance and understanding are absent. The relationship is stark and cold. A husband may find that he does not even compliment his wife when she has taken obvious efforts to please him. A wife may fail to offer a word of encouragement to her husband when he is going to an important job interview. Daddy may buy his daughter a new dress instead of taking the time to see her perform in the school play. Mama may conveniently forget her son's big day as star pitcher and go off to her volunteer work.

In the rush for individual self-esteem and satisfaction, this mate or parent becomes insensitive to the legitimate needs of the other person. He/she inflicts egocentric demands in situations where only some degree of mature and selfless giving could restore the serious imbalance in the relationship. If this destructive response continues, the husband/wife will eventually find that he/she does not need the mate. The two of them can literally become strangers, because they have never cultivated mature interdependence based on mutual supportiveness. Similarly, Daddy and Mama may be shocked one day to discover they have become estranged from a son/daughter. The child may honestly prefer a kindly uncle or aunt or teacher who offers him/her the enthusiasm and supportiveness he/she needs to develop normal self-esteem.

Individual Differences

The more mature a husband/wife is, the less likely it is that he/she will refuse to allow the other person to be himself/herself. A counselor sees all kinds of people—the educated and the uneducated, the sophisticated and the naive—who cannot tolerate in a mate any characteristics that distinguish him/her as a unique, separate being. The resistances may range from petty to monstrous, depending upon the pervasiveness and upon the depth of the fear that the husband/wife or parent/child experiences.

The more intimate the relationship, the more the immature man/woman will demand that the other individual be merely a reflection of his/her egocentric personality. In less personal relationships this destructive trait can become a problem if one human being has some authority over another: teacher-pupil, employer-employee relationships. If the relationship is comparatively impersonal and temporary, the destructive possibilities may be transferred into the home arena, where more intense demands can be acted out.

This inability to respect and encourage individual differences that do not seriously undermine the marital or parental intimacy has its most severe impact when one individual achieves unusual success or distinction.

It is not uncommon for a husband and wife—or, less frequently, a parent and child—to have a problem that revolves around some unique recognition afforded to one individual and not to the other. For example, an ambitious woman married to a passive man may find out that her earnings or status is a bone of contention. Her husband may not overtly demand that she quit work, but he may tell her how sloppy the house is, how badly neglected the children are, all while sitting in front of the television with a can of beer in his hand. This sort of passive resistance is a common barrier to the realization of a sustained relationship, for it prevents one individual from enjoying the legitimate rewards of his/her uniqueness.

Infantile Dependency

Few adult relationships survive the far-reaching consequences of infantile dependency, unless a counselor is called in early in the disruptive chain of events.

Despite the emphasis today on individuality and independence, our culture actually encourages infantile dependency by supporting the "perpetual youth phenomenon," which inhibits and discourages independent decision-making and responsibility. Moreover, infantile dependency is often seen as sexually appealing, because it enhances the notions of male strength and female "helplessness"—to the detriment of both sexes.

In any interpersonal relationships, from the most intimate to the most impersonal, an overly dependent individual can never realize his full worth as a human being. Infantile dependency frustrates the mature marital partner, the parent or the child.

All reciprocal human relationships can tolerate occasional bouts of infantile dependency, but a marital or parental relationship will suffer considerable stress if the practice continues for very long. An individual generally perceives this infantile dependency within himself/herself; he/she is uncomfortable and apprehensive about his/her ability to deal harmoniously with other human beings. A dependent person is usually aware of the unnecessary limitations he imposes on himself.

However, a mate or a parent may, because of his own personality problems, unconsciously nurture this response. Two people may be deadlocked in a relationship in which neither is very happy, but neither is so miserable that he/she will take positive action to diminish the tension and learn to interact in a more mature way.

Ignoring the Need for Individual Growth

Today individuality constitutes both the ultimate achievement in and the ultimate threat to our society. Individual growth is not—and need not be—a deterrent to marital harmony and parent-child closeness and understanding.

Practically speaking, however, we are living in a time when Daddy goes his way, Mama goes her way, and the children are "abandoned" to the impersonal "security" of schools, social services, churches and government agencies. The Mama who stays at home is looked upon as an incompetent, unable to compete with "achieving" women. The Daddy who gains recognition in his business or professional field may still be a lamentable parent.

What room does this leave within close personal relationships for human growth? Must one person grow at the expense of all other family members? Must one individual stagnate mindlessly while another mate flourishes?

We do not think so. The essence of marriage, parenthood and friendship is the kind of interdependence that encourages the partner, child or friend to realize his creative potential. Every human being should receive an affirmation of his individual merits. Compare the husband who applauds his wife's efforts to earn a college degree with the man who deliberately discourages his wife from seeking individual achievement. Who is happier, and who is a more creative human being? Consider the son/daughter whose Daddy and Mama encourage him/her to develop a talent. The individual as well as the family benefits from this growth process.

Too often, however, the search for individuality becomes a threat to marital intimacy and parental harmony because it is viewed as a competition that one person "wins" and the other "loses." The nonverbal message is that "I don't want him/her to find success [enjoy recognition or achievement] if I don't have it, too." The more immature and egocentric a man/woman/child is, the more destructive this attitude can be.

Keys to an Altruistic Life

We are truly free when we are capable of interior self-regulation; that is, when our inner feelings and motives are in harmony with a religious/ philosophical ethic that recognizes both the individual dignity of human beings and the collective good of humanity.

Self-regulation and self-determination are learned in the Daddy's girl/Mama's boy relationship. Detrimental societal forces may later arouse adverse responses in the child; however, these tend to have minimal effects if the parental influence is constructive and stable.

As the child accommodates himself to the gradual shift of authority from Daddy and Mama to himself, he becomes his own self-regulator. He develops a conscience and an ability to respond to other human beings in an honest and responsible manner. He learns that he cannot have one set of values for himself and another set for others.

It is no accident of fate that those men and women who are at peace with themselves—through interior self-regulation and possession of an external objective religious/philosophical ethic—are the ones who are capable of cooperative and harmonious social, marital and parental relationships.

Therefore, how we adjust in our interpersonal lives is dependent primarily on the maturation process within the family. A second factor is our understanding of the role of frustration and disappointment in life. These experiences come not only to those who are disadvantaged in some material way, but to all men and women, whatever their human condition. It is imperative that we gain a proper comprehension of these factors so that we can constructively utilize the aggressive energies that result from these universal experiences.

The "how" and "why" of frustration and disappointment are only partially understood. We say, for example, that some people have a low tolerance for frustration. This is customarily linked to impulsive destructive acts. We observe that others are capable of enduring considerable frustration and disappointment; these individuals divert their pent-up aggressive feelings into activities that result in some personal and/or societal benefits.

Whether you are single, married, a child, an adolescent, a husband, a wife, a Daddy or a Mama, you can systematically pursue a course of action that will deepen the sense of love-security in all your human relationships. Just as you make a conscious choice to take good care of your health, so, too, can you make responsible decisions regarding your interpersonal, marital and parental relationships.

There are certain constructive traits that provide a foundation for love-security in all human relationships, especially in the intimate milieu of marriage and parenthood. When Daddy and Mama commit themselves to parenthood, these traits become the building blocks with which the son/daughter creates the inner resources necessary for self-regulation and self-direction.

Although we have generally discussed these inner resources within the parent-child context, they are vital to all human relationships. Genuine friendships are nurtured on the same value system, although the impact is less intense than in marriage or parenthood.

Love-Service

No one can really take the place of Daddy/Mama in creating and sustaining the vital life-affirming intimacy that is the foundation of a wholesome parent-child relationship. Love-service includes those innumerable tasks and opportunities to give that weld a bond of trust, loyalty and understanding—a gift of self to one's own flesh and blood in reverence and awe of life created through marital love. Love-service comprises the whole range of maternal and paternal efforts involved in educating a child and preparing him/her for a responsible and useful life.

A husband and wife must have an abiding commitment in order to establish the consistency of behavior essential for optimum stability. A child must know that Daddy and Mama can be "counted on" above and beyond all other human beings. Love-service is this dedication to the dependent infant and child.

This does not mean that Daddy and Mama must become slaves or martyrs to a son/daughter. That is a distortion of the mature love-service relationship. Parents who are absorbed in the world of work and creativity generally enjoy self-esteem and have the capacity to transmit love and assurance to their children. Work outside the home does not in itself have an adverse effect on the Daddy's girl/Mama's boy relationship. Rather, the important factor is the maturity of the parents' attitude toward the child. If Daddy or Mama is selfish and feels that parenthood does not fit in with his or her life goals, there will be many indications to the child that he/she is a burden.

While not everyone may wish to become a parent, it is important that those men and women who choose this life task do so with some vision of the exalted and at times frightening powers for good or evil that they possess by virtue of their influence over sons and daughters. One way that Daddy and Mama can perceive love-service is through the deepening sensitivity that is revealed to them as their sons and daughters grow. The child is the same and yet different at each phase of maturation. The son/daughter is constantly unfolding and becoming as Daddy and Mama intangibly shape his/her life. Love-service requires a series of adjustments and a philosophical vision.

In effect, Daddy and Mama need to see their children with an inner eye in order to be aware of who they are and what they can eventually become. The eighteenth-century poet Goethe described this intricate unfolding: "If you treat an individual as he is, he will stay as he is. But if you treat him as if he were what he ought to be and could be, he will become what he ought to be and could be."

Self-Regulation

The concept of discipline and self-discipline in our society is largely negative. Discipline is thought of as a means of preventing and restricting the child "for his own good." In its extreme form, it is found in the Daddy and Mama who abuse their children.

As a consequence of this notion of discipline, another equally extreme position has emerged in which any and all "restrictions" are considered "bad" because they inflict physical and/or psychological pain in the form of guilt. A complex metamorphosis has taken place within one generation, in which the equation "discipline equals bad equals guilt" has been swept away in a wave of permissiveness based on the premise that if everyone's behavior is okay, there will be an elimination of guilt. Self-regulation or self-discipline is repudiated because of its association with rigidity, authority, inhumaneness.

It is not surprising that this course of events has taken place, for it parallels the crumbling and rejection of objective religious/philosophical ethics. It is not possible, nor is it desirable, for each human being to develop his own individual ethical system. The role of discipline, or self-regulation, as a positive and constructive tool has existed ever since men and women began to live in intimate family units. Its success or failure as a means of encouraging one pattern of behavior over another is related to the maturity or immaturity of the individuals who utilize it.

It is primarily through the fostering of self-regulation and love-service that the Daddy's girl/Mama's boy relationship prepares sons and daughters to become useful, productive and self-directed men and women. Self-regulation might be described as doing what you know you should do when no one else is around to see you do it. It is essential to achievement in intellectual and athletic endeavors. Men and women who strive to attain recognition in these fields understand that self-regulation is crucial to their success—it separates the dilettante from the professional.

Self-regulation gives meaning and direction to human relationships. Daddy and Mama teach their sons/daughters to accept discipline not in order to restrict or prevent behavior, but in order to give them the strength to make mature life decisions in all sorts of unforeseen circumstances. The child looks to his parents to teach him the self-direction that will shape his life and control his future destiny. Without this capacity for self-regulation, he/she will drift aimlessly from one set of unsatisfying life circumstances to another.

The process of transferring authority from Daddy and Mama to daughter/son is manifested in a long chain of acts and decisions that gradually give the child confidence in his/her own ability to choose among several courses of action. As the son/daughter learns that there is a relationship between his/her decision and future rewards or penalties, he/she becomes his/her own self-regulator. In effect, he/she accepts responsibility for his/her own acts. This is the ultimate goal of self-regulation.

When interpreted in this context, self-discipline can be an extremely effective technique with which to improve human relationships and parent-child interaction during any phase of the child's development. Contrary to current beliefs, it is not a self-limiting technique, but a systematic procedure that affords an individual optimum control over his life circumstances.

Ability to Forgive and Forget

How do Daddy and Mama persuade their children that they love them? How do Daddy and Mama help their sons and daughters develop confidence and trust in human beings outside the family? What is the vital balm of all human relationships?

When we reinforce the self-esteem of a child by the comforting act of forgiving and forgetting, we are strengthening his/her capacity to be a compassionate human being. When forgiveness is practiced within the family and in daily interpersonal relationships outside the home, a network of hope is established. The child learns to acknowledge human frailties, and by so doing encourages others to respond in a like manner. Daddy and Mama should convey to their children the notion that other human beings can add immeasurably to their happiness if they do not expect unrealistically perfect behavior. In this way children learn to develop the emotional resiliency so necessary to human relationships.

One childish or adolescent misunderstanding need not be the end of a friendship. On all levels of human interaction, this ability to forgive and forget provides the groundwork for sustained relationships in marriage and family life. One does not abandon or desert a husband/wife because of some human frailty. One has to learn to forgive.

This capacity is the bedrock of all abiding relationships. No satisfying relationship can exist without forgiveness. It is the balm that heals the unintentional psychic wounds that human beings are heir to in everyday encounters with their fellowman.

Ability to Perform a Satisfying Life Work

Attitudes toward work and the choice of a personal career are to a great extent influenced by the propensities, interests and aversions of Daddy and Mama. Parents who visualize work as an expression of their creative and intellectual energies subtly transfer their fervor to sons and daughters. Those who consider work to be a "necessary evil" instill a complex emotional frame of reference in their children. This includes apathy, indifference, irresponsibility, aimlessness and skepticism about the value of work as a reflection of individuality.

By helping their children to choose a life work, Daddy and Mama make yet another positive contribution to their self-esteem. Each member stands to gain in a family where parents have learned to cooperate and combine their work talents for the benefit of the family. Moreover, the constructive effect of work on the total human personality cannot be overemphasized. It is in man's/woman's nature to rely on the fruits of his/her efforts for a substantial part of the self-esteem he/she needs to function positively in human relationships.

Counselors are familiar with family situations in which one or both parents are indifferent to work and go through the motions of a job only to receive a paycheck that has no symbolic value to the recipient. It is under these circumstances that the dissatisfactions in the world of work spill over into human relationships.

The more desirable environment is one in which a mature Daddy and Mama have learned to cooperate with each other. Their mutual respect, dedication to children and work, and willingness to adapt are all formidable influences on sons' and daughters' attitudes. Realistically, of course, much work is performed without unusual recognition or acclaim of any sort. Routine and anonymity are part of working. However, we are thinking here in terms of a philosophical appreciation of the constructive aspect of work and the impact of this attitude on the relationship between parent and child. It is not a coincidence, for example, that the energetic and goal-oriented Daddy and Mama have daughters and sons who have enthusiastic attitudes toward work.

One's attitude toward work, with all of its complex symbolic and pragmatic aspects, is a crucial clue to a man's or woman's vital attitudes toward himself/herself. This is why work is an intrinsic building block in the human personality and in interpersonal relationships. The attitude a person has toward work and the satisfaction he/she derives from it reveal how the individual appears to himself/herself. Daddy and Mama can consciously prepare their sons and daughters to face work with enthusiasm, self-direction and an understanding of its profound significance in their lives.

Belonging

Belonging might be thought of as that dimensionless area in human relationships between intense intimacy and involuntary entanglement. Our heart belongs to someone, but we do not wish to be possessed. A human being yearns to be involved and committed, but not smothered or submerged in someone else's personality. The more intense the relationship, the more important it is to maintain this fragile balance between individuality and unity.

Belonging is a positive trait in the sense that it constitutes a continuing commitment of individuals to an interdependent relationship. When a child understands emotionally that she can rely on Daddy and Mama to help, guide and sustain her under any condition, she has a positive and unique awareness of belonging.

A strong sense of belonging implies that Daddy and Mama have given ample attention to a child. The son/daughter does not hesitate to approach Daddy or Mama because he/she enjoys a unique feeling of belonging. This feeling can only be based on an exclusive relationship. A child must not feel jeopardized by a constant succession of "Daddy" or "Mama" partners temporarily associated with the natural parent. The cohesiveness and strength derived from this one-to-one relationship enables the child to venture into the complicated world outside the home with self-assurance and decisiveness. Particularly in the parent-child relationship, this caring response must be expressed in a mature fashion so that it does not appear as overprotectiveness, possessiveness or parental superiority, all of which can be destructive to the personality of the child.

When all members of a family are interacting constructively, this feeling of belonging can provide the basis for much inner strength. The child learns that he/she can count on others, and he/she learns to be counted on. Self-reliance and mutual trust are derivative benefits of this continuing interpersonal experience.

Helping Those Who Cannot Help Themselves

All human relationships are inevitably tested by crisis situations. To put it another way, men and women in their marital, parental and individual life roles are bound to find that there are times when they cannot help themselves.

To go out of one's self into the life of another, to "walk in his/her shoes," goes against the grain of the idolatry of individuality that prevails today. Only through the childhood Daddy's girl/Mama's boy relationship does an individual learn that man/woman does not, and cannot, live for himself/herself alone.

Today we pay lip service to the notion of helping others and point to complex social and governmental agencies that assist individuals and families after the damage has been done. After Daddy and Mama have gone their separate ways, after a son/daughter has become a ward of the court or shown antisocial behavior, then all the machinery for helping those who cannot help themselves is put into action. This assistance is essentially impersonal, and as such is much less effective than the personal caring and concern of family and friends.

The capacity and desire to help those who cannot help themselves clearly "costs" us something. It involves a recognition that some other member of our family or community is in need in some way. But if that need can be met in a personal family way, positive benefits will come to both the giver and the recipient. Compassion, when it is deliberately cultivated, orients each parent-child relationship away from the self. A concern for others results in healthy self-respect.

In constructive interpersonal relationships, where each member has been taught to lend a helping hand to those who are afflicted in some way, there is an acute sensitivity to the needs of others. Helping others actually reduces the inner tensions caused by self-centeredness, the enemy of enduring and harmonious relationships.

Every family member must appreciate the fact that the pursuit of happiness is a collective endeavor and is experienced only when each person is committed to helping all others in the family group. This attitude stimulates mental health.

Learning to Make Decisions

One of the characteristics of an effective human being is the ability to make decisions. In order for a child to become a healthy, self-directed adult, Daddy and Mama must be committed to promoting altruistic decision-making.

Decision-making is based on the joining together of subjective experience and objective information—at first under the legitimate and benign authority of the parents. Many problems in relationships are inadvertently created by the person who, because he is fearful of making decisions, refuses to choose one course of action over another. The indecisive individual may then have feelings of rage, vindictiveness, dissatisfaction or frustration. He/she may accuse the decisive person of being an obstacle to his/her personal happiness.

Happy and enduring relationships reflect a high degree of maturity and commitment and hence a positive decision-making ability. A son/daughter whose Daddy/Mama makes effective decision-making a facet of family relationships will be self-assured. And because the child feels secure, he or she will gain inner strength. In adulthood he/she will not mull over alternative possibilities interminably. Moreover, he or she will be free of the emotional debris that invariably comes with a lifetime habit of indecision and self-created negative human experiences.

Naturally there will be some mistakes made in the decision-making process along the way, but the significant point is that interpersonal relationships will be improved and clarified. Joint decision-making will give added direction and meaning to marital and parental interaction. Two people, whether husband and wife or parent and child, are no longer just casually bound together in an aimless and apathetic relationship. Instead, this decision-making ability provides a foundation for love-service, self-regulation and all the other positive traits that promote and continuously vitalize human relationships.

Today counselors are seeing more and more families destroyed by impulsive decision-making and unilateral self-serving decisions. Although these decisions may appear superficially to be benign, they are in essence manipulative and self-destructive. An example that is fairly common is the decision of an individual to choose another husband/wife because he/she has a "right" to personal happiness. This person is carefully ignoring the profound repercussions such a decision will have later in life on a son/daughter. Usually the reason given for such a decision is a rationalization and conceals motives hidden in the individual's unconscious. In counseling this man may declare that he is capable of making decisions, but he will follow quickly with the observation that he is miserable and undecided about the future.

To this individual the necessity of making decisions seems to diminish happiness. Actually what is occurring is a process of self-deception. A counselor can, in such instances, guide the individual toward a true understanding of decision-making as a positive act that can be used to prevent future unhappiness. The counselor's task is to help the individual realize that responsibility (accepting the rewards and consequences) is the other side of the decision-making coin.

The integration of the ability to make decisions into the human personality makes possible predictable and secure life-affirming relationships.

Conscious Replacement

How does one realistically alter the human personality so as to enjoy optimum happiness in personal relationships?

We believe that this process is sparked from within the individual by his/her self-perception, sense of unhappiness or frustration with present relationships, and degree of motivation to transform his/her personality. This process then involves redirecting one's energies within a program of self-help and/or professional counseling.

There are a couple of important considerations one must look at if one is to be realistic about such personality changes.

First, if the negative personality traits are of long-standing duration and the human relationships are in an extremely precarious condition, a great deal of individual effort and counseling skill will be required to help the person redirect destructive energy.

Second, when an individual is troubled, he/she is likely to want to escape and to blame the other person for all existing conflict. For example, a husband or wife may seek a divorce; a parent may abdicate parental responsibility with the statement "I've done all I can for him." The tendency is for the unhappy person to wish to abandon all troublesome human relationships and begin again with someone new. Our society tacitly endorses a thesis of human obsolescence through high divorce rates and high incidence of child abuse and assorted forms of assault, all of which indicate a lack of comprehension of the dignity and value of all human beings. Only when an individual understands the full significance of this devastating philosophy can he/she begin to mend the ruptured relationships in his/her personal life.

Reconstructing, redirecting and transforming processes occur when the individual voluntarily and deliberately chooses to believe and act on the conviction that he/she has limited himself/herself by restricting the growth of the other individual in a one-to-one relationship. As the individual sets himself free from the bondage of self-limiting and destructive personality traits, two subtle changes become apparent. The individual voluntarily replaces negative traits with life-affirming habits that generate greater self-esteem and more altruistic relationships with others. And as the person grows in self-understanding, he/she becomes more profoundly aware of cause and effect patterns in human behavior. Consequently, the other individual in the troubled relationship finds that he/she too has contributed resistance and manipulative destructive traits to the relationship. These can then be eliminated in order to reestablish an improved relationship based on love-service and its by-products, love-security and happiness.

Inner tensions and feelings of destructive aggression are gradually reduced or diverted into other activities. The individual's new-found inner peace, based on his recognition of his own humanity and mortality, serves as a new frame of reference for his interpersonal behavior. Personality alteration should not be thought of as a fixed or static goal, but rather as a continuing and deepening life experience. The intricate and subtle unfolding of the personality in everyday human activities will strengthen marital and family relationships.

Today there are many different kinds of counseling that can be used to supplement self-help. Because no individual's actions are isolated from those of other family members, family counseling is one of the most effective ways of treating husbands/wives, Daddies/Mamas, children, and their respective interrelationships. When a man/woman enjoys deeper satisfaction in one area of interpersonal relationships, he/she may be encouraged to examine and improve other social relationships as well. A husband/father may find that once he learns not to dominate his daughter by treating her in a servile manner, he can then express love in his marital relationship without exploiting his wife.

An individual's success is largely dependent on his own capacity to envision the happiness inner personality transformation can bring. From this vision will come the crucial motivation and sensitivity.

Learn to Live with Yourself

The solution to the problem of self-acceptance lies in our recognition both of free will and of the fact that we cannot live for ourselves alone. An individual is not likely to find intense self-fulfillment outside of human relationships. Fame, status, power and recognition are usually fleeting.

Marriage, family and friendship provide opportunities for self-fulfillment by first requiring each of us to give of ourselves. The seeds of love and nurturing that we plant in our human relationships as a husband, wife, Daddy or Mama will be harvested, for good or for evil. Self-esteem is not a magic gimmick invented by behavioral scientists to lure men and women hungry for love and enduring relationships into a haven of egocentric individuality. We "feel good" when we give of ourselves in all relationships. Our greatest inner happiness comes from those personal encounters where there is sharing on all levels of interaction. This is possible chiefly through marital and family ties.

The way to self-acceptance is not found in glib, superficial formulas for self-improvement, but in a profound scrutiny of our inner lives. This means that we must not be dependent on the prevailing culture, with its constantly changing customs and fads. A man or woman cannot literally accept and love in a religious/philosophical sense until he/she relates his/her life to that of other human beings in intimate, nurturing, enduring relationships. It is impossible to learn to love and forgive oneself without first entering deeply into the lives of others and then maintaining that commitment through good times and bad. Marriage and parenthood teach one how to live with oneself in a vital, productive and committed manner. Learning to live with oneself implies a commitment to self, family and community—to promoting the good of the individual as well as that of the group.

When an individual has really made great strides in personality alteration, he/she begins to acknowledge his/her responsibility for feelings and decisions. If there has been an error in judgment or if feelings have been hurt in a marital or parent-child relationship, the individual has enough self-esteem that he does not wish to blame the other person in the relationship. He/she can take the initiative in mending the problem, and the relationship can continue on a new basis of improved understanding and love-service. Therefore, the individual, as he gains self-esteem, is building a stronger bridge to other human beings.

Allegiance to an Objective Religious/ Philosophical Value System

A man or woman cannot live happily within a family on the basis of a random ethical value system authenticated by feelings alone. The trend toward creating one's own ethical system has led to self-serving ersatz "religions" and to disillusionment with human relationships. The common idea that "marriage is only a piece of paper" and that parenthood is in a somewhat similar category is an outgrowth of this trend. Friendships, too, suffer, because a man's or woman's word no longer transmits the sense of honor and loyalty that in the past was crucial to any continuing relationship.

Indeed, there has been a mindless repudiation of ideals that have served as a beacon to humankind for centuries by sustaining civilization through family life. Certain individuals have distorted traditional objective religious/philosophical value systems in an attempt to confuse and demoralize young people on the brink of forming enduring marital and parental commitments. Many young people have been led to believe that an objective religious/philosophical value system constitutes a restriction on an individual's ability to find genuine fulfillment in various life roles.

We have found quite the contrary to be true. Those patients who have even a nominal allegiance to an objective religious/philosophical value system are more likely to be motivated toward personality alteration. This objective religious/philosophical value system, along with their subjective feelings, serves as a vital guide to interaction in all human relationships. The personal ego is neither ignored nor exaggerated. It is recognized as a facet of one's character that must be integrated into life so that every individual has significance and dignity.

This framework encourages conviction and loyalty in marriage, family life and all other human relationships. The greatest life accomplishment of the vast majority of men and women is the creation and sustenance of human life—the nurturing of children who re-create this link with past and future.

With the widespread acceptance of permissive individuality and rejection of an objective religious/philosophical value system, marriage and family life have come upon nightmarish times. Relationships are entered into casually. Commitments are meaningful only when they are pleasure-filled. Children are burdens in our self-oriented culture. Is it any wonder that there is a proliferation of self-destructive, antisocial and even criminal behavior among children today, symbolic of parental rejection and disavowal of an objective religious/philosophical value system?

If we think of allegiance to an objective religious/philosophical value system as one of the cornerstones of family life and individual human happiness, it is because an abandonment of such standards leads to confusion and human suffering on a vast scale. This is evident today in deteriorating marital and parental relationships. On a practical level, allegiance to this value system can be thought of as a positive personality trait, because the fact that both individuals subscribe to a common conviction gives dimension, predictability and stability to relationships.

Belief in a traditional value system is, in effect, an affirmative statement about a man and woman, parent and child; it ennobles their relationship by translating the vision of what they can be to each other into the mundane acts of daily life. It is a positive declaration that what they sow together, they will reap. If they sow mutually strengthening acts of love, they will reap happiness, tranquillity and self-direction. If they acknowledge that duties and responsibilities are an essential facet of their relationship, they will reap the privileges and rewards. An objective religious/philosophical value system makes possible this continuing process of fulfilling oneself through enhancing the lives of others.

Which Way, Daddy and Mama?

Child-rearing practices today have been substantially adjusted to reflect the self-orientation of contemporary parents. The intimate, dedicated love and care of past generations of Daddies and Mamas seems to run counter to an overwhelming movement away from the life-affirming family unit and toward individuality.

Are we presently moving toward a society that wishes to be free of all concerns about children? Are we moving toward a society where parenthood is something you "do" only because you can't find a paying job and have no other talents?

On the one hand, some behavioral scientists seem to be saying that the tasks of parenthood are beyond the capacities of the average man and woman. Another equally compelling message is that parenthood is not worthy of our time and attention. These conflicting and demoralizing attitudes are reinforced by trendy ideologies that regard marriage as a self-fulfilling sensate experience that has no relevance to the larger society beyond the man and the woman involved in the relationship. These self-oriented attitudes, instead of leading to promised land, have yielded baffled men, women and children who have been utterly destroyed by their experiences with marriage and family life. This is the inevitable consequence of society's increasingly hostile attitudes toward marriage, family life and all other interpersonal relationships that require dedication and effort.

Today a growing number of men and women are reluctant to make the commitment that is essential to enduring marital and parental relationships. They are unconvinced of the innate value of these relationships to

245

the self. The increasing number of divorce cases in which neither Daddy nor Mama wishes to assume custody of the children indicates this preference for self above all. These individuals want to be assured that they are "taken care of" first before they make any investment of self in another human being. The intimate relationships of marriage and parenthood do not work that way.

Are we fearful of committing ourselves to these enduring reciprocal relationships because we want more than we are willing to give? Is the ultimate betrayal of self tangled within this snare of commitment?

There are, of course, a great number of men and women who make the commitment in good faith. Somewhere between the "super" Mom and Dad and the child abusers are those multitudes of parents who inconspicuously devote themselves with quiet valor to the task of rearing children.

Today there are literally millions of Daddies and Mamas who are giving their daughters/sons that love-security which only comes when Daddy and Mama enter fully into the lives of their children for the purpose of creating and sustaining a life beyond their own. This act of faith is their link with immortality.

There are millions of other Daddies and Mamas who are destroying the next generation, unintentionally perhaps, but just as surely as if they were poisoning their children a little at a time. These men and women are not "monsters" or obvious psychotics. Some of them have been caught in life circumstances beyond their control, and they do not understand that frustration and disappointment come not only to those men and women who appear to be disadvantaged in some material way, but to everyone, irrespective of individual human condition.

The chief difference between the Daddy and Mama who create and sustain a loving and secure relationship with a son/daughter and those who do not is that the former understand that they have freedom of choice, whereas the latter do not. Troubled, narcissistic parents invariably consider themselves "victims of fate." They do not envision any other kind of human relationship for their children or for themselves, and, moreover, they are unaware that their energies can be redirected toward a better life.

In these difficult times, marital and parental relationships can be strengthened, we believe, primarily by revitalizing two interrelated life-affirming principles. We are convinced that marriage must be a lifelong commitment in order to provide the ideal framework for the continuous caring for and molding of those lives entrusted to a husband and wife as parents. We further believe that parenthood is a privilege. It is an opportunity for individuals to achieve optimum self-fulfillment by dedicating themselves to their own flesh and blood. This is the means by which authentic and lasting happiness can be realized by Daddy and Mama and their children.

Men and women who are committed to each other and to their children are not afraid to grow up and accept the responsibilities of marriage and child-rearing. They acknowledge, as the self-oriented do not, that their needs need not come first. They have grown beyond their childish needs and frustrations into a supportive, life-affirming capacity. And it is through marriage and parenthood, within the context of positive traits as guiding life principles, that they forge a destiny of love-security and human happiness.

Suggested Readings

Alderson, Bernard. *Andrew Carnegie, the Man and His Work.* New York: Doubleday, Page, 1902.

"All American Boy." *Newsweek,* August 15, 1966.

Alliluyeva, Svetlana. *Only One Year.* Translated by Paul Chavchavadze. New York: Harper & Row, 1969.

————. *Twenty Letters to a Friend.* Translated by Priscilla Johnson McMillan. New York: Harper & Row, 1967.

Alpert, Hollis. *The Barrymores.* New York: The Dial Press, 1964.

Axelrad, Jacob. *Anatole France: A Life Without Illusions.* New York: Harper & Row, 1944.

Barrymore, Diana, and Gerold Frank. *Too Much, Too Soon.* New York: Holt, 1957.

Beauvoir, Simone de. *Memoirs of a Dutiful Daughter.* Translated by James Kirkup. Cleveland and New York: World Publishing, 1959.

————. *The Prime of Life.* Translated by Peter Green. Cleveland and New York: World Publishing, 1962.

Bergler, Edmund, M.D. *Homosexuality: Disease or Way of Life.* New York: McGraw-Hill, 1956.

Boulton, Agnes. *Part of a Long Story.* New York: Doubleday, 1958.

Carnegie, Andrew. *Autobiography.* New York: Houghton Mifflin, 1920.

Chevalier, Maurice. *With Love.* Boston: Little, Brown, 1960.

Coles, Robert. "American Amok." *The New Republic,* August 27, 1966.

Darwin, Sir Francis, ed. *Charles Darwin's Autobiography, with His Notes and Letters Depicting the Growth of the Origin of the Species.* New York: Schuman, 1950.

Davis, John H. *The Bouviers—Portrait of an American Family.* New York: Farrar, Straus & Giroux, 1969.

Drakeford, John. *Forbidden Love.* Waco, Tex.: Word Books, 1971.

Dugdale, Blanche E. C. *Arthur James Balfour, First Earl of Balfour.* New York: G. P. Putnam, 1937.

Freud, Anna. *Normality and Pathology in Childhood.* New York: International Universities Press, 1965.

Freud, Martin. *Glory Reflected: Sigmund Freud, Man and Father.* New York: Vanguard, 1958.

Hoffman, Martin. *The Gay World.* New York: Basic Books, 1968.

Howard, Sidney. "The Silver Cord." In *Representative Modern Dramas,* edited by Charles Huntington Whitman. New York: Macmillan, 1940.

Irvine, William. *Apes, Angels, and Victorians.* New York: McGraw-Hill, 1955.

James, Henry. *Wings of the Dove.* New York: Penguin Books, 1974.

Jenkins, Elizabeth. *Elizabeth the Great.* New York: Coward-McCann & Geoghegan, 1958.

Jones, Ernest. *Life and Work of Sigmund Freud.* New York: Basic Books, 1953.

MacArthur, General Douglas. *Reminiscences.* New York: McGraw-Hill, 1964.

"Madman in the Tower, The." *Time,* August 12, 1966.

Maurois, Andre. *Proust: Portrait of a Genius.* New York: Harper & Row, 1950.

O'Casey, Eileen. *Sean.* Edited with an Introduction by J. C. Trewin. New York: Putnam-Coward-McCann & Geoghegan, 1972.

O'Neill, Eugene. *Nine Plays.* New York: Liveright, 1932.

Rutter, Michael, M.D. *Children of Sick Parents. An Environmental and Psychiatric Study.* London: Oxford University Press, 1966.

Shaw, G. B. "Getting Married." In *Makers of the Modern Theatre,* edited by Barry Ulanov. New York: McGraw-Hill, 1961.

Sheaffer, Louis. *O'Neill, Son and Artist.* Boston: Little, Brown, 1973.

————. *O'Neill, Son and Playwright.* Boston: Little, Brown, 1973.

Sparrow, Judge Gerald. *The Great Assassins.* New York: Arco Publishing, 1968.

Stearn, Jess. *The Grapevine.* New York: Doubleday, 1964.

Thomson, Elizabeth H. *Harvey Cushing, Surgeon, Author, Artist.* New York: Schuman, 1950.

Wright, Frank Lloyd. *An Autobiography.* New York: Duell, Sloan & Pearce, 1943.